MANAGING FOR QUALITY
INTEGRATING QUALITY AND BUSINESS STRATEGY

THE BUSINESS ONE IRWIN/APICS LIBRARY OF INTEGRATED RESOURCE MANAGEMENT

Integration Functions

Managing Information: How Information Systems Impact Organizational Strategy
Gordon B. Davis and Thomas R. Hoffman

Managing Human Resources: Integrating People and Business Strategy   *Lloyd Baird*

Managing for Quality: Integrating Quality and Business Strategy   *V. Daniel Hunt*

World-Class Accounting and Finance   *Carol J. McNair*

Customers and Products

Marketing for the Manufacturer   *J. Paul Peter*

Field Service Management: An Integrated Approach to Increasing Customer Satisfaction
Arthur V. Hill

Effective Product Design and Development: How to Cut Lead Time and Increase Customer
Satisfaction   *Stephen R. Rosenthal*

Logistics

Integrated Production and Inventory Management: Revitalizing the Manufacturing Enterprise
Thomas E. Vollmann, William L. Berry, and D. Clay Whybark

Purchasing: Continued Improvement through Integration   *Joseph Carter*

Integrated Distribution Management: Competing on Customer Service, Time, and Cost
Christopher Gopal and Harold Cypress

Manufacturing Process

Integrative Facilities Management   *John M. Burnham*

Integrated Process Design and Development   *Dan L. Shunk*

Integrative Manufacturing: Transforming the Organization through People, Process, and
Technology   *Scott Flaig*

MANAGING FOR QUALITY
INTEGRATING QUALITY AND BUSINESS STRATEGY

V. Daniel Hunt
President
Technology Research Corporation

BUSINESS ONE IRWIN
Homewood, Illinois 60430

This publication is designed to provide accurate and
authoritative information in regard to the subject matter
covered. It is sold with the understanding that neither the
author nor the publisher is engaged in rendering legal, accounting,
or other professional service. If legal advice or other expert
assistance is required, the services of a competent
professional person should be sought.

From a Declaration of Principles jointly adopted by a Committee
of the American Bar Association and a Committee of Publishers.

Sponsoring editor: Jeffrey A. Krames
Production manager: Mary Jo Parke
Designer: Larry J. Cope
Compositor: Carlisle Communications, Ltd.
Typeface: 11/13 Times Roman
Printer: Book Press

Library of Congress Cataloging-in-Publication Data

Hunt, V. Daniel.
    Managing for quality : integrating quality and business strategy /
V. Daniel Hunt.
        p.   cm. — (The Business One Irwin/APICS library of integrated
resource management)
    Includes bibliographical references and index.
    ISBN 1-55623-544-5
    1. Total quality management—United States.   2. Success in
business—United States.   3. Total quality management—Awards—
United States.   I. Title.   II. Series.
    HD62.15.H858   1993
    658.5′62—dc20   92–26133

Printed in the United States of America
1   2   3   4   5   6   7   8   9   0   BP   9   8   7   6   5   4   3   2

To James E. Wise, Jr.
An Officer, Gentleman, and Friend

FOREWORD

Managing for Quality is one book in a series that addresses the most critical issue facing manufacturing companies today: integration. Integration is the identification and solution of problems that cross organizational and company boundaries and, perhaps most important, the continuous search for ways to solve these problems faster and more effectively. The genesis of the series is the commitment to integration made by the American Production and Inventory Control Society (APICS). A few years ago, I attended several brainstorming sessions in which the primary question for discussion was this: What jobs will exist in manufacturing companies in the future—not at the very top of the enterprise and not at the bottom, but in between? The prognostications included these:

- The absolute number of jobs will decrease, as will layers of management. Manufacturing organizations will adopt flatter organizational forms with less emphasis on hierarchy and less distinction between white collars and blue collars.
- Functional "silos" should become obsolete. The classical functions of marketing, manufacturing, engineering, finance, and personnel will be less important in defining work. More people will take on "project" work focused on continuous improvement of one kind or another.
- Fundamental restructuring, meaning much more than financial restructuring, will become a way of life in manufacturing enterprises. The primary focal points will be a new market-driven emphasis on creating value with customers, as well as greatly increased flexibility, a new business-driven attack on global markets—which includes deployment of new information technology—and fundamentally new jobs.

- Work will become much more integrated. The payoffs will be seen through connections across organizational and company boundaries. Included in the trend are customer and vendor partnerships, with an overall focus on improving the value-added chain.
- New measurements that focus on the new strategic directions will be required. Metrics will be developed that incorporate the most important dimensions of the environment. Similar metrics and semantics will be developed to support the new uses of information technology.
- New "people management" approaches will be developed. Teamwork will be critical to organizational success. Human resource management will become less of a "staff" function and more closely integrated with the basic work.

Many of these prognostications are already a reality. APICS has made the commitment to leading the way in all of these change areas. The decision was both courageous and intelligent. There is no future for a professional society not committed to leading-edge education for its members. Based on the society's experience with the Certification in Production and Inventory Management (CPIM) program, the natural thrust of APICS was to develop a new certification program focusing on integration. The result, Certification in Integrative Resource Management (CIRM), is a program composed of 13 building-block areas, which have been combined into four examination modules, as follows:

1. Integration functions.
   Total Quality Management.
   Human resources.
   Finance and accounting.
   Information systems.
2. Customers and products.
   Marketing and sales.
   Field service.
   Product design and development.
3. Manufacturing processes.
   Industrial facilities management.
   Process design and development.
   Manufacturing (production).

4. Logistics.
   Production and inventory control.
   Procurement.
   Distribution.

As can be seen from this topical list, one objective in the CIRM program is to develop educational breadth. Managers increasingly must know the underlying basics in each area of the business: who are the people who work there, what are day-to-day *and* strategic problems, what is state-of-the-art practice, what are the expected improvement areas, and what is happening with technology. This basic breadth of knowledge is an absolute prerequisite to understanding the potential linkages and joint improvements.

But it is the linkages, relationships, and integration that are even more important. Each CIRM examination devotes approximately 40 percent of the questions to the connections among the 13 building-block areas. In fact, after a candidate has successfully completed the four examination modules, he or she must take a fifth examination (Integrated Enterprise Management), which focuses solely on the interrelationships among all functional areas of an enterprise.

The CIRM program has been the most exciting activity on which I have worked in a professional organization. Increasingly, manufacturing companies face the alternatives of either restructuring proactively to deal with today's competitive realities or just sliding away—giving up market share and industry leadership. Education must play a large role in making the necessary changes. People working in manufacturing companies need to learn many new things and "unlearn" many old ones.

The educational materials available to support CIRM once were very limited. There were textbooks in which basic concepts were covered and bits and pieces that dealt with integration, but there simply was no coordinated set of materials available for this program. Creating these materials has been the job of the CIRM series authors, and it has been my distinct pleasure as series editor to help develop the ideas and facilitate our joint learning. All of us have learned a great deal, and I am delighted with every book in the series.

Thomas E. Vollmann
Series Editor

PREFACE

Producing high-quality goods and services is crucial not only to continued economic growth, but also to national security and the well-being and the standard of living of each family.

Reasserting quality leadership will require a firm commitment to the Total Quality Management principles.

Improving quality takes time and resources and can be achieved only through a combination of factors. It is a long-term commitment by top management that involves working with suppliers to improve performance; educating, training, and motivating workers; developing accurate and responsive management systems; and establishing targets for quality improvement.

Quality improvement principles apply to small companies as well as large corporations, to service industries as well as manufacturing, and to the public sector as well as private enterprise. Improving the quality of goods and services goes hand in hand with improving productivity and lowering costs. It is also essential to the process of enhancing worker fulfillment and customer satisfaction.

Private-sector organizations and government institutions around the world are joining forces in promoting a national commitment to Total Quality Management. Business executives are working together again to develop the skills and techniques needed for producing goods and services of higher quality.

V. Daniel Hunt
Springfield, Virginia

ACKNOWLEDGMENTS

This book contains major portions of *Quality in America*—chapters 1 through 7, and 10. *Managing for Quality* shifts the focus to integrating quality and business strategy based on the Total Quality Management methodology.

Managing for Quality also has been developed based on the expertise of a wide variety of authorities who are specialists in their respective fields.

The following publications were used as the resources for this book. Portions of these publications may have been included. Those definitions or artwork that have been reproduced are reprinted with the permission of the respective publisher.

Quality in America, V. Daniel Hunt. Business One Irwin, Homewood, Ill., 1992.

A Better Idea—Redefining the Way Americans Work, Donald E. Peterson. Houghton Mifflin, Boston, 1991.

AT&T Quality Improvement Process Guidebook. AT&T, Basking Ridge, N.J., 1988.

Deming Management at Work, Mary Walton. G. P. Putnam, New York, 1990.

The Deming Prize Guide—For Overseas Companies. Deming Prize Committee, Union of Japanese Scientists and Engineers (JUSE), (Revised October 1991), Tokyo, Japan.

The Deming Route to Quality and Productivity, William W. Scherkenbach. CEE Press, Washington, D.C., 1988.

1991–1992 CIRM Study Guide. American Production and Inventory Control Society, Stock No. 09015, May 1991, Falls Church, Va.

Diffusion of Innovations, Everett M. Rogers. The Free Press, New York, 1983.

Excellence in Government: Total Quality Management in the 1990s, David K. Carr and Ian D. Littman. Coopers and Lybrand, Washington, D.C., 1990.

Federal Total Quality Management Handbook. U.S. Government Printing Office, Washington, D.C., May 1991.

A Guide to Benchmarking in Xerox. NTIS Publication PB91-780106, 1990.

State-of-the-art report, *A Guide for Implementing Total Quality Management.* Reliability Analysis Center, Report SOAR-7, 1990.

Handbook of Cost Management, Barry J. Brinker. Warren, Gorham & Lamont, 1992.

In Search of Excellence, Thomas J. Peters and Robert H. Waterman, Jr. Harper and Row, New York, 1982.

An Introduction to the Continuous Improvement Process, Principles and Practices, Brian E. Mansir and Nicholas R. Schacht, Logistics Management Institute, Bethesda, Md., August 1989.

Juran on Quality by Design, J. M. Juran. The Free Press, New York, 1992.

Juran on Planning for Quality, J. M. Juran. The Free Press, New York, 1988.

Juran's Quality Control Handbook, 4th Edition, J. M. Juran, Editor-in-Chief, and Frank M. Gryna, Associate Editor, McGraw-Hill, New York, 1988.

Made in America: Regaining the Productive Edge, Michael L. Dertouzos, Richard K. Lester, and Robert M. Solow. The MIT Commission on Industrial Productivity, MIT Press, 1989.

Obtaining EC Product Approvals After 1992—What American Manufacturers Need to Know, Sarah E. Hagigh. U.S. Department of Commerce, "Business America," February 1992.

Out of the Crisis, W. Edwards Deming. MIT Center for Advanced Engineering Study, Boston, 1986.

A Passion for Excellence, Tom Peters and Nancy Austin. Random House, New York, 1985.

Quality Is Free, Philip B. Crosby. McGraw-Hill, New York, 1979.

Quality and Productivity Self-Assessment Guide for Defense Organizations. Department of Defense, Washington, D.C., 1990.

Quality Without Tears. Philip B. Crosby. New American Library, New York, 1985.

Total Quality: An Executive's Guide for the 1990s, Ernst & Young Quality Improvement Consulting Group. Business One Irwin/APICS, 1990.

Total Quality Control, Third Edition, Armand Feigenbaum. McGraw-Hill, New York, 1983.

Total Quality Management Guide, Volumes 1 and 2. Office of the Deputy Assistant Secretary of Defense for Total Quality Management, DoD 5000.51-G, February 15, 1990.

USMG Partnership: The Way We Work. Xerox, USMG Printing Office, Rochester, N.Y., 1988.

The preparation of a book of this kind is dependent on an excellent staff, and I have been fortunate in this regard. Special thanks to Ronald Fraser and Donald Keehan for research assistance of the material for this book.

I appreciate the careful and conscientious editing by Lori Ackerman. This manuscript has been prepared by James C. Foulk.

Many individuals provided material, interview comments, and their insights on improving quality in their businesses. I appreciate their input and help in defining the message of this book. Special recognition is noted for Peter Angiola, Office of the Undersecretary of Defense for Acquisition, Total Quality Management; Laurie A. Broedling, deputy undersecretary of defense for Total Quality Management; Richard Bueton, senior vice president and director of quality, Motorola Inc.; David K. Carr, partner, Coopers & Lybrand; Jeffrey M. Clark, Cadillac Motor Car Division; James C. Cline, corporate quality manager, Globe Metallurgical Inc.; Karen A. Collard, Xerox Corporation; John F. Cooney, manager, National Quality Award Office, Xerox Business Products and Systems; Mary A. Hartz, Total Quality Management section leader, IIT Research Institute; Newt Hardie, vice president, Quality, Milliken & Company; Sandi Janssen, International Business Machines Corporation; Paul A. Noakes, vice president and director, External Quality Programs, Motorola Inc. William Smith, vice president and senior quality assurance manager, Communications Sector, Motorola Inc.; Frank Voehl, vice president of QualTec; Chuck Vogel, manager, Total Quality, Westinghouse Electric Corporation, Commercial Nuclear Fuel Division; John R. West, manager, Corporate Quality Improvement, Federal Express.

CONTENTS

CHAPTER 1

GLOBAL QUALITY TODAY

QUALITY IS GOOD BUSINESS

Quality pays. Quality gets results. Quality sells. Quality increases profit. The first question business leaders ask when they evaluate whether they need to improve their quality program is, What's in it for the business?

All too often, businesses ask this question in times of crisis. Their markets are changing, global competitors have sneaked up on them, and then they are forced to change the way they do business to survive.

Consider why some business leaders improved their quality, and what they got in return.

William Smith, vice president and senior quality assurance manager at Motorola Inc., tells us, "We put Motorola's quality process in place to satisfy customers. The real payoff from our quality improvement program is that it has certainly been instrumental in helping us to increase market share, to increase sales, to increase profitability."

Globe Metallurgical Inc. also demonstrates that any firm, large or small, can develop an excellent quality program, and one that pays off. James C. Cline, corporate quality manager for Globe Metallurgical, gives this account of his company's renewed commitment to quality begun in 1984:

> That was our turning point from what we call the detection mode to the prevention mode. The benefits, we found, are both measurable and unmeasurable, and in many ways the unmeasurable ones are the most significant. We have been able to increase our market share tremendously. Before 1984 we shipped virtually no products overseas, less than a truckload a year. Today one of our biggest customers is in Europe, and we also ship to Australia, Korea, and Taiwan.

1

We have a much more stable work force because of employee satisfaction and have not laid off a single employee in seven years. Absenteeism has been virtually eliminated, and workers leaving Globe to go to work somewhere else is virtually unheard of. The climate in our company is no longer "us and them." It's not workers and management. It's just "us."

Chuck Vogel, quality manager for Westinghouse, Commercial Nuclear Fuel Division, reiterated that "total quality is people." You should not look at quality improvement as a marketing tool, but as a management tool. Lots of companies are shortsighted. They concentrate too much on near-term profits and fail to see the long-term impact of quality improvement on their global markets. Westinghouse recognized the changing global market and made quality a priority in their business.

If you don't care where your industry and your business are headed in the 1990s, if you think your quality performance cannot be improved, or if you're still in a state of "global marketplace denial," this book won't help you.

On the other hand, if you are not so sure business-as-usual is the wave of the future, read on. This book can help you. Because the 1990s are shaping up as a change-filled period full of opportunities—and risks—this book is designed to help make sure you and your firm are well positioned not only to cope in the increasingly competitive global marketplace of the 1990s, but to prosper in it.

Unlike the overly optimistic quality rhetoric of the 1980s, this down-to-earth book seeks a middle ground. It recognizes that in the 1990s business leaders must strike a balance between the quick-fix approach of the past and the fact that widespread ignorance concerning the real level of quality performance in business is still found in many parts of the manufacturing and service sectors. Improved quality is not a cure-all for all business ills, but it is an essential first step in the right direction.

A very few companies are counted among the world-class leaders in quality improvement. But thousands upon thousands of other companies have yet to take that all-important first step to ensure their products and services deliver to each customer a dependable, high level of quality. Drawing in part on the lessons learned by the early quality leaders, this book is a no-nonsense guide for the next wave of firms—some large, some small—that must adopt quality management practices in the next five to ten years if they are to survive.

QUALITY DRIVEN BY GLOBAL COMPETITION

Since World War II, the world has been "shrinking." Advances in telecommunications have linked all parts of the world electronically and, to a lesser extent, politically. Over the years a new economic infrastructure has replaced the old one. As national companies serving primarily domestic markets expanded into the international marketplace, a "global web," as Robert Reich calls it, of economic interconnectedness formed and is today a dominant economic force shaping the economic scene.

Without question, the coming decade will see a further extension of these trends and become an economic turning point for the world. During the 1980s, two significant events—in addition to the coming of age of the global economy—have set the stage for the 1990s. First, under growing pressure from foreign competition, corporations rediscovered "quality." After decades of indifference to, and neglect of, what was happening in Japan and elsewhere in the world, the global business community began its turnaround in the early 1980s when a few large corporations became convinced that good-quality products and services were their ticket to the future. By the mid-1980s, talk about quality became the "in" topic.

The end of the 40-year Cold War and the collapse of the Soviet economy in the early 1990s is the second fundamental sea change that will make the coming decade unique. With the "evil empire" dismantled and preoccupied with its own internal economic turmoil, both the United States and Europe could redirect their energies from military confrontation to worldwide commercial competition. A new Germany serving as the economic core of a unified European Community will soon become the world's third regional economic superforce. In addition to the United States and the Pacific Rim, including Japan, these three regions will dominate the international economy of the 1990s.

Manufacturing and service companies cannot afford to remain passive in the coming years. The business community will either fully integrate itself into new and evolving global markets, or large parts of it are likely to be left behind as foreign competitors absorb greater and greater shares of the only market that really matters anymore: the global market. Economic isolationism means stagnation and slow economic death. The time is ripe for virtually all businesses to adopt a new world view built on proven quality improvement practices.

FIGURE 1–1
Shift to Global Integration

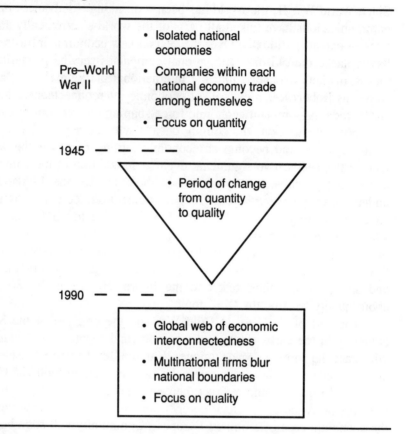

Figure 1–1 illustrates the scope of the shift to global integration and the renewed importance of quality. The message it delivers loud and clear is this: Because of these intricate global webs in which international companies are now full-fledged partners, businesses have little or no choice but to keep up with the other global competitors in the web if they want to remain competitive. *Whether* or not to adopt improved quality practices is no longer a real option for most companies. The only option, really, is *when* to shift and whether your company will do it soon enough to remain competitive.

Still, many companies have been slow to accept and adapt to the realities of a highly competitive global marketplace, and slow to regard the industrial development of competing countries as a challenge to, as well as an opportunity for, their own economic growth. Consequences of this failure to adapt are measured in terms of loss of market share, unnecessary plant closings, high unemployment, and noticeable deterioration in the quality of jobs available to workers. Most observers of this condition have long since concluded that any successful challenge to these problems requires the business community to acknowledge the erosion of the comparative advantage of its manufacturing and service industries—in such important activities as quality, technology, innovation, investment, and productivity—and then to take the needed corrective actions.

Figure 1–2 graphically shows that the number of companies in the United States that have aggressively adopted quality management practices lags far behind global competitors, such as Japan. Japanese firms, on average, have also attained a higher level of quality in their products and services.

FIGURE 1–2
Level of Quality Adoption in Japan and the United States

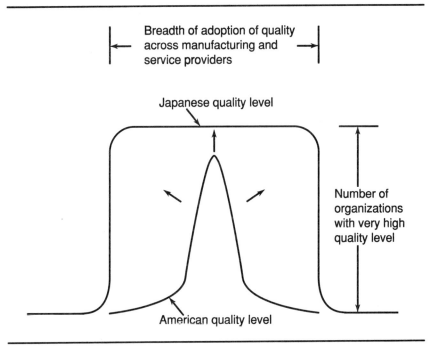

Experts all have a slightly different view of the global business in the 1990s. The common thread, however, is clear and strong: Nearly every manufacturing and service sector will be increasingly vulnerable to imports in the foreseeable future. Automation isn't the answer, for it would only quicken the production of poor-quality products. Import barriers and protection are not the answer, either. You can no longer hide from foreign competition. The only way out is through the door marked Quality.

HOW ARE YOU DOING?

Your global competitors create and produce items of high quality because it pays! Continual improvement in quality leads to reduced costs because of less rework, fewer mistakes, fewer delays, and better use of time and materials. In the United States, for example, 20 to 25 percent of production costs is spent in finding and correcting mistakes. Add the additional costs incurred in repairing or replacing faulty products in the field, and the total cost of poor quality may approach 30 percent. In Japan it is about 3 percent. The cost of ignoring quality is enormous. Businesses all too often try to achieve quality by setting acceptable quality levels and using "tailgate" inspection to measure compliance. With this passive-reactive approach, improving quality results in increased scrap and rework, and in increased costs. Your competitors do not do it that way. First, they do not subscribe to the notion of an acceptable quality level because it assumes that some defects are acceptable. Their goal is one of no defects, which is achieved through a process of continuous improvement. Second, they have adopted a proactive or preventive approach to quality. They consider quality to be an integral part of product and process design, not something that is achieved through management oversight or inspection. To achieve designed-in quality, your global competitors use systematic product and process techniques based on statistical process control analyses to identify sources of process or material variation, to decide when it is economical to reduce these sources of variation, and to ensure the product is robust in light of remaining variability. They then continue to closely monitor process performance.

World-class, quality-focused companies declare that quality is the concern and responsibility of every employee, "from the president to the janitor," and quality concerns are pervasive from product inception through customer support. Top management is directly involved in quality, as contrasted with just support quality or committing the business to it. Managers in quality-focused businesses accept responsibility for quality, direct and participate in quality education, establish quality goals, and take management action required to help realize these goals. Managers direct and participate in quality policy, conduct self-assessments, direct allocation of resources for quality efforts, and spend substantial time with workers on the projects. Quality teams provide the principle mechanism for workers to meet frequently with their colleagues on improvement projects and for periodic and frequent meetings with management, so that management can find concrete ways to help.

While global competitors believe that quality is a design and process issue, they still recognize the need for inspection as part of an overall process control strategy. The responsibility for in-process inspection and analysis is assigned primarily to individual production workers, not to quality assurance personnel. Although quality assurance personnel are staffed by such companies, their role generally is limited to participation in the concurrent design teams and to carrying out quality planning and higher-level analyses. The workers carry out the elementary statistical process control analyses to detect unacceptable process variability and in most cases are authorized to take corrective action when indicated by the analyses. Only if the worker cannot solve the problem does it get referred to a higher level.

By placing so much quality emphasis on the individual worker, your competitors generate individual pride in workmanship and quality with a resulting major gain in employee motivation. They have also achieved a closed-loop operation in which variations in process quality are determined very early and corrected at the lowest level of the organization at which such a correction can be made.

Coopers & Lybrand have developed a set of "World-Class Metrics" for manufacturing companies, as shown in Table 1–1. In terms of quality, you can see the disparity between the quality performance of American companies and of your competitors.

Closing the Competitive Gaps: The International Report of the Manufacturing Futures Project states, "Each part of the world (Europe, Japan, and America) believes that it has an advantage over its competitors in a different dimension. The Europeans believe they are ahead in product performance, the Japanese in flexibility, and the Americans (to their surprise) in price." As these competitors approach parity on the fundamentals of quality in the 1990s, performance, price, and especially flexibility will become more important elements of business strategies.

TABLE 1–1
World-Class Metrics

Attribute	World-Class Standard	U.S. Average
Setup time	System < 30 minutes Cell < 1 minute	2–4 hours
Quality	1500 PPM captured 300 PPM escapes	3–5% captured 2–5% in warranty
Cost of quality	3–5%	15–25%
Ratio of manufacturing space to total space	> 50%	25–35%
Work as a function of time	20%	1.75–5%
Material velocity	> 100 turns	2–4 turns
Material residence time	3 days	3 months
Flexibility	270 parts/machine tool	25 parts/machine tool
Distance	300 feet	> 1 mile
Uptime	95%	65–75%

Source: Ronald R. Barris, national director of industrial automation, Coopers & Lybrand.

Global competitors have made significant changes in their strategic plans over the past decade. European and American manufacturers have improved their manufacturing capabilities in order to hold or attempt to regain a viable market-share position depending on type of products. Their strategy often has been based on a return to the fundamentals of effective product and process development integration, with a special focus on quality improvement and organizational restructuring. In contrast, the Japanese, feeling confident that they produce the best-quality products in the world, have emphasized flexibility through the use of automation (CAD, robots, CIM) and price reduction of their products.

Table 1–2 lists, in rank order of importance, programs that companies in Japan, Europe, and the United States stress as their near-term priorities. The Europeans and Americans are focused on quality improvement programs such as statistical process control, zero defects, and supplier quality enhancement efforts. The Japanese appear to be aggressively advancing their lead in flexible production by their emphasis on computer-aided flexible systems (CAD, CAM, CIM), and creating new production processes for new products.

TABLE 1-2
Enhancement Priorities in Japan, Europe, and the United States

Japan	Europe	United States
Lead time reduction	Zero defects	Supplier quality
Computer-aided design	New product information	Statistical process control
Value analysis	Supplier quality	Systems integration
New process/product development	Systems integration	Lead time reduction
Systems Integration	Team motivation	Worker safety
New product introduction	Lead time reduction	Zero defects
Job enlargement	Supervisor training	Defining strategy
Supplier lead time reductions	Just-in-time	Supervisor training
FMS/CIM/EIS	Statistical quality control*	New product introduction

*Flexible Manufacturing Systems, Computer Integrated Manufacturing, Enterprise Integration Systems

Source: Reproduced with permission of Manufacturing Roundtable, Boston University.

NO QUICK FIX

What to do? The key to competitiveness in the 1990s is to avoid emulating one nation's approach: Keep an honest set of business priorities firmly fixed in your minds, and allow them to guide your actions. You should not be drawn into playing another nation's game.

Perhaps the most daunting part of the challenge facing the business community is the nature of the change that is required in the years ahead. If the problem were just slow production, we could design faster machines. If the problem were simply one of poorly trained workers, we could redesign the education system to accommodate the needs of the modern worker. As we will see in the pages that follow, businesses are facing the prospect of massive changes in the basic culture that directs how we do business.

Unlike mechanical fixes, cultural change takes time and hard work. When it comes to building quality into a company where it does not now exist, there simply is no quick fix. Interviews with business leaders have repeatedly confirmed how difficult it is for a company to shift from a culture that condones poor quality to one that insists on high-quality processes, products, and services. Many firms simply don't have sufficient energy and leadership to make the change, and for them the future is bleak. Change may be difficult, but what's the alternative? In the 1990s, as we shall demonstrate repeatedly in this book, the quick-fix mentality is the problem, not the cure.

When confronting a new crisis or problem, individuals and organizations characteristically react in a similar way: They deny that a problem exists. The denial period may last a brief moment or it may never end. Nonetheless, until the individual or organization overcomes this initial stage in the problem-solving process and faces reality, the crisis will remain unsolved. Those firms entering the 1990s with a business-as-usual attitude are unwilling to acknowledge reality and are stuck—for a moment or forever—in denial. Until they get over or go around this barrier, they are setting themselves up for failure in the coming years.

TOTAL QUALITY MANAGEMENT

The concept of Total Quality Management is used in this book as a shorthand way of stressing two fundamental tenets: First, quality must become the company's *number one* business strategy priority. Quality is not a sprint; it is a long-distance event that takes top management attention and persistence, and lots of it. If you have world-class quality products, services and people, you will also generate world-class profits. Second, a company's quality program must address its own unique needs. Off-the-shelf, canned, "just add water" quality solutions cannot generate the level of human commitment within the organization needed to succeed. In fact, you may substitute your company's quality initiative name in place of the term *Total Quality Management* when thinking about the concepts presented in this book.

Total Quality Management is both a philosophy and a set of guiding concepts, principles, and practices that represent the foundation of a continuously improving organization. It applies human resources and quantitative methods for improving the materials and services supplied to your company, for improving all of the processes within your company, and for improving your company's ability to meet the needs of the customer now and in the future. It integrates fundamental management techniques, existing improvement efforts, and technical tools in a disciplined, focused, and continuous improvement process.

Total Quality Management addresses the quality of management as well as the management of quality. It involves everyone in an organization in a systematic, long-term endeavor to develop processes that are customer-oriented, flexible and responsive, and constantly improving in quality. Quality includes all aspects of every product or service of value to a customer. Ultimately, Total Quality Management is a means through which an organization creates and sustains a culture committed to continuous improvement.

Thousands of American firms are still employing the tools, management techniques, and paradigms of the machine age as we begin to deal with the problems and complexities of the 21st century. The management methods that still predominate are based on the theories of F. Taylor, B. F. Skinner, and other pioneers of scientific management. Those approaches were reductionist in nature and were patterned on the very machines that shaped the age. They were appropriate for their time, but they are excess baggage today.

Russell Ackoff illustrates the point with this example: Suppose you were to acquire all the makes of automobiles produced in the world and then systematically select from the set the best carburetor, transmission, brakes, and so forth. When you attempt to assemble the world's best possible automobile from the collection of the best parts, you would not even be able to produce an automobile, because the parts would not fit together. The performance of the whole—its quality—is not the sum of the performance of the parts; it is a consequence of the relationship between the performance of the parts.

Under Total Quality Management, your organization will deliberately seek to create a positive and dynamic working environment, foster teamwork, apply quantitative methods and analytical techniques, and tap the creativity and ingenuity of all of your people. You will focus on collective efforts to better understand and meet internal and external customer needs and to continuously increase customer satisfaction.

The Total Quality Management philosophy provides a comprehensive way to improve total organization performance and quality by examining each process through which work gets done in a systematic, integrated, consistent, organization-wide manner. It includes understanding the concept of variation and its implications for process improvement. Total Quality Management addresses all forms of work and applies equally to every person in the organization, including top management, marketers, service providers, designers, production workers, white-collar workers, and laborers.

Whoever we are in an organization, we can easily fall into the trap of thinking that our company is too big to be affected by our individual actions. That perception is common and frustrating, and fortunately, it is a false one. Only through the collective efforts of their individual members do companies change; companies are incapable of changing themselves.

Whatever your position in your company, your efforts to perform a job and to improve that performance directly affect the influence you will have in the company, the control you will have over your personal situation, and your ability to manage and lead. Combined with the efforts of others, your effectiveness directly influences the company's overall ability to meet its mission and ultimately affects our performance as a nation. Furthermore, how we perform today will also affect future generations.

Total Quality Management is a means for improving personal effectiveness and performance and for aligning and focusing all individual efforts throughout an organization. It provides a framework within which you may continuously improve everything you do and affect. It is a way of leveraging your individual effort and extending its effect and its importance throughout an organization and beyond.

Total Quality Management is not a destination but a journey toward improvement. This book will help you get started on that journey. It will help you understand not only the benefits of continuous improvement and your role and responsibilities in leading the improvement effort in your company, but why continuous improvement is important to each of us. This book will serve as a frame of reference for the ongoing dialogue about Total Quality Management, and it will help you set the direction for your own path to improvement. As you read these words, your journey has begun.

If you care about where industry in general—and your company in particular—are headed in the 1990s, now is the time to act. Companies that procrastinate and delay taking the first step toward the Total Quality Management concept, or stay in a state of denial too long, risk failure in the competitive years ahead.

The choice is yours. You can pick a smooth, planned transition to your competitive future, or you can wait for the coming crisis to force your company into the quality arena. It's in your hands. Read on!

CHAPTER 2

RESOURCE INTEGRATION: THE ENDURING CHALLENGE

THE CHALLENGE

During the age of the craftsman, the period when virtually all goods and services were the product of a lone individual, the problem of how to best integrate complex human activities in large organizations was simply unknown. Each craftsman personally possessed all of the skills and knowledge needed to produce a product or service. With the arrival of the industrial revolution and the rise of large manufacturing organizations, however, the craftsman was largely pushed aside and replaced with specialists who could perform more efficiently a limited number of steps in the total manufacturing process.

Because specialists, by definition, deal with only a small slice of a larger whole, the need to reunite—or *integrate*—the activities and outputs of many individual specialists into a complete product or service became an enduring challenge for 20th-century manufacturers. During most of this century the favored method of integration has been one form of standardization or another. Over the years managers have tried to solve their integration challenges in many ways, including standardization of work, standardization of skills, and standardization of output. Only when standardization began to lose its ability to satisfy customer needs and had to compete with a new, post–World War II form of integration pioneered in Japan did manufacturing managers begin to seriously search for better resource-integration tools.

RESOURCE INTEGRATION AND
TOTAL QUALITY MANAGEMENT

The American Production and Inventory Control Society's (APICS) Integrated Resource Management (IRM) certification program is an inevitable link in this long chain of historical events. Its appearance in the early 1990s is hardly accidental, but instead in harmony with the flow of developments. While the need for an IRM certification program was probably not yet fully recognized in the United States in 1980, by 1990 the introduction of Total Quality Management (TQM) practices in a significant number of American firms created a pressing demand for better integration methods. My own estimates are that early in the 21st century, quality management will have become the dominant resource-integration method and the accepted way of doing business for firms around the world. We are now in a transition period in which old integration methods are being replaced by new ones.

Quality management evolved, largely unnoticed, from simply a novel industrial engineering concept to full fruition during the industrial redevelopment of post–World War II Japan. But following its introduction into the United States in the early 1980s and its adoption among innovative firms in the middle to late 1980s, interest in Total Quality Management grew rapidly.

In addition, because Total Quality Management calls for the introduction of innovative approaches for the involvement of workers in the operation of industrial enterprises, the demand for training in new, Total Quality Management–related management skills also will continue to rise during the coming decade. As corporate leaders in the 1980s began to sense the true magnitude of the shift in management techniques being ushered in with the rise of quality management, they began looking for ways to tailor broad quality management concepts to the particular needs of their firms. In this respect the IRM certification program is the natural result of the long evolutionary development of management thought, and serves to link past managerial practices with those of the future.

On a more sober note, the IRM program may well be *the* means for many industrial firms to both survive and prosper in a change-filled future environment. In the years to come, firms will either adopt Total Quality Management–based integration techniques, or, in all likelihood, they will fade away under pressures from competitors at home and abroad.

WHAT IS TOTAL QUALITY MANAGEMENT?

Total Quality Management is not a minor refinement of past managerial practices: What sets Total Quality Management apart from other approaches to management is a genuinely new perspective of how to best combine the resources that make up an organization. Total Quality Management involves a unique set of organizing principles, a new role for top management and workers alike, and an array of practices and techniques designed to implement these organizing principles. In other words, Total Quality Management is both a comprehensive managerial philosophy and a tool kit for its implementation.

Some feel that Total Quality Management is a radical departure from traditional management practices because of its analytic focus on statistical process control and work-flow processes rather than on function or product. Others question its insistence that the customer, not the marketing department or the R & D department, is best equipped to define quality.

Still other critics worry about the new roles assigned to the "empowered" worker in a Total Quality Management organization. Because workers and processes are the basic sources from which quality flows, every worker in a Total Quality Management firm, from president to custodian, and every process, from the handling of invoices to processing customer complaints, has one central and common purpose: to improve the quality of the firm's products and services to best satisfy the customer.

According to the Federal Quality Institute:

> In a Total Quality Management context, the standard for determining quality is meeting customer requirements and expectations the first time and every time. There are many potential requirements and expectations that customers have, depending upon the particular product or service and needs of the customer. Rather than the organization attempting to specify what it views as quality, a Total Quality Management approach to quality systematically inquires of its customers what they want, and strives to meet, and even exceed, those requirements. Such an approach helps to identify the elements of quality that are of paramount importance to customers. It also recognizes that customers' expectations may change over time.
>
> Total Quality Management is a strategic, integrated management system for achieving customer satisfaction. It involves all managers and employees and uses quantitative methods to improve continuously an organization's

processes. It is not an efficiency ("cost cutting") program, a morale-boosting scheme or a project that can be delegated to operational managers and staff specialists. Paying lip service to quality improvements, by merely using quality slogans to exhort workers, is equally dangerous.

At the foundation of Total Quality Management are three principles of action: to focus on achieving customer satisfactions, to seek continuous improvement, and to encourage full involvement of the entire work force.

In a Total Quality Management context, the standard for determining quality is meeting customer requirements and expectations the first time and every time. There are many potential requirements and expectations that customers have, depending upon the particular product or service and needs of the customer.

To illustrate how customers' quality expectations may vary, consider two automobiles: a four-wheel-drive vehicle, such as a Jeep Cherokee, and a luxury four-door sedan, such as a Cadillac. Which is of higher quality? If you want a vehicle for use on camping and fishing trips or to fight the snow in the Northeast, you might prefer the Cherokee. If, on the other hand, you want the vehicle for touring on the highway or to impress your business clients, the Cadillac might be considered of higher quality.

The basic Total Quality Management message sent to managers in all product and service lines is this: To remain responsive to changing customer demands, the organization itself must be ready and able to both detect the need for change, *and* to maintain the ability to quickly make the needed changes to continue to satisfy the customer.

The Federal Quality Institute's description of Total Quality Management is particularly useful for our purposes because it represents a general point of view and one that is not specifically aimed at a particular industrial sector. On the other hand, APICS is specifically concerned with how Total Quality Management can best be applied in manufacturing firms. By APICS's definition, Total Quality Management supports the roles of the quality department and other employees charged with ensuring quality. There is growing worldwide recognition of how critical quality management is to the success of a product and the company that produces and markets the product. This recognition is accompanied by a greater role for the quality organization and increased involvement in quality issues at all levels of management. APICS addresses quality management from this broader, more proactive and more integrated perspective.

The process of Total Quality Management begins with the determination of customer requirements. From these requirements, evaluations can be made on the methods and processes that are proposed for manufacturing the product. The requirements also are used to determine appropriate measurements and tests as well as the specific ranges of data values to be verified. Finally, these requirements are used to evaluate the product's performance and serviceability in the field.

Total Quality Management starts with the product concept and spans the entire product life. Significant shifts in the way that quality is being managed are evident in organizations that are striving to be world-class competitors. There is an emphasis on the generic issues of design for producibility and process control, rather than on inspecting specific items. Statistical tools can be used to identify and reduce process variability and avoid defects. And high quality is recognized as a strategic advantage. All of these shifts reflect the fact that Total Quality Management is a key requirement for companies to survive in the future and to compete worldwide.[1]

TOTAL QUALITY MANAGEMENT OPERATING PRACTICES

To define Total Quality Management is one thing; to implement it is another. As we shall see, quality management is far more than tinkering with an organization's structure.

At the single-firm level, quality management is often compared to the adoption of a new work culture or philosophy. Shifting from a traditional, functional view of a business enterprise to one based on work-flow processes is not an easy task—and the transition will take years in most cases. For this reason, Total Quality Management's guiding principles emphasize:

- A constancy of purpose among the organization's leadership.
- A long-term, never-ending commitment to higher quality.
- The development of a single, integrated, systems view of the organization.
- The involvement of every worker—from top to bottom—in the quest for quality.
- A focus on work processes.

---

[1]1991–1992 CIRM Study Guide (Falls Church, Va.: American Production and Control Society), May 1991, Stock No. 09015, p. 36.

These principles are important because they give a clearly stated, unifying meaning to the entire organization—its workers, suppliers, and customers. They are met by integrating seven key operating practices:

- Demonstrating personal leadership of Total Quality Management by top management.
- Strategically planning the short- and long-term implementation of Total Quality Management throughout the organization.
- Ensuring that everyone focuses on customers' needs and expectations.
- Developing clearly defined measures for tracking progress and identifying improvement opportunities.
- Providing adequate resources for training and recognition to enable workers to carry the mission forward and reinforce positive behavior.
- Empowering workers to make decisions and fostering teamwork.
- Developing systems to assure that quality is built-in at the beginning and throughout operations.

Put another way, the essence of Total Quality Management is involving and empowering the entire work force in the continuous improvement of the quality of goods and services that satisfy, and even delight, the customer. To achieve this goal, organizations must identify customers and their needs, have a clear idea of how to go about meeting expectations, and make sure that everyone in the organization understands the customers' needs and is empowered to act on their behalf.

As stated earlier, there are few quick fixes for improving quality. Experience shows that it takes years to create a new environment, or "culture," that places a premium on excellence. Building structures that will sustain and manage change, and an education system that will support the expanded role for workers, is a time-consuming process.

Top Management Leadership and Support

The primary and perhaps single most critical element in the Total Quality Management equation is the role of top management leadership and support. Top business managers must be directly and actively involved in establishing a new environment that encourages change, innovation, risk taking, pride in work, and continuous improvement on behalf of all customers. These top-level leaders set the tone, determine the theme, and provide the impetus for action throughout the organization. They assert a clear vision of what the organization can achieve, and they communicate the quality policies and goals throughout the organization.

Total Quality Management–style strategic business planning becomes a cross-functional process and the responsibility of a team of senior managers. Strategic planning drives the organization's continuous process improvement efforts and helps to identify which processes will be targeted for improvement. In this way, quality improvements are integrated into the strategic business planning process so that planning and action become a part of the day-to-day management of the firm.

During the early stages of the quality planning process, all employees—including union leadership, where applicable—must be an integral part of the transition to Total Quality Management. The Total Quality Management leader will empower workers on the line to make decisions. Leaders will shift their efforts from directing and controlling how the operations will be carried out to identifying and removing barriers that prevent employees from meeting customer requirements and expectations. They lead the fundamental cultural change in the organization from crisis management to continuous improvement.

In a Total Quality Management organization, worker "empowerment" means that the supervisory and control responsibilities, which are commonly reserved for senior managers in traditionally organized firms, are entrusted to cross-functional teams of workers that, on a day-to-day basis, transform inputs into outputs. Top leaders empower workers by giving each process team the freedom to set goals and the tools to achieve them. Ideally, the inspection department will no longer be needed in a Total Quality Management plant because each worker will be committed to doing his or her job right the first time.

Focus on the Customer

High-performance organizations seek not only to meet customer expectations, but also to go the extra mile and delight both their internal and external customers. Actively involving customers in the improvement process and finding out exactly what they want is central to a quality management effort. A strategy based solely on an organization's internal perception of its customers' needs is not likely to accurately measure what customers really want or what they think of current services and products. Only the customers know, and their expectations are likely to change over time.

Depending on its special needs, each organization should have a wide range of methods for obtaining and assessing customer feedback, including customer surveys, in-depth interviews of groups of customers, follow-up of customer complaints, collection of customer feedback at the time of service delivery, and third-party analysis of customer feedback. Customers should have easy access to the organization for obtaining information and resolution of their problems. Quality-focused organizations adopt a service orientation as the primary means of achieving their mission.

Teamwork and Employee Empowerment

Once top management has made the long-term commitment to Total Quality Management, the most important and critical ingredient to achieving a quality commitment throughout an organization is employee involvement, empowerment, training, and teamwork. Improving work processes can be successful only when all people in the organization, top to bottom and horizontally across functions, are involved in making the changes. When the intelligence, imagination, and energies of the entire work force are engaged in the pursuit of the organization's goals, lasting results can be realized. People closest to the problems usually have the best information sources and solutions.

The idea of employee involvement and empowerment is not unique to Total Quality Management. Indeed, many management practitioners claim to support the idea. Efforts often fall short not because of the absence of good intentions on the part of managers or employees, but because managers have not adopted specific systems and procedures to make employee involvement a routine part of the new way of doing business.

The first step in achieving employee empowerment is to involve employees in the systematic identification of and solution to problems, through teams of employees working on specific process or operating issues, cross-functional problem-solving teams, and self-managing teams. The key is that employees be empowered to make real and lasting changes.

Employee involvement in quality improvement teams must be supported and reinforced by building into the organization's management system explicit recognition and support for the team concept. Management councils and other management bodies must be established and take responsibility for approving employee teams at the outset, assigning resources to let the teams perform their mission, and perhaps most importantly, authorizing changes in overall systems and policies necessary to implement the solutions.

Employees are an almost unlimited source of knowledge and creativity that can be used not only to solve problems, but to continuously improve the quality of the products and services they produce.

Continuous Process Improvement

One of Total Quality Management's overall implementing methodologies is continuous process improvement. Each process team is constantly trying to improve the performance of the work process—from input from the supplier to output to the customer. The tools used in this never-ending quest for improvement are simple, yet effective.

In order to ensure that processes are continuously improved, statistical data should be collected and analyzed on an ongoing basis, with particular attention to variations in work processes. The causes behind these variations are important, because different strategies are applied to sporadic variations than to chronic variations that signal deeply seated problems in a process.

Statistical control methods are used to reduce rework, waste, and cycle time, and to measure the extent to which the firm is satisfying its customers' demands.

Commitment to Training and Recognition

Often the key element that is missing in efforts to improve work-flow processes is the training that will enable empowered teams of employees to do their jobs. Classroom and on-the-job training ensures that employees are adequately equipped with the skills to perform their work, and includes training in quality management concepts and skills such as teamwork, problem solving, and methods for collecting and analyzing data using basic statistical tools.

Employees who make contributions to quality improvement should be recognized and rewarded in ways that are meaningful and timely. Reinforcing positive performance is a key ingredient for developing service excellence. An organization that claims to be focused on quality but, in fact, measures and rewards other things sends conflicting messages to its employees.

Measurement and Analysis

Many managers depend on intuition and seat-of-the-pants judgments to solve problems. In a Total Quality Management organization, however, decisions must be based on hard data whenever possible. Statistical process control systems are crucial, and must be put in place to allow each process improvement team in the organization to systematically measure the degree to which it is achieving its quality goals and the degree to which its output satisfies their customers' expectations. Judgment is best replaced with objective data.

Data should be collected on a wide selection of customer satisfaction factors such as responsiveness, reliability, accuracy, and so forth. Measurement systems also should focus on internal processes, especially on key processes that generate variation in quality and cycle time.

Quality Assurance

In order to meet customer quality requirements, the work processes used to produce products and services must be designed to prevent problems and errors from occurring in the first place. Quality assurance in a Total Quality Management environment focuses on the front end of each process—its inputs—rather than on the traditional method of inspecting and checking products at the end of operations, after errors are made. Processes are designed both to prevent errors and to detect and correct them as they occur throughout the process. As part of the emphasis on prevention and early detection, employees are trained to analyze incoming supplies. Suppliers are asked to assess and improve their processes to make sure that their incoming products or services are error-free. Successful Total Quality Management organizations establish a partnership with both suppliers and customers to assure continuous improvement in the quality of the end products and services.

HISTORICAL CONTEXT OF TOTAL QUALITY MANAGEMENT

Traditional mass production methods worked reasonably well for the United States for many decades. U.S. industrial power was built on a unique combination of natural resources, advanced technology, a productive labor supply, and a favorable political and economic climate. Americans produced goods and services efficiently, in large volumes, and at levels of quality unmatched in the world.

All of that began to change in the 1950s. Japanese industrialists asked several Americans to help them convert their war-devastated industries in an effort to serve their growing domestic consumption needs and to develop a strong export market by improving the poor-quality image then associated with Japanese products.

Ironically, W. Edwards Deming was the first American to have a major impact on Japanese industries. During World War II Deming worked with war production industries where he refined his statistical quality control methods. But after the war, the United States lost interest in quality management.

Through a series of lectures given in the 1950s to members of the Japanese Union of Scientists and Engineers, Deming convinced Japanese business leaders of the critical importance of statistical techniques for controlling work processes and for improving product quality. For the next 40 years he remained a driving force in the Japanese industrial revolution.

Joseph Juran also was invited to advise top- and mid-level Japanese executives. He emphasized the broad management aspects of quality and focused on planning, organizational issues, management's responsibility for quality, and the need to set goals and targets for improvement.

Other Americans, including Philip B. Crosby and Armand V. Feigenbaum, made important early contributions. These individuals stressed the importance of top management in establishing a favorable organizational climate and the role of technical systems for assuring that quality is *the* primary mission of the organization.

The results of the quality movement in Japan are now well known. Japanese products, such as automobiles, advanced electronics, electric appliances, air conditioners, toys, and so forth, are now widely recognized for their high quality, as shown in Table 2–1. As a consequence, many markets once dominated by the United States have been taken over by Japanese enterprises. For example:

- Since 1960, the United States has lost 40 percent of its market share to foreign competitors; during the same period, Japan has increased the size of its foreign market by 500 percent.
- The nine largest banks in the world are now Japanese.

TABLE 2-1
U.S. Competitiveness Relative to Japan and Europe

A	Pharmaceuticals
A	Forest products
B+	Aerospace
B	Chemical manufacturing
B	Food
B	Scientific and photographic equipment
B	Petroleum refining
B-	Telecommunications equipment
C+	Computers
C	Industrial and farm equipment
C	Motor vehicles
C-	Metals
D	Electronics

Source: *Fortune,* March 1992.

- The two largest companies in the world are Japanese; 50 of the world's 100 largest companies are now Japanese.
- The United States used to make 90 percent of the color television sets in the world. We now make 5 percent.
- There are no American-made VCRs, compact disc players, or single-lens reflex cameras.

Once American managers and firms made a commitment to Total Quality Management, they too have shown a remarkable ability to regain lost ground. A major impetus for the U.S. response is the same that initially led the Japanese to embark on their quality effort: survival in the world marketplace. By the middle to late 1970s, major companies such as Westinghouse, Ford Motor Company, Xerox, Motorola, and Corning had lost significant market share. Some were concerned about their very survival. Before it began to implement Total Quality Management, Xerox Corporation was in imminent danger of going out of business, according to its former CEO David Kearns. Xerox had lost 65 percent of its copy machine market share to its Japanese competitors. The Xerox response was to launch an all-out effort to improve quality in its Business Products and Systems Division, guided by the Total Quality Management principles described above. Xerox determined customer needs and requirements through extensive data-collection efforts. New products and services were based on detailed analyses of data. A key element of Total

Quality Management at Xerox is benchmarking. In all key areas of product, service, and business performance, the company compares itself with the performance levels achieved by world leaders, regardless of industry. The result: Xerox has now regained the market share it had lost and can once again claim the title of "the industry's best" in most copier markets.

THE GLOBAL CHALLENGE

The so-called global challenge is composed of two fundamental parts. First, the U.S. economy is no longer a self-contained market in which goods and services are produced by Americans for consumption by Americans. Today more than ever, the U.S. economy is integrated into a worldwide economy, and a significant portion of the U.S. gross national product is composed of foreign transactions. This means that American firms increasingly must compete not just with other American firms, but with firms around the world that produce similar products. Second, this global challenge is particularly identified with the rise of Japan as a world-class competitor. And much of Japan's success is directly linked to their early development and refinement of Total Quality Management practices. But Japanese workers don't work harder than Americans; they simply learned how to work smarter.

In order for American firms to deal successfully with the global challenge, we must abandon outdated managerial techniques and adopt new ways of manufacturing American products. We need not copy the Japanese experience, but we must carefully adopt for American use many of the quality-based management practices adopted by Japan. Just as mass production management techniques replaced cottage craft industries, Total Quality Management techniques are now replacing mass production manufacturing methods, which until recently dominated manufacturing processes.

THE TRANSITION TO TOTAL QUALITY MANAGEMENT

The following three-phase description of the transition from a functionally integrated organization to a Total Quality Management integrated organization will provide the reader a snapshot of where the Total Quality Management journey is headed. While a bit oversimplified, this encapsulated view of Total Quality Management will supply a framework around which the remainder of this book will be built.

Functional Integration

Figure 2–1 is a graphic representation of a functionally designed, hierarchical organization. Each box represents separate functions or departments—such as accounting, engineering, or operations—found in most organizations. Functions and departments are linked vertically in a formal hierarchy. Each department or function has been assigned the responsibility to perform one or more activities—for example, pay invoices, draft product specification, build and ship light bulbs, and so on. As required, departments and functions build horizontal relationships with one another, depending on work-flow patterns.

Each functional subunit naturally develops its own view of the world, its own standard way of doing its work, and a minimum level of interaction with other functional departments. In other words, over time, each department or function tends to build bureaucratic barriers between

FIGURE 2–1
Functional Business Organization

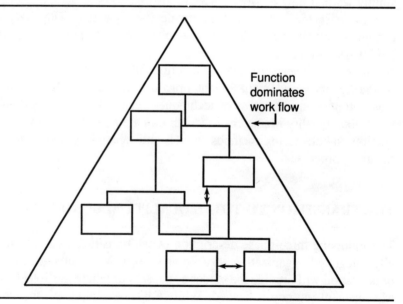

itself and the rest of the organization. Special committees often are formed to temporarily break through a barrier, and other coordination mechanisms are regularly put into place to maintain a minimum level of interdepartmental communication and cooperation.

In most functionally oriented organizations, the net effect of this organizational structure is that work units not only become isolated from one another, but, even more debilitating, the organization becomes isolated from and less responsive to its customers.

The Organization in Transition

In its evolution from a functionally designed organization to a Total Quality Management–oriented organization, three basic changes must take place: (1) Process must replace function as the fundamental unit of analysis, (2) workers must shift their loyalty from functional departments to process-focused (cross-function) teams, and (3) responsiveness to customer needs and quality must replace responsiveness to department and functional rules.

As these changes take place, bureaucratic barriers begin to disappear and the energies of individuals and teams of workers are refocused on the work processes over which they have control (see Figure 2–2). Supplier-customer linkages are also clarified and strengthened.

Total Quality Management Integration

Just as the functionally organized firm contains many functions and departments, the quality-organized firm is made up of a number of different processes, each with an input and an output. Some processes may be large and complex, others small and simple. Yet in each process, the workers must be sensitive to the quality of the inputs they receive from their suppliers, and to the quality of the outputs they deliver to their customers. Workers are responsible, as individuals and as members of a process improvement team, for making sure their efforts convert each unit of input into a customer-satisfying unit of output—every time and on the first try.

In Figure 2–3, the accent is no longer on organizational departments, nor on the skills and expertise associated with a particular functional bureau in the organization. Rather, in the Total Quality Management–integrated business, customer-satisfying, input-output transformation processes are what really matter.

FIGURE 2–2
Interdepartmental Integration

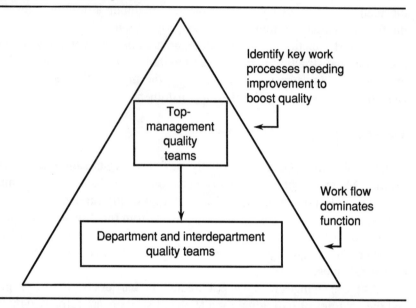

THE SOLUTION: BETTER RESOURCE INTEGRATION

All change, whether at the individual or organizational level, requires first a recognition of the need to abandon old ways of doing business for new ones, and second, a step-by-step plan for actually putting the new design into place. While both parts are equally important, the second part of the change process—its implementation—is often the more difficult of the two because it means substituting unfamiliar practices for familiar practices, which can be daunting. For this reason, an understanding of where Total Quality Management is likely to take your organization is needed up-front. The following snapshot of how a functionally organized firm differs from a quality-organized firm—and the transition between the two—will help you appreciate the scope of the implementation program needed to get from where your firm is today to Total Quality Management tomorrow.

The Starting Point

Most manufacturing firms today are still organized along functional lines and depend on managerial techniques developed and popularized during

FIGURE 2–3
Cross-Functional Total Quality Management Process

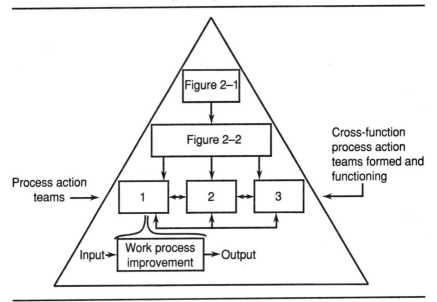

the era of mass production. Mass production techniques are ideally suited as a means to lower the unit costs of rather standard products that typically enjoy relatively long design and product-life cycles. Long design and product-life cycles afforded ample time for the relationships among the functional parts of an organization's management process to carefully and slowly evolve. Once worked out, these relationships remained stable for long periods and were routinized and reinforced with habitual use and standard operating procedures.

In the new, global marketplace, however, the organizational stability that permitted these mass production techniques to flourish is no longer commonplace. Today's customer demands change rapidly, product-life cycles are getting shorter all the time, and product runs are becoming smaller.

Consequently, manufacturing firms must purposefully build more flexibility into their managerial and operating processes. Like its products, a firm's work force also must be more responsive than ever to constantly changing environments both inside and outside of the organization.

In response to this new reality, APICS's IRM certification program has established as its objective "to develop multifaceted persons" who

(1) can work effectively in teams across functional areas, (2) have the knowledge to cut across functional management areas, (3) can influence and manage change in the organization, and (4) will positively affect the management of an organization and position it for continuous success. Such a multifaceted manager is ideally suited to play a key role in an organization's transition to quality management and in its ongoing quest to remain a quality leader.

CHAPTER 3

A BUSINESS EXECUTIVE'S
GUIDE TO QUALITY

WHAT IS QUALITY?

Why All the Fuss about Quality?

After the United States rediscovered quality in the 1980s, suddenly the word quality seemed to appear everywhere—here as an adjective, there a noun. Parents were expected to spend quality time with their children, kids were going to receive high-quality educations, and everyone was concerned about the declining quality of life in the United States. In the business community, Management By Objectives was out. Total Quality Control and Total Quality Management were suddenly in. Even President Bush got into the act, declaring that if American business was to be a world-class player, it would have to "look at quality first."

The purpose of this chapter is threefold. First, it will acquaint you with the language and key concepts of Total Quality Management. Second, it will serve as a primer, raising your awareness of quality to a level sufficient to ensure you will benefit fully from the remainder of the book. Finally, it is hoped this chapter will develop in you a personal desire to assume a leadership role in your company's Total Quality Management efforts.

Definitions Galore

Table 3–1 is a good place to start our search for the meaning of quality. Notice that business people do not have a monopoly on the term. The quotations from Robert Pirsig, a novelist, and Barbara Tuchman, a his-

TABLE 3–1
Definitions of Quality

1. Customer-based

    "Quality is fitness for use."

    J. M. Juran

    "Total Quality is performance leadership in meeting customer requirements by doing the right things right the first time."

    Westinghouse

    "Quality is meeting customer expectations. The Quality Improvement Process is a set of principles, policies, support structures, and practices designed to continually improve the efficiency and effectiveness of our way of life."

    AT & T

2. Manufacturing-based

    "Quality [means] conformance to requirements."

    Philip B. Crosby

    "Quality is the degree to which a specific product conforms to a design or specification."

    Harold L. Gilmore

3. Product-based

    "Difference in quality amount to differences in the quantity of some desired ingredient or attribute."

    Lawrence Abbott

    "Quality refers to the amount of the unpriced attribute contained in each unit of the priced attribute."

    Keith B. Leffler

4. Value-based

    "Quality is the degree of excellence at an acceptable price and the control of variability at an acceptable cost."

    Robert A. Broh

    "Quality means best for certain customer conditions. These conditions are (a) the actual use and (b) the selling price of the product."

    Armand V. Feigenbaum

5. Transcendent

    "Quality is neither mind nor matter, but a third entity independent of the other two . . . even though Quality cannot be defined, you know what it is."

    Robert Pirsig

    ". . . a condition of excellence implying fine quality as distinct from poor quality. . . . Quality is achieving or reaching the highest standard as against being satisfied with the sloppy or fraudulent."

    Barbara W. Tuchman

torian, indicate how far the quality idea has infiltrated into other parts of society. The so-called quality movement in the United States has become a society-wide issue.

The table also shows how broadly and subtly the term is being defined within the business community. Quality is not just a product-based term or a service-based term or a manufacturing-based term. As you read over this array of definitions, ask yourself this question: Is quality resident only in a firm's product or service, or is quality also found in the process that produces the product or service?

The answer to this question will bring you to a new level of awareness concerning the real meaning of quality, and to the realization that quality *is* actually present in, or missing from, every aspect of a firm's operation from top to bottom and side to side. And remember, there is no one "right" definition of quality. The definition adopted by your firm will be right only if it fits the firm's unique managerial conditions and competitive requirements.

For the Total Quality Management concept we define *quality* as the extent to which products and services produced conform to customer requirements. Customers can be internal as well as external to the organizational system (e.g., products or services may flow to the person at the next desk or work area rather than to people outside of the immediate organization).

The days of limiting the definition of quality to the "soundness" of the product—its hardness or durability, for example—are gone. The new kind of quality American firms rediscovered in the 1980s is far more cultural than physical, far more the way things are done than the nature of the things themselves.

THE LANGUAGE OF QUALITY

Like any other field of study, Total Quality Management brings with it a new set of ideas and a new vocabulary to express these ideas. But be careful. While the quality management literature is full of familiar-sounding business terms, many take on a somewhat different meaning when used in a Total Quality Management context. The language of quality vocabulary includes the following terms:

Process. The familiar definition of process is simply an agreed-upon set of steps. But in the Total Quality Management context, *process* also means "the logical way things are done" in an organization. Total Quality Management is based on a "continuous process improvement" approach, meaning it is a never-ending, cyclical search for ways to do things better.

Customer. In traditional management lore, attention is usually given only to the external customers. In Total Quality Management, however, a second, equally important customer is the internal customer— the end user of a firm's product or service located inside the firm.

Patrick Townsend, in his book *Commit to Quality,* provides a simple model that splits quality into two halves. In Table 3–2, "quality in fact" represents the view of quality from the perspective of a supplier, while "quality in perception" is how a customer looks at quality. A firm is located between its suppliers and its customers, and if the company is to serve as a world-class organization linking the two, it must also adopt a quality-focused—a Total Quality Management—approach as its principal business objective.

But this seemingly simple supplier-customer model is complicated by the fact that the company is *both* a customer of its suppliers (internal and external) and a supplier to its customers (both internal and external). A Total Quality Management approach is the means for bringing the views of the suppliers and the views of the customers into harmony with each other. In graphic form, this relationship of the company to its many suppliers and customers is shown in Figure 3–1.

TABLE 3–2
Quality: Fact and Perception

Quality in fact
    Doing the right thing
    Doing it the right way
    Doing it right the first time
    Doing it on time

Quality in perception
    Delivering the right product
    Satisfying your customer's needs
    Meeting your customer's expectations
    Treating every customer with integrity, courtesy and respect

Source: Patrick Townsend, *Commit to Quality* (John Wiley & Sons, 1990).

FIGURE 3–1
Total Quality Management Customer/Supplier Relationships

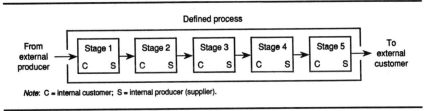

Note: C = internal customer; S = internal producer (supplier).

Source: *Continuous Improvement Process: Principles and Practices* (Bethesda, Md.: Logistics Management Institute, 1989).

Customer Requirements. The needs of the customers—both internal and external users—constitute a company's customer requirements. The ultimate aim of the company is to satisfy these requirements, as shown in Figure 3–1, and thereby satisfy its customers.

Supplier Specifications. Once a firm determines its customer requirements, it can then establish supplier specifications. Total Quality Management companies reject the idea that their suppliers should be picked mainly on the basis of price. Far more emphasis is placed on whether a supplier can meet the company's customer-driven specifications on a continuous basis, thus avoiding the introduction of defects into the company's production process.

Conformance. This term is closely linked to customer requirements. In the Total Quality Management context, conformance demands that products and services be measured against known and reliable customer requirements to ensure they will, in fact, meet customer needs. Guesswork is not allowed. Dependence on historical data only is rejected. Conformance must be based on continuously updated data that reflects current, objective measures of customer needs.

Data. Total Quality Management is a data-driven approach to quality improvement. Information or a set of facts is presented in descriptive form. There are two basic kinds of data: measured (variable data) and counted (known as attribute data).

Statistical Process Control.   Statistical process control (SPC) is a disciplined way of identifying and solving problems in order to improve performance. It involves use of fishbone diagrams to identify causes and effects of problems. Data are then collected and organized in various ways (graphs, Pareto charts, and/or histograms) to further examine problems. The data may be tracked over time (control charts) to determine variation in the process. The process is then enhanced in some way, and new data are collected and analyzed to determine whether the process has been improved.

Variation.   While studying process data in the 1920s, Walter Shewhart of the Bell Laboratories first made the distinction between controlled and uncontrolled variation due to what he called common and special causes. He developed a simple but powerful tool to dynamically separate the two: the control chart. Since that time, control charts have been used successfully in a wide variety of process control situations, both in the United States and other countries, notably Japan. Experience has shown that control charts effectively direct attention toward special causes of variation when they appear and reflect the extent of common-cause variation that must be reduced by management action.

Several types of control charts have been developed to analyze both variables and attributes. According to Shewhart, however, all control charts have the same two basic uses: First, a control chart serves as a *judgment*—to give evidence whether a process has been operating in a state of statistical control, and to signal the presence of special causes of variation so that corrective action can be taken. Second, it is used as an *operation*—to maintain the state of statistical control by extending the control limits as a basis for real-time decisions.

Cross-Functional Teams.   These teams are similar to quality teams, but the members are from several work units that interface with one another. These teams are particularly useful when work units depend on one another for systems integration, materials, information, and so forth.

Employee Empowerment.   In many companies, employees, by design, are doers not thinkers. They are expected only to perform to minimum standards. In Total Quality Management companies, on the other hand, every single employee is expected to solve problems, participate in team-building efforts, and generally expand the scope of their role in the organization. The goal of employee empowerment is to stop trying to motivate workers with extrinsic incentives, as is the case in traditional practices, and build a work environment in which all employees take pride in their work accomplishments and begin motivating themselves from within.

This enhanced role of the worker draws on the work of Douglas McGregor during the 1950s and his familiar Theory X and Theory Y assumptions about the nature of the worker. He argues that the Theory X view is fundamentally flawed. His Theory Y assumptions, on the other hand, underlie the Total Quality Management approach and invite a wider and more responsible role for the worker in an organization. A review of McGregor's two sets of assumptions, shown in Table 3–3, will facilitate a better understanding of the expanded role of the worker in Total Quality Management firms in the 1990s.

Culture.   Culture does not mean going to the opera. Rather, it is the prevailing pattern of activities, interactions, norms, sentiments, beliefs, attitudes, values, and products in your company. Many executives want to ignore culture. It is too nebulous, too difficult to "fix." Some believe all is well, or "if it's not broke, don't fix it."

Recently a vice president for a large American company became a born-again quality advocate. He met late Friday with the CEO to outline his plan to improve the organization's quality by changing the corporate culture and adopt Total Quality Management concepts. All was well until the CEO jumped up, full of enthusiasm, and said he wanted the corporate culture changed by close of business Monday!

One of the most difficult tasks for top management is to understand the impact of culture modification on their near-term and long-term business strategy. Changing your corporate culture takes years, not days.

FUNDAMENTAL CONCEPTS OF QUALITY

The fundamental concepts and principles of Total Quality Management include (1) need for a single interdependent system, (2) adoption of the Total Quality Management paradigm, (3) enhanced leadership for management's new role, (4) constancy of purpose, (5) commitment to quality, (6) customer focus, (7) benchmarking, (8) process orientation,

TABLE 3–3
McGregor's Theory X and Y

Theory X Assumptions of the Worker

1. The average human being has an inherent dislike of work and will avoid it if he can.

2. Because of this human characteristic of dislike of work, most people must be coerced, directed, threatened with punishment to get them to put forth adequate effort toward the achievement of organizational objectives.
3. The average human being prefers to be directed, wishes to avoid responsibility, has relatively little ambition, wants security above all.

Theory Y Assumptions of the Worker

1. The expenditure of physical and mental effort in work is as natural as play or rest.
2. External control and the threat of punishment are not the only means for bringing about effort toward organizational objectives. Man will exercise self-direction and self-control in the service of objectives to which he is committed.
3. Commitment to objectives is a function of the rewards associated with their achievement.
4. The average human being learns, under proper conditions, not only to accept but to seek responsibility.
5. The capacity to exercise a relatively high degree of imagination, ingenuity, and creativity in the solution of organizational problems is widely, not narrowly, distributed in the population.
6. Under the conditions of modern industrial life, the intellectual potentialities of the average human being are only partially utilized.

Source: Douglas McGregor, *The Human Side of Organizations* (New York: McGraw-Hill, 1960), pp. 33–34; pp. 47–48.

(9) continuous process improvement, (10) system-centered management, (11) investment in knowledge, (12) teamwork, (13) total involvement, and (14) long-term commitment. These synergistic concepts and principles of Total Quality Management work together in a logical and holistic manner to give substance and vitality to the continuously improving corporate culture. Figure 3–2 illustrates this holistic view.

A Single Interdependent System

In traditional management, a company's product or service—its output—is the focal point of attention. Typically, the company's goal is to make sure its output is error-free before it leaves the plant. This is usually

FIGURE 3–2
Holistic View of Total Quality Management Integration

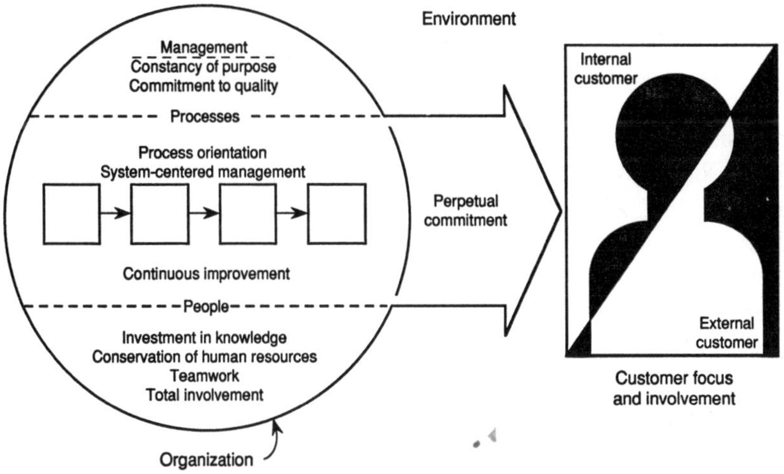

Source: An Introduction to the CIP Principles and Practices (Bethesda, Md.: Logistics Management Institute, 1989).

accomplished with an in-house inspection department designed to spot defective products. In other words, because each work unit is treated separately, the mistakes of one department can easily become the input for another department. Mistakes are not avoided, but detected and corrected.

In a Total Quality Management–focused business, all work units, suppliers, and customers are viewed as part of a single, interdependent system. From a quality perspective, either the whole system is working well, or the whole system is not working well. Total Quality Management rejects the notion that one unit's defects can be passed along to another unit and become its inputs. Total Quality Management insists that each work unit does its job correctly—the first time around, every time around. When the total process is designed to perform its tasks correctly, the system is said to be healthy, the customer is satisfied, and the cost of maintaining the system is reduced to its minimum level.

A New Business Paradigm

A few of the characteristics associated with the traditional way of managing a company have already been mentioned. Underlying these characteristics is a set of generally held but largely invisible beliefs and values, such as "The job of top management is to find answers to company problems" and "Workers must be closely monitored if they are to be productive" and the like. The sum of the common beliefs held by a majority of managers today comprises what is called the traditional management paradigm.

A different set of beliefs and assumptions about the nature of life in the business organization underlies the Total Quality Management practices described throughout this book. Total Quality Management is a paradigm shift. A paradigm, according to futurist Joel Barker, is a set of values and regulations that first establishes boundaries and then establishes how to be successful in solving problems within those boundaries. A paradigm shift for the individual requires a profound change in one's thinking. For your company, it requires cultural change. And as everyone knows, cultural change does not come easily. For example, a quality management company assumes that workers are capable of managing themselves (once given the tools to do so) and that solutions to most problems faced in the work place can be found within the work force itself, not in the CEO's office. Clearly, the belief systems of traditional management and Total Quality Management are not compatible. That is, a company operating under the traditional paradigm cannot fully adopt Total Quality Management practices without first replacing the old belief system with a new one. A company shifting its belief system is said to be undergoing a change in its internal culture.

As the number of American business firms shifting from the old to the new Total Quality Management paradigm grows in the 1990s, there will come a point—somewhere around the 50 percent mark—when the entire competitive American business community will have made the paradigm shift (see Figure 3–3). After that point any laggard firms wishing to remain competitive will, out of necessity, have to shift to the new paradigm or retire their business. My estimate is that the turning point from the old to the new Total Quality Management paradigm in the American business community will take place around the year 2000. After that point, the pros and cons of Total Quality Management will no longer be debated as they are today. After 2000, Total Quality Management will become the operative belief system of the entire American business community, and the shift from only a bottom-line mentality to a customer-first way of corporate life will be complete.

Unfortunately, the Total Quality Management concept is all too frequently advocated without sufficient substance or understanding. It is

FIGURE 3-3
American Business Adopts Total Quality Management Principles by the Year 2000

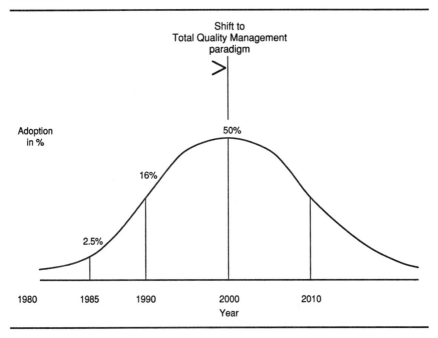

much easier to jump on particular aspects of the concept—such as statistical process control, employee involvement, structured problem solving, and other tools and techniques—than it is to understand and embrace the concept in its holistic sense. If the number of U.S. government and industry organizations that claim to be implementing quality improvement in its fundamental sense were really doing it, for example, our world-class competitors would be begging for mercy. We in business cannot afford to settle for the easy way. We cannot take shortcuts. And we cannot pretend that buzzwords, slogans, rhetoric, and posturing are enough to meet the competitive challenges American business faces.

Leadership and Management's New Role

Total Quality Management is destined to alter both the definition of what constitutes leadership in an organization and the role of top management. Listen to what *A Guide for Implementing Total Quality Management,* by the ITT Reliability Analysis Center (RAC), has to say on the role of top management in implementing a Total Quality Management process:

> RAC recommends the top-down model because it has the highest probability for success, although it doesn't guarantee success. The top-down model fosters management commitment, the single most important requirement for . . . success. . . . Top-down implementation requires management leadership as well as commitment. Management must lead the effort, providing . . . vision and philosophy for the organization. Management must lead the cultural change required.
>
> The top-down approach assures the availability of the resource support that is crucial for success. Time, money, and people are going to be required. . . . The bottom-up approach sends the message that quality management is something for the employees, but not necessarily for management.

Vision and Philosophy. Leadership is the key role for top managers. In more traditional management cultures, the meaning given to the term *leadership* is somewhat amorphous. In a Total Quality Management culture, however, leadership takes on a more precise definition. A quality leader must first establish a common vision of what the company is all about, its purpose. He or she must also realize that vision through his or her unique Total Quality Management philosophy—a set of guiding principles and practices—that will form a top-to-bottom, organization-wide belief system of the way in which the company will go about its business.

Management's New Role. Traditional management methods—the accepted norm today in the United States—are in conflict with Total Quality Management practices. For example, traditional management practices require managers to hold employees accountable; yet in a firm practicing Total Quality Management, the customer, not top management, controls the actions of the workers. In traditionally managed firms, fighting daily fires consumes management's energies, and competition among work groups is encouraged. In Total Quality Management organizations, however, these practices are replaced with a managerial focus on teamwork and continuous process improvement to permanently put out brush fires.

W. Edwards Deming describes the new role for top management in *Out of Crisis*:

> The job of management is not supervision, but leadership. Management must work on sources of improvement, the intent of quality of product and

of service, and on the translation of the intent into design and actual product. The required transformation of Western style of management requires that managers be leaders. The focus on outcome (management by numbers, Management by Objectives, work standards, meeting specifications . . .) must be abolished, and leadership put in place.

Changing the Corporate Culture.   Table 3–4 gives you a realistic idea of the magnitude of change often required when your company moves from a traditional to a Total Quality Management culture. Don't underestimate the initial resistance to change that is likely to be generated in an organization once it is clear to its employees how deeply the proposed changes will alter the old way of doing things.

Constancy of Purpose

The constancy of purpose principle is a core Total Quality Management concept. For the Total Quality Management organization, constancy of purpose is generally articulated by management through a broad statement of corporate purpose, which provides individuals with a steady and consistent vision of where they are going, what is expected of them, and what they expect of themselves. Likewise, a constancy of purpose demonstrated consistently by management's behavior enables each individual

TABLE 3–4
Culture Change from Traditional to Total Quality Management Implementation

Total Quality Management Is . . .	Total Quality Management Is Not . . .
• Demonstrating executive leadership and commitment.	• Assigning responsibility for quality to others.
• Listening to customers to determine their requirements.	• Assuming you know your customers' requirements.
• Doing the right thing right the first time.	• Doing it over to make it right.
• Identifying cost of quality and focusing on prevention.	• Overlooking the hidden costs of poor quality.
• Continuous process improvement.	• A one-time fix.
• Taking ownership at all levels of the organization.	• Assigning responsibility for quality to one department.

to construct a reliable mental road map on which to base decisions and actions.

Top management is responsible for providing constancy of purpose. It must be provided from the highest possible level so that it can be infused throughout all parts of an organization. It is conveyed by a clear statement of a vision for the company with a set of consistent goals and objectives, and it is supported by strategic and tactical plans. The constancy of purpose is reinforced by an ongoing stream of management signals and actions that nurture and support the realization of the vision.

Commitment to Quality

Commitment to quality is a cornerstone of the Total Quality Management concept. The concept of quality improvement must encompass both measurability and the customer's perceptions of usefulness. Improvement implies a comparison with past performance. Quality improvement implies increasing degrees of excellence with reference to specific and accepted points of reference. Those points of reference include specifications, cost, performance, schedule, responsiveness, and product or service improvement based on competitive benchmarks.

A commitment to quality must begin with top management. Guided by its constancy of purpose and its corporate philosophy, top management must identify the external customers for the organization's products and services. Top management must understand the customer's needs and expectations and assure that those needs are translated into the attributes and characteristics of the products or services. Top management must direct the resources of the organization toward continuously improving the product or service with respect to the customer-relevant attributes.

Customer Focus and Involvement

Without customer focus and involvement, both constancy of purpose and commitment to quality become meaningless. Attracting, serving, and retaining customers is the ultimate purpose of any company, and those customers help the organization frame its quality consciousness and guide its improvement effort. A process, product, or service has no relevance without customers; everything done in an organization is done for the customer. The quality of a product or service is defined by customer behavior and response. Process improvement must be guided by a clear understanding of customer needs and expectations.

Increased customer satisfaction is the ultimate result of customer focus and involvement. The responsibility for assuring customer focus and involvement starts with a top management focus on the organization's external customer and extends down through every level of activity to involve all customers in the improvement process. Total Quality Management emphasizes satisfying all customers, internal and external.

Just as a company is dynamic, so are its customers. Customer requirements change for a variety of reasons, often uncontrollable and unpredictable. To serve its customers adequately, therefore, the organization must continually reassess its customers' needs and requirements and factor them into its improvement efforts. Failure to consider customers and to actively involve them in the improvement effort is a fatal flaw in a company's quality philosophy.

Benchmarking

A benchmark is a standard of excellence or achievement against which other similar things must be measured or judged. Simply speaking, benchmarking is the process of:

- Figuring out what to benchmark.
- Finding out what the benchmark is.
- Determining how it's achieved.
- Deciding to make changes or improvements in one's own business practices to meet or exceed the benchmark.

These four questions—while sounding fairly simple—require thinking and analysis. They require that you know your own business processes and practices down to the smallest detail. Benchmarking is a process of comparing—comparing results, outputs, methods, processes, or practices in a systematic way. One of the purposes of this book is to help you through the process of self-assessment.

Process Orientation

The most effective means for an organization to address customer needs and improve itself is to focus improvement efforts on its processes. Process orientation requires a significant change in thinking for many American managers. American management practices—particularly quality functions—have traditionally focused primarily on the post-production identification and rejection of defective products. While that approach may be reasonably successful in preventing most unsatisfactory products from reaching customers, it does little to change the processes that create defects.

Total Quality Management forces management to think in terms of process rather than in terms of finished product. Everything that is done in an organization is accomplished through a process comprising definable stages, steps, or activities. Each step of a process is a producer and a customer. The customer is always the step subsequent to the producer. Hence, the principle of customer focus and involvement provides a precise means for defining the purpose (and often the means) of the process.

Continuous Process Improvement

The central, unifying concept in the Total Quality Management approach is the idea that everything a firm does is part of a continuous improvement process. Here is how Brian E. Mansir and Nicholas R. Schacht of the Logistics Management Institute describe this key concept in a report titled *An Introduction to the Continuous Improvement Process: Principles & Practices:*

> Continuous improvement process is the fundamental principle around which quality is centered. It complements and animates the principles of process orientation and customer focus and involvement with the certain recognition that no process, product, or service ever attains perfection and that neither the customer's expectations nor the quality of the competition remains static. A deliberate positive change (improvement) is required to win and hold a customer base or to remain economically competitive. Devotion to continuous improvement is a demonstration of constant, purposeful commitment to quality.

Continuous improvement depends on both innovative and small incremental changes. Innovation is characterized by large dramatic changes (see Figure 3–4) resulting from new technologies or new ways of thinking and is often the product of research and development.

American management has traditionally focused on innovation as the primary engine of improvement. The organization also recognizes the importance of innovation for developing new processes, products, and services. It also recognizes small incremental improvements (see Figure 3–5) as essential for maintaining and building on the new performance

FIGURE 3–4
The Large-Step Innovation-Driven Improvement Process

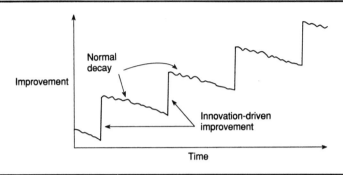

Source: *Continuous Improvement Process: Principles and Practices* (Bethesda, Md.: Logistics Management Institute, 1989).

FIGURE 3–5
The Small-Step Improvement Process

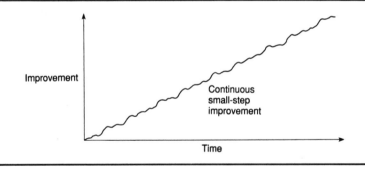

Source: *Continuous Improvement Process: Principles and Practices* (Bethesda, Md.: Logistics Management Institute, 1989).

standards achieved through innovation. Total Quality Management organizations seek a better balance between innovation and small incremental improvement.

Eventually the opportunities from small incremental process improvements reach a point of diminishing returns. Before that occurs, the company should be prepared to introduce the next level of innovation and to begin again the incremental improvement cycle. The balance between innovation and incremental improvement is key and is illustrated by the growth curves in Figure 3–6.

FIGURE 3-6
Balance between Innovation and Incremental Improvement

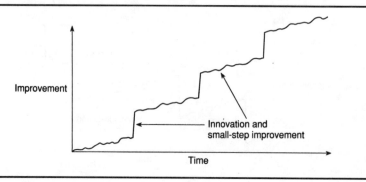

Source: *Continuous Improvement Process: Principles and Practices* (Bethesda, Md.: Logistics Management Institute, 1989).

System-Centered Management

System-centered management requires managers to actively improve the system within which they work. Management's new job is to study and reform the processes by which work is accomplished. This concept is anathema to many American managers. Many managers come to their positions with the idea that their job is to ensure that work is accomplished in accordance with the established processes. They tend to see their role as keeping people busy and processing the paper that constitutes their deliverable products. True, a substantial part of their job is motivating the work force, providing better discipline, hiring better people, or performing administrative tasks. However, when managers assume that the fundamental structure and processes of the system are fixed and correct, they fail to address their most important job: improvement of the system.

The traditional attitude about management's role leads managers to deal with a continuous stream of momentary demands for attention. The demands of the in-basket never cease, squeaky wheels constantly need oiling, and most managers get bogged down in detail and are unable to step back and deal with the entire process or system. The manager becomes a mechanic, so busy tinkering with the sources of noise that he cannot see that the machine—the organizational system—is becoming obsolete and incapable of performing to modern standards.

Investment in Knowledge

Personal knowledge, teamwork, security, and personal involvement are among the key factors that govern how individuals function and interact within the company. Expanding knowledge is both a personal and a company responsibility. Both the individual and the company must commit to investing in knowledge.

Investment in knowledge is aimed at maximizing human potential and capital. All planned improvement comes from growth in understanding. Improvement is achieved through questioning why things are done and the ways they are done, by trying new ways of doing things, and by learning. Increased education and knowledge should be a lifelong opportunity and experience. In the work place, every employee should be challenged to grow in value to the organization and in self-worth. An organization that practices Total Quality Management makes this growth happen!

Teamwork

Although knowledgeable, skilled employees are crucial to the Total Quality Management improvement process, the individual skills they provide may be substantially leveraged when employed in the context of teamwork. Teamwork is essential to the success of the Total Quality Management culture in an organization. One universal goal is ultimately to involve every member of the organization in relevant process improvement team activity.

Teamwork does not necessarily imply that new organizational entities must be created. Rather, in most applications it means that existing groups will begin working as teams, using the techniques that take advantage of interpersonal dynamics.

Most process improvement teams mirror the natural function or work group structures and thus overlay the existing organizational hierarchy. Additional teams are created to ensure cross-functional process improvement and attention to processes of special interest or broad application, such as reward and recognition or quality-of-work-life issues.

For the most part, creation of the team network flows from the top down. Training team members within the team setting, an integral part of the deployment process, produces what H. James Harrington, author of *The Improvement Process,* calls a ''waterfall effect'' of systematically washing out the counterproductive ideas and signals as the culture is deployed down into the organization.

Each team, once created, engages in ongoing process improvement activity that is appropriate to its level and area of responsibility. These activities include customer recognition, process definition, performance requirements definition, performance measurement and assessment, and process improvement cycle activity. Statistical information provides a common language for the examination of process performance and for the assessment of improvement efforts.

Conservation of Human Resources.   To be true to its constancy of purpose, the organization must recognize that its people are its most important asset. This recognition is rooted in the principle of conservation of human resources. Often management behavior does not reflect an appreciation of this principle. Work force reduction is frequently the first avenue of cost reduction. Rank-and-file employees are too frequently perceived as pairs of hands or strong backs with too little regard for the available mind.

An enlightened and consistent approach to leadership is a cornerstone of every successful Total Quality Management application. All of the leaders in the field—including Deming, Juran, Drucker, and Crosby—stress the importance of creating a stimulating, secure, and supportive environment in which teamwork, creativity, and pride of workmanship can thrive. Without this environment none of the other elements of Total Quality Management can be totally successful.

A key message of the principle of human resource conservation is, "We expect the best from our people and we give them our best in return." The creation and maintenance of a work environment that is compatible with a Total Quality Management culture is absolutely a top management responsibility.

Total Involvement

Ultimately, all the Total Quality Management principles will guide the actions of every person in the organization. The principle of total involvement (participation and empowerment) addresses this universal involvement in Total Quality Management. It is concerned with ensuring continuity of appropriate signals throughout the organization and realizing process improvement benefits in every area of activity. Total participation means that every individual gets involved and has a responsibility to seek continuous improvement at both the individual and team level. Total empowerment means that individuals are given the necessary authority to make decisions and initiate improvement actions within their own work areas and expertise. Employees are encouraged through respect and trust to exercise self-direction and self-discipline. Empowerment is a source of pride, a wellspring of creativity, and an engine for improvement action.

This empowerment is essential if the principle of total involvement is to be followed. Participation and empowerment are stimulated, nurtured, and guided by management involvement, teamwork, clear objectives, and vigorous open communication.

Perpetual Commitment

Perpetual commitment makes it clear that Total Quality Management is not a program that has starting and finishing points, but rather a process that, once begun, will be used by the company to conduct all future business. Commitment is a management action that implies a management responsibility to encourage and facilitate positive change even when such change is difficult, time-consuming, or lacking immediate return on the investment. Commitment is measured by behavior: It means holding a steady long-term course in the face of short-term pressure; making improvement the top agenda item in communications and decisions; being willing to invest for the long-term benefit; supporting the creative improvement initiatives of the work force; structuring the recognition system to reward initiative and improvement; providing for extensive education and training, including everyone in the process; and becoming personally involved in improvement activity. In sum, it means making Total Quality Management the company way of life.

Initial deployment of Total Quality Management in an organization requires a considerable amount of time and effort. Many changes must occur—ways of thinking, individual and group behavior, methods of accomplishing tasks, attitudes, priorities, relationships, signals, and knowledge levels. These changes will not, and indeed cannot, happen overnight. Experience indicates that three to five years, depending on your current state of practice for quality, may be required for an organization to reach Total Quality Management maturity—that is, fully in place and accepted as the standard way of doing business.

The length of time required to reach maturity should not be perceived as a reason for you to not begin the transition process to Total Quality Management. Experience shows that positive results and significant returns on investment start very early in the process. Total Quality Management, when managed correctly, should essentially pay for itself even in the first year. Companies that are only two or three years into the process have reported returns on investment of $4 or $5 for every $1 invested.

Top management in an organization is responsible for ensuring that Total Quality Management is a perpetual commitment. Every member of the organization should know with certainty that Total Quality Management is not just another fad that management will soon forget. Everyone should understand that getting on board is mandatory and that it is not possible to "wait until this Total Quality Management thing blows over." The responsibility for knowing what is going on and for providing the leadership to shape and guide the change process cannot be delegated. Each manager and each individual must recognize a personal role and responsibility and must be given a personal, intrinsic incentive in the Total Quality Management effort.

THE COST OF QUALITY

One of the more compelling reasons prompting early quality leaders to trade in traditional practices for Total Quality Management practices was the projected cost of poor quality if they did business as usual. Once CEOs realize how costly their old way of doing business is, mainly because it actually builds poor quality and unnecessary costs into the process, shifting to a new, defect-free process becomes very attractive costwise. According to *A Guide for Implementing Total Quality Management,* of the Reliability Analysis Center:

> The cost of poor quality has been quoted by various sources as being between 15 percent to 50 percent of the cost of doing business. . . . One of the most effective actions management can take to improve productivity in any organization is to improve the quality of its processes. Quality saves, it does not cost. . . . Reducing the cost of poor quality directly affects the bottom line. Improving quality is the most direct way for an organization to increase profit.

More specifically, in *Quality Is Free,* Philip B. Crosby zeros in on the cost of quality:

> Quality is free. It's not a gift, but it is free. What costs money are the unquality things—all the actions that involve not doing jobs right the first time.
>
> Quality is not only free, it is an honest-to-everything profit maker. Every penny you don't spend on doing things wrong, over, or instead becomes half a penny right on the bottom line. In these days of "who knows what is going to happen to our business tomorrow" there aren't many ways left to make a profit improvement. If you concentrate on making quality certain, you can probably increase your profit by an amount equal to 5 to 10 percent of your sales. That is a lot of money for free.

The key event then in a company's journey toward Total Quality Management is an awareness among top management that their financial statements already reflect the costs of not doing things right the first time around, that they must change their definition of quality, and that to be successful, the Total Quality Management program must be organization-wide and involve everyone at all levels.

Simply stated, the cost of quality aims at spending capital wisely and avoiding wasting it. Xerox defines Cost of Quality as the measurement of what your division, department, teamwork group or family group is spending for its overall Quality. According to Xerox, there are three kinds of measurements in Cost of Quality:

1. *Conformance.* Spending that is in conformance with customer requirements. Conformance means that work outputs are being measured against known customer requirements.
2. *Cost of nonconformance.* Spending that is not in conformance with customer requirements. It is measured in time needed to go back and do a job over. Nonconformance can also cost money by exceeding your customer requirements.
3. *Lost opportunities.* A profit not earned because a customer is lost because of lack of quality.

Figure 3–7 will help you visualize the cost shifts that can be expected before and after a company adopts a Total Quality Management approach to management. Implicit in this cost of quality diagram is the notion that the firm will continuously set and achieve higher and higher quality standards.

FIGURE 3-7
The Cost of Quality: Before and After Total Quality Management

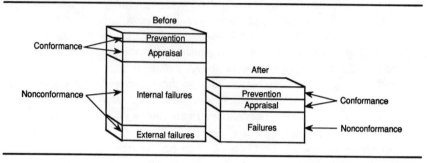

THE CORPORATE QUALITY CHAMPION

Earlier in this chapter we discussed the anticipation of the coming paradigm shift from traditional management to Total Quality Management practices. Once this shift takes place, Total Quality Management practices will quickly displace existing practices—that is, they will become standard operating procedures—in most American firms. Until that paradigm shift takes place, however, the process of introducing and institutionalizing a set of new management ideas in an existing company is a very difficult task.

Each new procedure introduced into a firm is certain to upset an existing status quo. Workers who identify personally with the existing status quo will, in turn, feel vulnerable and insecure. Their response is likely to be resistance to the new ideas and the changes in behavior required to implement them. For this reason, if a new idea is to pass from simply a new concept to actual practice in an organization, it needs a boost from a champion.

A full-time champion is needed to overcome the resistance the change process will generate and to settle the myriad of problems and barriers that will crop up from day to day. In the absence of a dedicated champion, the initiation of a new idea will soon falter before it is routinized. A Total Quality Management champion—an individual that leads by his or her own participation—is needed to inspire others to participate fully in the change process. A successful Total Quality Management champion will (1) visibly support the company's Total Quality Management strategy, (2) insist on the team approach, (3) measure his or **her** success by customer satisfaction, (4) build feedback loops within the firm and to suppliers and customers, and (5) meet goals.

A new idea such as Total Quality Management must pass through four stages (see Figure 3–8) before it is institutionalized in your company.

FIGURE 3–8
The Total Quality Management Idea-Adoption-Implementation Process

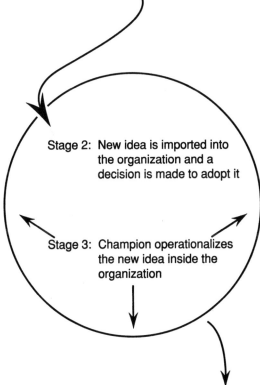

Stage 1: New idea originates outside of the organization and captures the interest of a leader inside the organization

Stage 2: New idea is imported into the organization and a decision is made to adopt it

Stage 3: Champion operationalizes the new idea inside the organization

Stage 4: The new idea becomes routinized and becomes the "way business is done" in the organization

Stage 1: The source of the new ideas such as the Total Quality Management concept are located *outside* of the target organization. The Total Quality Management concept captures the interest of an organizational *insider,* such as the CEO or Quality Manager.

Stage 2: An insider, (or group of insiders) makes the decision to adopt the new idea.

Stage 3: Once the decision to adopt the idea is made, an internal change process must then be set in motion to operationalize the new idea. Characteristically, a champion—a person with strong personal convictions concerning quality management, sufficient formal or informal authority, expertise, or some other mix of desired qualities—is given responsibility for the day-to-day implementation process.

Stage 4: Only when the new idea is finally internalized and accepted as the "way things are done" in an organization is the champion's job complete.

In their book *In Search of Excellence,* Thomas Peters and Robert Waterman, Jr., identified the "fired-up champion" as an indispensable ingredient present in all of the best-run companies:

> The champion is not a blue-sky dreamer, or an intellectual giant. The champion might even be an idea thief. But, above all, he's the pragmatic one who grabs onto someone else's theoretical construct if necessary and bull-headedly pushes it to fruition. . . . Champions are pioneers, and pioneers get shot at. The companies that get the most from champions, therefore, are those that have rich support networks so their pioneers will flourish. This point is so important it's hard to overstress. No support system, no champions. No champions, no innovation.

The question now is this: Does your company have a Total Quality Management champion? If not, why not you?

CHAPTER 4

DIFFERENT QUALITY STRATEGIES

MORE THAN ONE WAY

The Innovators

At the turn of the century, most Americans believed that leaders were born, not made. The idea that anyone could develop leadership traits was only gradually accepted. Today, however, the study of leadership is a part of most business school curricula. The diffusion of Total Quality Management practices throughout American manufacturing and service industries has followed a similar path, as managers cautiously redefine how they view, and perform, their work.

Like innovators before them, Philip Crosby, W. Edwards Deming, and Joseph M. Juran are change agents—spreading the notion that business and government leaders can and must learn to build quality performance into their enterprises, and that quality is neither a matter of chance nor an act of magic. But because change involves risks for individuals and organizations alike, each new idea is accompanied by resistance to change. Familiar habits and beliefs are traded in slowly for new ones. Research has shown that the diffusion of new ideas and successful change processes—whether occurring society-wide or just within individual companies—pass through predictable stages. Everett M. Rogers has grouped innovation adopters into five categories, ranging from "innovators" to "laggards" (see Figure 4–1).

Rogers's classification scheme helps us better appreciate the process of quality management change in several ways. First, it places the quality movement in the United States into a longer-range, historical context, and

FIGURE 4–1
Distribution of Adopters of Innovations

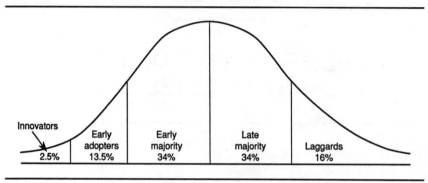

Source: Everett M. Rogers, *Diffusion of Innovations* (New York: Free Press, 1983).

suggests that Crosby, Deming, and Juran—the "innovators" of new ideas—are the starting points of a society-wide change process. Second, we also learn from Rogers that the "early adopters," the risk-taking companies (such as the Malcolm Baldrige Award winners) that first embraced the new ideas, represent only a fraction of the potential adopters.

Finally, as quality management ideas spread into the business population at large, dependence on the guru-dominated diffusion process used by the relatively few early adopting firms will probably be complemented by customized, mix-and-match approaches to better accommodate the needs of thousands upon thousands of adopting companies in the years ahead.

Toward Customized Adoption

In Japan in the 1950s, quality management innovators achieved a charismatic appeal. Only in the early 1980s, as these innovators spread their ideas among American clients who were also feeling the impact of global competition, did quality management begin to gain a similar appeal in the United States. Under the influence of a single innovator, firms tended to adopt a more or less pure approach—à la Deming, Juran, or some other guru. Not until the middle and late 1980s were the ideas of these innovators popularized and their various approaches adopted.

Today, business and government organizations throughout the United States are on the verge of mass adoption of Total Quality Management practices. In this emerging era, the one-on-one, guru-dominated approach will become less and less able to keep up with the demand as the number of adopters skyrockets. Now that both the experiences of the early adopters and the wide variations in methodology promoted by the gurus have percolated through the business community, it seems only natural that mix-and-match, customized approaches to Total Quality Management will replace the original, guru-dominated approach.

Is There One Best Approach?

The remainder of this chapter introduces the basic ideas and concepts of a few leading quality management experts. These experts, it should be stressed, are just a sampling of a still larger community of quality management thinkers, including Armand V. Feigenbaum, Kaoru Ishikawa, and Rosabeth Moss-Kanter. The three quality management experts highlighted here do, nonetheless, offer the reader a wide range of approaches to better understand quality today.

W. Edwards Deming's approach is selected because of his well-known role in the reconstruction of Japan's industrial base following World War II and his broad, philosophical approach to change with an emphasis on a statistically based implementation process and concern for empowerment. Joseph M. Juran's contribution, on the other hand, contains a distinct product-development flavor and a systematic, three-step methodology for helping managers zero in on quality management. Finally, Philip Crosby stresses a well-structured, stage-by-stage development of an organization's culture. Therefore, his model may have greater appeal for those executives interested in a more incremental road-map approach.

Caution: Don't assume that a single best method should, or does, exist. Maybe it does, maybe it doesn't. Only you can decide. If, after comparing the Crosby approach to those of Deming and Juran, for example, you conclude that Crosby's model fits exactly the needs of your firm, you might consider adopting it wholesale. On the other hand, after a careful comparison of the strengths and weaknesses of each approach, you may decide that a pick-and-choose approach is the way to go. For example, you might use a version of Crosby's maturity grid at the organization-wide level, and a version of Deming's control chart approach at the subunit level.

The challenge facing U.S. business executives in the 1990s is not simply to decide whether to adopt any quality management program, but to adopt one that best fits their specific competitive business environment.

THE CROSBY SCHOOL

Like Chester Barnard, a 40-year veteran of American Telephone and Telegraph and author of the 1938 classic study of management, *The Functions of the Executive,* Philip Crosby's quality management ideas also followed a long corporate career. Rising through managerial ranks, Crosby was a vice president of ITT for 14 years. Crosby's insider corporate perspective is reflected in a down-to-earth approach to quality management. He believes an organization can "learn" and that top management should adopt a quality management style not because it is the right thing to do, but because it is "free" and good for the bottom line.

The Problem Organization

Crosby believes "the problem organization" will benefit most from his quality management program. In his book *Quality Without Tears,* Crosby identifies a problem organization by the presence of five symptoms:

- The outgoing product or service normally contains deviations from the published, announced, or agreed-upon requirements.
- The company has an extensive field service or dealer network skilled in rework and resourceful corrective action to keep the customers satisfied.
- Management does not provide a clear performance standard or definition of quality, so the employees each develop their own.
- Management does not know the price of nonconformance. Product companies spend 20 percent or more of their sales dollars doing things wrong and doing them over. Service companies spend 35 percent or more of their operating costs doing things wrong and doing them over.
- Management denies that it is the cause of the problem.

In other words, virtually every business firm is, by Crosby's definition, a problem organization. Why? Because managers traditionally attack problems as they crop up in the organization and seek random improvements. Top management, according to Crosby, is too quick to "send everyone else to school, set up programs for the lowest levels of the organization, and make speeches with impressive-sounding words. It is not until all the problems are pulled together, particularly the financial ones, that the seriousness of the situation is exposed."

Crosby's View of Quality

The real meaning of quality, Crosby asserts in *Quality Is Free,* suffers from several erroneous assumptions. Quality is not:

- Goodness, or luxury, or shininess.
- Intangible, therefore not measurable.
- Unaffordable.
- Originated by the workers.
- Something that originates in the quality department.

Quality is conformance to requirements; nonquality is nonconformance.

To put this definition into practice, Crosby assumes that quality either is or is not present in the whole organization; that quality is the responsibility of everyone in the organization; and that quality is measurable. In addition, he cautions the quality-bound executive, "The process of instilling quality improvement is a journey that never ends. Changing a culture so that it never slips back is not something that is accomplished quickly."

Crosby's Quality Management Maturity Grid

The first step for an organization moving toward a quality management profile is to determine its current level of "management maturity." Crosby's Quality Management Maturity Grid, shown in Table 4–1, is used for this purpose. Along the left-hand margin are six measures of the sophistication of an organization's management style, including how the organization handles problems, the attitude of top management, and the cost of quality to the firm. Across the top are five levels, or stages, of quality management maturity. These range from Stage I, "Uncertainty," in which an organization is characterized by the statement, "We don't know why we have quality problems," to Stage V, "Certainty" reserved for organizations in which top management can proclaim, "We know why we don't have quality problems."

Once a firm has located its current maturity stage on the grid, it then implements a quality improvement program based on Crosby's 14 steps of quality improvement delineated in Table 4–2. Each step is designed as a building block to move the organization's management style through progressively higher level maturity stages—titled "Awakening," "En-

TABLE 4–1
Crosby's Quality Management Maturity Grid

Measurement Categories	Stage I: Uncertainty	Stage II: Awakening	Stage III: Enlightenment	Stage IV: Wisdom	Stage V: Certainty
Management Understanding and Attitude	Fails to see quality as a management tool.	Supports quality management in theory but is unwilling to provide the necessary money or time.	Learns about quality management and becomes supportive.	Participates personally in quality activities.	Regards quality management as essential to the company's success.
Quality Organization Status	Quality activities are limited to the manufacturing or engineering department and are largely appraisal and sorting.	A strong quality leader has been appointed, but quality activities remain focused on appraisal and sorting and are still limited to manufacturing and engineering.	Quality department reports to top management, and its leader is active in company management.	Quality manager is an officer of the company. Prevention activities have become important.	Quality manager is on the board of directors. Prevention is the main quality activity.
Problem Handling	Problems are fought as they occur and are seldom fully resolved; "fire fighting" dominates.	Teams are established to attack major problems, but the approach remains short term.	Problems are resolved in an orderly fashion, and corrective action is a regular event.	Problems are identified early in their development.	Except in the most unusual cases, problems are prevented.

Cost of Quality as Percentage of Sales	Reported: unknown Actual: 20%	Reported: 5% Actual: 18%	Reported: 8% Actual: 12%	Reported: 6.5% Actual: 8%	Reported: 2.5% Actual: 2.5%
Quality Improvement Actions	No organized activities.	Activities are motivational and short term.	Implements the 14-step program with full understanding.	Continues the 14-step program and starts Make Certain.	Quality improvement is a regular and continuing activity.
Summation of Company Quality Posture	"We don't know why we have quality problems."	"Must we always have quality problems?"	"Because of management commitment and quality improvement programs, we are identifying and resolving our quality problems."	"We routinely prevent defects from occurring."	"We know why we don't have quality problems."

Source: Adapted from Philip B. Crosby, *Quality is Free* (New York: McGraw-Hill, 1979).

TABLE 4-2
Crosby's Fourteen-Step Program

Step 1. *Management commitment.* Top management must become convinced of the need for quality improvement and must make its commitment clear to the entire company. This should be accompanied by a written quality policy, stating that each person is expected to "perform exactly like the requirement, or cause the requirement to be officially changed to what we and the customers really need."

Step 2. *Quality improvement team.* Management must form a team of department heads (or those who can speak for their departments) to oversee quality improvement. The team's role is to see that needed actions take place in its departments and in the company as a whole.

Step 3. *Quality measurement.* Quality measures that are appropriate to every activity must be established to identify areas needing improvement. In accounting, for example, one measure might be the percentage of late reports; in engineering, the accuracy of drawings; in purchasing, rejections due to incomplete descriptions; and in plant engineering, time lost because of equipment failures.

Step 4. *Cost of quality evaluation.* The controller's office should make an estimate of the costs of quality to identify areas where quality improvements would be profitable.

Step 5. *Quality awareness.* Quality awareness must be raised among employees. They must understand the importance of product conformance and the costs of nonconformance. These messages should be carried by supervisors (after they have been trained) and through such media as films, booklets, and posters.

Step 6. *Corrective action.* Opportunities for correction are generated by Steps 3 and 4, as well as by discussions among employees. These ideas should be brought to the supervisory level and resolved there, if possible. They should be pushed up further if that is necessary to get action.

Step 7. *Zero-defects planning.* An ad hoc defects committee should be formed from members of the quality improvement team. This committee should start planning a zero-defects program appropriate to the company and its culture.

Step 8. *Supervisory training.* Early in the process, all levels of management must be trained to implement their part of the quality improvement program.

Step 9. *Zero Defects Day.* A Zero Defects Day should be scheduled to signal to employees that the company has a new performance standard.

Step 10. *Goal setting.* To turn commitments into action, individuals must establish improvement goals for themselves and their groups. Supervisors should meet with their people and ask them to set goals that are specific and measurable. Goal lines should be posted in each area and meetings held to discuss progress.

TABLE 4–2 (concluded)

Step 11. *Error cause removal.* Employees should be encouraged to inform management of any problems that prevent them from performing error-free work. Employees need not do anything about these problems themselves; they should simply report them. Reported problems must then be acknowledged by management within 24 hours.

Step 12. *Recognition.* Public, nonfinancial appreciation must be given to those who meet their quality goals or perform outstandingly.

Step 13. *Quality councils.* Quality professionals and team chairpersons should meet regularly to share experiences, problems, and ideas.

Step 14. *Do it all over again.* To emphasize the never-ending process of quality improvement, the program (Steps 1–13) must be repeated. This renews the commitment of old employees and brings new ones into the process.

---

lightenment," and "Wisdom"—toward "Certainty" at right-hand side of the management grid. Only at this final stage is conformance to the firm's stated quality requirements assured. A zero-defects culture—a set of beliefs held throughout the organization that says, in effect, "Do it right the first time"—is established, and the cost of quality is reduced to its lowest possible level.

The Crosby Quality College

A mood of intellectual progress established by the labels Crosby has given to each stage on his management maturity grid reinforces the role of organizational learning in his "do it right the first time" approach to quality management. Wishful thinking won't work. Only constant, top-level effort will move an organization toward the right-hand side of the grid. To make sure this happens, the Crosby Quality College offers a no-nonsense environment that reinforces again and again one basic theme: Zero-defect management is possible.

As Crosby states in *Quality Without Tears:*

> The main problem of quality as a management concern is that it is not taught in management schools. It is not considered to be a management function, but rather a technical one. . . . However, with the pressure on quality erupting worldwide and the difficulty in getting senior management to do something about it, it becomes apparent that a new measurement is

needed for quality. The best measurement for this subject is the same as for any other—money.

The Crosby Quality College does not educate individuals per se. According to Crosby, "The college deals with whole companies, not with individuals." While at this college, every action taken by the student, from the manner in which he or she registers at the hotel upon arrival to ownership of problems in class, is designed to reinforce *the* central message: Conformance to requirements—the definition of quality—is both beyond compromise and financially wise.

THE DEMING PHILOSOPHY

Born in 1900, and recipient of a Ph.D. in mathematics and physics from Yale, W. Edwards Deming was first introduced to the basic tenets of traditional management principles in the late 1920s as a summer employee at Western Electric's famous Hawthorne plant in Chicago. Here the revolutionary human relations studies of Harvard Professor Elton Mayo began to raise a fundamental question: How can firms best motivate workers? Deming found the traditional motivation system in use at that time to be degrading and economically unproductive. Under that system, worker incentives were linked to piecework to maximize worker output, followed by an inspection process in which defective items were subtracted from the worker's piecework credits. The virtues of an egalitarian work place is an enduring theme found throughout Deming's philosophy.

During the 1930s, Deming's collaboration with Walter A. Shewhart, a statistician working at Bell Telephone Laboratories, led to his conviction that traditional management methods should be replaced with statistical control techniques. Deming recognized that a statistically controlled management process gave the manager a newfound capacity to systematically determine when to intervene and, equally important, when to leave an industrial process alone. During World War II, Deming got his first opportunity to demonstrate to government managers how Shewhart's statistical quality control methods could be taught to engineers and workers and put into practice in busy war production plants.

Following the war, Deming left government service and set up a private consulting practice. The State Department, one of his early clients, sent him to Japan in 1947 to help prepare a national census in that devastated country. While American managers soon forgot their wartime quality control lessons and continued their prewar love affair with traditional management practices that prized production over quality, Deming's evolving quality control methods received a warm reception in Japan.

In fact, the Japanese now credit much of their postwar industrial renaissance to Deming's statistical process control–based philosophy of quality. Each year in his name, the Union of Japanese Scientists and Engineers awards the Deming Prize to companies that have demonstrated outstanding contributions to product quality and dependability. In addition, in 1960 the Japanese emperor awarded Deming Japan's Second Order Medal of the Sacred Treasure, a tribute rarely paid to a foreigner.

The Quality Crisis

In his book *Out of the Crisis*, Deming holds American managers responsible for causing a society-wide quality crisis:

> Western style of management must change to halt the decline of Western industry, and to turn it upward. . . . There must be an awakening to the crisis, followed by action, management's job. . . . The transformation can only be accomplished by man, not by hardware (computers, gadgets, automation, or new machinery). A company cannot buy its way into quality.

Deming's philosophy is prone to put quality in human terms. When a firm's work force is committed to doing a good job and has a solid managerial process through which to act, quality will flow naturally. A more practical, composite definition of quality might read as such: Quality is a predictable degree of uniformity and dependability at low cost, and suited to the market.

Because Japan adopted statistical-based control techniques in the early 1950s, it has a 30-year head start on the United States. Deming estimates it will take American managers another 30 years to achieve the advanced level of statistical control now in wide practice in Japan. While Western managers have focused on outcome and practiced "retroactive management," such as Management By Objectives, the Japanese have perfected quality. In 1985, as quoted in *The Deming Management Method*, by Mary Walton, Deming summed up his indictment this way: "Failure to understand people is the devastation of Western management." The American quality crisis is being prolonged by what Deming calls the Seven Deadly Diseases (see Table 4–3) associated with traditional management practices.

TABLE 4-3
The Seven Deadly Diseases

1. *Lack of constancy of purpose.* A company that is without constancy of purpose has no long-range plans for staying in business. Management is insecure, and so are employees.
2. *Emphasis on short-term profits.* Looking to increase the quarterly dividend undermines quality and productivity.
3. *Evaluation by performance, merit rating, or annual review of performance.* The effects of these are devastating—teamwork is destroyed, rivalry is nurtured. Performance ratings build fear and leave people bitter, despondent, beaten. They also encourage defections in the ranks of management.
4. *Mobility of management.* Job-hopping managers never understand the companies they work for and are never there long enough to follow through on long-term changes that are necessary for quality and productivity.
5. *Running a company on visible figures alone.* The most important figures are unknown and unknowable—the "multiplier" effect of a happy customer, for example.
6. *Excessive medical costs for employee health care, which increase the final costs of goods and services.*
7. *Excessive costs of warranty, fueled by lawyers who work on the basis of contingency fees.*

Deming's Fourteen Points

To eliminate these underlying managerial diseases, Deming prescribes his own 14-point cure, found in Table 4-4. Both the philosophical foundation for Deming's managerial transformation and the role assigned to statistical quality control in the execution of that philosophy are present in his 14-point program of quality management. These points are so central to his approach, Deming will not accept a new company client until its president has promised to faithfully implement *all* 14 points. Halfway measures will not do. If a company is unwilling to change its management philosophy 100 percent to the Deming way, Deming passes that client by. Why? Because Deming is convinced that about 85 percent of all quality problems are caused by harmful management practices. Consequently, a CEO intent on changing the way production workers perform *without* changing the obsolete management system will, at best, address only 15 percent of the problems.

TABLE 4-4
Deming's Fourteen Points

1. *Create constancy of purpose for improvement of product and service.* Deming suggests a radical new definition of a company's role: Rather than to make money, it is to stay in business and provide jobs through innovation, research, constant improvement, and maintenance.

2. *Adopt the new philosophy.* Americans are too tolerant of poor workmanship and sullen service. We need a new religion in which mistakes and negativism are unacceptable.

3. *Cease dependence on mass inspection.* American firms typically inspect a product as it comes off the assembly line or at major stages along the way; defective products are either thrown out or reworked. Both practices are unnecessarily expensive. In effect, a company is paying workers to make defects and then to correct them. Quality comes not from inspection but from improvement of the process. With instruction, workers can be enlisted in this improvement.

4. *End the practice of awarding business on the price tag alone.* Purchasing departments customarily operate on orders to seek the lowest price vendor. Frequently, this leads to supplies of low quality. Instead, buyers should seek the best quality in a long-term relationship with a single supplier for any one item.

5. *Improve constantly and forever the system of production and service.* Improvement is not a one-time effort. Management is obligated to continually look for ways to reduce waste and improve quality.

6. *Institute training.* Too often, workers have learned their job from another worker who was never trained properly. They are forced to follow unintelligible instructions. They can't do their jobs well because no one tells them how to do so.

7. *Institute leadership.* The job of a supervisor is not to tell people what to do, nor to punish them, but to lead. Leading consists of helping people do a better job and of learning by objective methods who is in need of individual help.

8. *Drive out fear.* Many employees are afraid to ask questions or to take a position, even when they do not understand what their job is or what is right or wrong. They will continue to do things the wrong way, or not do them at all. The economic losses from fear are appalling. To ensure better quality and productivity, make sure workers feel secure.

9. *Break down barriers between staff areas.* Often a company's departments or units are competing with each other, or have goals that conflict. They do not work as a team so they cannot solve or foresee problems. Worse, one department's goals may cause trouble for another.

10. *Eliminate slogans, exhortations, and targets for the work force.* These never helped anybody do a good job. Let workers formulate their own slogans.

11. *Eliminate numerical quotas.* Quotas take into account only numbers, not quality or methods. They are usually a guarantee of inefficiency and high cost. A person, to hold a job, meets a quota at any cost, without regard to damage to the company.

TABLE 4-4 (concluded)

12. *Remove barriers to pride of workmanship.* People are eager to do a good job and distressed when they cannot. Too often, misguided supervisors, faulty equipment, and defective materials stand in the way of good performance. These barriers must be removed.

13. *Institute a vigorous program of education and retraining.* Both management and the work force will have to be educated in the new methods, including teamwork and statistical techniques.

14. *Take action to accomplish the transformation.* It will require a special top management team with a plan of action to carry out the quality mission. Workers cannot do it on their own, nor can managers. A critical mass of people in the company must understand the Fourteen Points, [and] the Seven Deadly Diseases.

Statistical Process Control

Identifying the Problem. The methodological core of Deming's quality management approach is the use of simple statistical techniques to continuously improve a firm's management process. Only through statistical verification, according to Deming, can the manager (1) know that he or she has a problem, and (2) find the cause of the problem. Deming uses quality control charts, like the one shown in Figure 4-2, to identify the absence or presence of a quality problem. Because all human activity will contain unavoidable variations—that is, every product or service is slightly different from all the others—an acceptable range of "random variations" must be established for every product or service.

Once measurable upper and lower control limits have been set for a product or service, and a control chart prepared to reflect these limits, the workers performing the activity periodically plot actual measurements on the chart. When these measurements fall outside of the acceptable, "random variation" range, the worker immediately knows a "nonrandom" quality problem exists.

Classifying the Problem's Cause. The next step is to identify the cause behind the problem. Two possibilities exist. The cause could be a "common cause," or one rooted in the basic management system in use and, therefore, a problem that is potentially company-wide in scope. Fundamental design errors or the use of imprecise machinery are examples of common causes. Alternatively, the problem could be the result of

FIGURE 4–2
A Typical Deming Control Chart

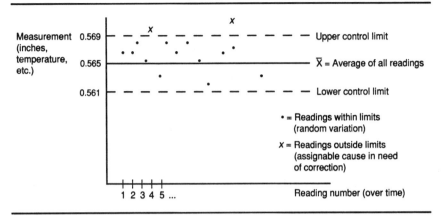

a "special cause," or one stemming from a more isolated source—a few poorly trained workers in one department, for example.

Deming recommends using several additional charting methods to learn more about the factors causing the quality problems exposed in a control chart. Mary Walton, in *Deming Management at Work*, sums up the crucial role of statistics this way: "American managers pride themselves on hunches and intuition. When they succeed, they take credit. When they fail, they find someone to blame. But a quality transformation rests on a different set of assumptions: decisions must be based on facts . . . [and] it is helpful to display information graphically." Figure 4–3 summarizes the full array of Deming's charting techniques. An elaboration on the specific uses of these charting methods is found in Chapter 7, "Tools and Techniques."

Correcting the Problem.   The final step in the quality management cycle is for the manager and the workers to eliminate the cause of the quality problem by taking the necessary actions contained in the 14 points. These actions may range from redesign of a faulty manufacturing assembly line, to a one-day training course for workers to learn how to operate a new machine or how to better serve a new type of customer.

Boosting Performance.   While finding and curing quality problems keep a firm's activities within *established* quality limits, Deming also uses control charts to actually boost a firm's performance. By narrowing

FIGURE 4-3
Doing It with Data—Seven Helpful Charts

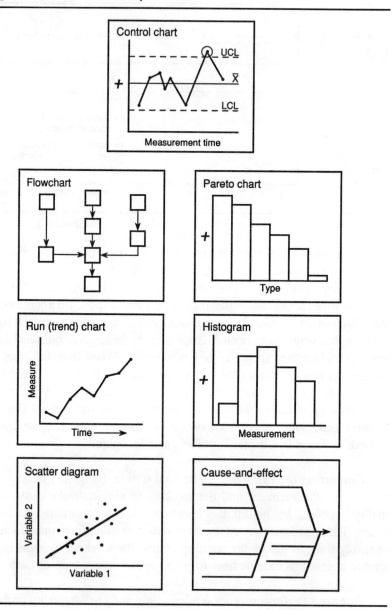

Source: Mary Walton, *Deming Management at Work* (New York: Putnam, 1990).

the established range between the upper and lower random variation limits for an activity, a firm will, in effect, artificially and deliberately create and then solve self-inflicted quality problems. The result is an increase in the firm's attainable level of quality. In this way, managers can plan for and implement a long-range quality improvement program to stay ahead of the competition.

The Plan-Do-Check-Act (PDCA) Cycle

Deming envisions a never-ending, circular management process. The Plan-Do-Check-Act (PDCA) Cycle, an adaptation of the work of Shewhart, links the seven diseases, the 14 points, and the statistical techniques into a continuous process—without a starting or ending point. Only through the ongoing application of the four-stage cycle shown in Figure 4–4 can an organization attain and retain a superior quality management process. There are no shortcuts.

THE JURAN TRILOGY

Joseph M. Juran was educated during the first quarter of this century in engineering and law. His outlook, in general, reflects a rational, matter-of-fact approach to business organization and one heavily dependent on

FIGURE 4–4
The Shewhart/Deming PDCA Cycle

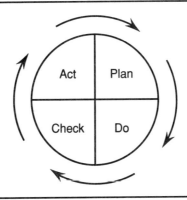

sophisticated "shop floor" planning and quality control processes. The focal point of Juran's quality management philosophy is the firm's individual product or service, not the organization per se. By making sure the building blocks—each individual product or service—meets the customers' requirements, a company-wide quality program will emerge.

Like Deming, Juran also played a significant role in rebuilding Japan after World War II, and he also received the Second Class of the Order of the Sacred Treasure for "the development of Quality Control in Japan and the facilitation of U.S. and Japanese friendship." His search for underlying principles of the management process led to his focus on quality as the ultimate goal. Before becoming a quality management consultant and lecturer, Juran worked in both government and business organizations.

A National Quality Crisis

The basic society-wide problem, according to Juran, is that American industry is caught up in a quality crisis; and while many U.S. managers agree with him on the existence of the crisis, too few understand how to end it. Juran identifies two widely held but wrong assumptions that are preventing American managers from finding solutions to their problems. First, many managers have not yet accepted the fact that they, not the workers, must shoulder most of the responsibility for the performance of their companies. Juran concludes that until top management redirects its energies toward planning quality into their products—rather than actually planning a lack of quality into them, as is presently the case—the quality crisis will continue. Second, this erroneous assumption is compounded by managers' failure to realize that great financial gains can be made once quality becomes their top priority.

The result of this obsolete mindset is summarized by Juran in his book *Juran on Planning for Quality:*

> Many companies are facing serious losses and wastes that have their main origin in deficiencies in the quality planning process:
>
> • Loss of sales due to competition in quality.
> • Costs of poor quality, including customer complaints, product liability lawsuits, redoing defective work, products scrapped, and so on.

- The threats to society . . . [since the ability of] the products of an industrial society . . . to lengthen the human life span; relieve people of drudgery; provide opportunities for educational, cultural, and entertainment . . . depends absolutely on the continuing and proper performance of those products, that is, on their quality.

Juran's Quality Trilogy

The challenge facing American managers, according to Juran, is to abandon the traditional approach to product planning, which carelessly introduces quality flaws into the product's original design. The traditional approach depends on an inspection and rejection process to find and correct quality problems in individual products, without ever redesigning the planning process itself.

Adoption of Juran's quality trilogy requires that a firm, once and for all, redesign its product and service planning and control systems and then, through an ongoing improvement program, ensure that the basic causes of quality flaws are permanently eliminated. This means a firm's planning system should contain a single, *universal* thought process that supersedes the *particular* processes used in the production of an individual product. It also requires the adoption of Juran's definitions of quality presented in *Juran on Planning for Quality:*

> Quality [is] (1) product performance that results in customer satisfaction; (2) freedom from product deficiencies, which avoids customer dissatisfaction. A shorthand expression that conveys both meanings is "fitness for use."

Conceptually, Juran divides quality management into this quality trilogy: quality planning, quality control, and quality improvement. While planning, controlling, and improving managerial processes have long been considered fundamental executive functions, Juran asserts they are seldom combined in a structured way—as they are in the quality trilogy—for managing product quality. Figure 4–5 describes the way in which Juran's three-part approach is designed to reduce the cost of quality over time.

Quality Planning.   In Juran's approach to quality management, the central task is "the activity of developing the products and processes required to meet customers' needs." To accomplish this task, he recommends the road map shown in Figure 4–6. During the quality planning

FIGURE 4–5
The Juran Trilogy Reduces the Cost of Quality

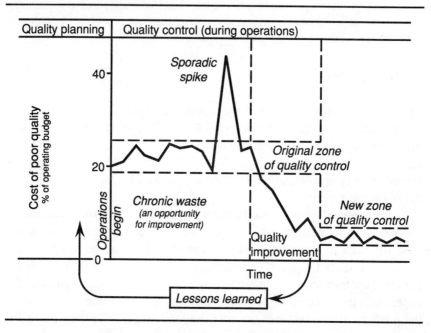

Source: J. M. Juran, *Juran on Planning for Quality* (New York: Free Press, 1988).

stage, a firm prepares to meet established quality goals. The result of the planning stage is a dependable process that can be trusted to perform as planned under operating conditions.

Quality Control.   Control processes are designed to ensure that the quality goals set in the planning stage are, in fact, being met during the actual production or rendering of the firm's products and services. Figure 4–7 illustrates Juran's quality control process.

Quality Improvement.   Unlike quality planning and quality control processes that logically fit together to form a step-by-step, product idea-to-quality-product continuum, quality improvement is the means by which a firm selectively identifies and implements change on a subsystem level. Quality planning and quality control establish a stabilized product quality "culture," or foundation, throughout an organization. The third part of the trilogy, however, known both as quality improvement and

FIGURE 4–6
The Quality Planning Road Map

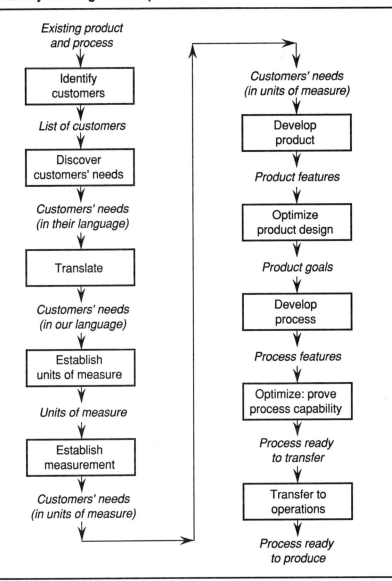

Source: J. M. Juran, *Planning for Quality* (New York: Free Press, 1988).

FIGURE 4–7
Juran's Quality Control Process

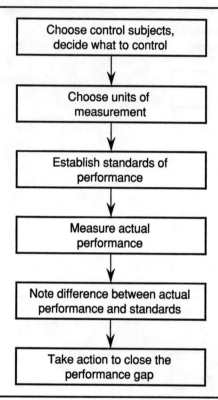

Juran's "breakthrough sequence," provides managers the means for finding and remedying the basic quality-limiting causes embedded in the organization. Juran expressly does not consider the improvement phase of his trilogy to be a quick-fix exercise. Instead, whenever a basic cause leading to a quality failure is identified, Juran insists that the planning-control processes be altered to permanently prevent that cause from occurring again in the future.

The breakthrough process described in Table 4–5 is used in conjunction with Juran's planning and control processes while the trilogy is first being installed in an organization, and as a trouble-shooting tool to keep the planning-control sequence running smoothly after it is established in the organization. Juran uses the term *breakthrough* to emphasize that this part of the trilogy is the means for achieving unprecedented

TABLE 4-5
Juran's Breakthrough Sequence

1. [Urge a] *breakthrough in attitudes.* Managers must first prove that a breakthrough is needed and then create a climate conducive to change. To demonstrate need, data must be collected to show the extent of the problem; the data most convincing to top management are usually cost of quality figures. To get the resources required for improvement, expected benefits must be presented in terms of cost and return on investment.

2. *Identify the vital few projects.* Pareto chart analysis is used to distinguish the vital few projects from the trivial many and to set priorities based on problem frequency.

3. *Organize for breakthrough in knowledge.* Two organizational entities should be established: a steering group and a diagnostic group. The steering group, composed of people from several departments, defines the program, suggests possible problem causes, gives the authority to experiment, helps overcome resistance to change, and implements the solution. The diagnostic group, composed of quality professionals and sometimes line managers, is responsible for analyzing the problem.

4. *Conduct the analysis.* The diagnostic group studies symptoms, develops hypotheses, and experiments to find the problem's true causes. It also tries to determine whether defects are primarily operator controllable or management controllable. (A defect is operator controllable only if it meets three criteria: operators know what they are supposed to do, have the data to understand what they are actually doing, and are able to regulate their own performance.) Theories can be tested by using past data and current production data and by conducting experiments. With this information, the diagnostic group then proposes solutions to the problem.

5. *Determine how to overcome resistance to change.* The need for change must be established in terms that are important to the key people involved. Logical arguments alone are insufficient. Participation is therefore required in both the technical and social aspects of change.

6. *Institute the change.* Departments that must take corrective action must be convinced to cooperate. Presentations to these departments should include the size of the problem, alternative solutions, the cost of recommended changes, expected benefits, and efforts taken to anticipate the change's impact on employees. Time for reflection may be needed, and adequate training is essential.

7. *Institute controls.* Controls must be set up to monitor the solution, see that it works, and keep abreast of unforeseen developments. Formal follow-up is provided by the control sequence used to monitor and correct sporadic problems.

levels of quality performance in an organization. Juran estimates that approximately 80 percent of the problems identified with breakthrough analysis, including defect rates, are correctable only by improving the management control system. The remaining 20 percent are attributable to the actions of the operating work force.

Cost of Quality Accounting System

To keep top management interested in and supportive of the department-level quality planning process, Juran uses a cost of quality (COQ) accounting system to demonstrate how cost-effective it really is to shift to a quality management process. Here is how it works.

By comparing the rising costs of implementing Juran's appraisal and prevention process to the decreasing costs of detecting internal and external product failures, an executive can determine his optimal level of effort. In the early stages of implementing a quality management process, every dollar invested in appraisal and prevention activities cuts the firm's external and internal failure costs by far more than one dollar. As the defect rate and failure costs drop in response to the widespread adoption of quality management processes, the firm's level of investment will be optimal whenever a dollar spent on appraisal and prevention equals one dollar reduction in detecting and fixing failures. Because the costs of finding and preventing the last few defects in a production system are extremely high—higher than the costs saved if these defects were eliminated—the optimal quality level is somewhat less than a 100 percent, defect-free system.

COMPARATIVE ASSESSMENT

Before comparing the specific quality management approaches of Crosby, Deming, and Juran, let's first place the ideas of these innovators into their larger, societal framework. As a group, they are all advocates of the need for a greater commitment to quality in the work place. But each holds a somewhat different view of what causes the quality vacuum. Table 4–6 attempts to identify the genesis, or the root causes, of the quality challenge facing the United States. Of the three, Crosby tends to locate the roots of the problem within the firm itself. Juran and Deming, on the other hand, seem to trace company-based quality problems back to the values found in the general, post–World War II American society.

TABLE 4–6
The Genesis of the Total Quality Management Movement

	Nature of the Crisis	*Cause of the Crisis*	*The Solution*	*Their Definition of Quality*
Crosby	Communication failure within the firm	Lack of commitment to quality	Company culture committed to quality	Conformance to company's own quality requirements
Deming	Loss of international competitiveness	Society and company acceptance of low quality	Society and company committed to quality	Dependable, customer-satisfying product or service at a low cost
Juran	Loss of international competitiveness	Company acceptance of low quality	Company committed to quality	Product or service that is fit for use

The Early Adopters

A measure of the adoption of Total Quality Management principles and practices in the last 10 years is shown in Table 4–7. The table provides a partial listing of some of the growing number of well-known companies that have adopted the ideas of Crosby, Deming, Juran, and other gurus.

Common Ground

The various Total Quality Management approaches explored here build on a solid base of commonly held expectations and assumptions. In many respects they are far more alike than they are different from one another. Each approach:

- Requires a very strong top management commitment.
- Shows that quality management practices will save, not cost, money.
- Places the responsibility for achieving quality primarily on the managers and the systems they control, not on the workers.

TABLE 4–7
Some of the Early Total Quality Management Adopters*

	Crosby	Deming	Juran
AT & T		X	
Bechtel	X		
Burroughs	X		
Campbell Soup		X	
Chrysler	X		
Dow Chemical		X	
Du Pont			X
Ford		X	
GM	X	X	
Hughes Aircraft		X	
IBM	X		
Johnson & Johnson	X		
Mobil			X
Monsanto			X
Texas Instruments			X
Xerox			X

*Reflects primary initial quality philosophy.

- Stresses that Total Quality Management is a never-ending, continuous improvement process.
- Is customer-oriented.
- Assumes a shift from an old to a new organizational culture.
- Is founded on building a strong management/worker problem-solving team.

But the differences do matter. The differences among the approaches will most influence a manager's decision to adopt portions of one over another. Let's compare and contrast Crosby, Deming, and Juran on a number of key issues in terms of balancing the strengths and weaknesses of each approach.

What Is the Nature of the Organization?

Crosby.   More so than the others, Crosby's approach has an unmistakable, organization-wide, team-building flavor. The organization is treated almost as if it were a whole, living organism that evolves through time toward higher and higher levels of self-awareness.

Deming.   Resident in Deming's view of the business organization is a deep current of social responsibility. The purpose of the organization is to stay in business. But why? It is not to make a lot of money, but to lend stability to the community it serves, to treat workers throughout the organization with the respect naturally due every human being. There is a moral tone to the Deming approach that is absent in the others.

Juran.   Of the three, Juran's outlook focuses more on the parts rather than the whole organization. The whole does matter, but the path to a healthy organization is to make sure each part is finely tuned. Juran seems to invite the use of his trilogy on an isolated, troubled department.

Is a Step-by-Step Implementation Process Readily Apparent?

Crosby and Juran.   In both of these approaches, we have a feeling that a starting point and an end point is visible. Crosby's maturity grid and Juran's trilogy might be called "user-friendly."

Deming.   With Deming, there is a feeling that a road map does not exist, that without a tutor's guiding hand one would not readily know where to start on the journey.

Can the Approach Be Implemented Piecemeal?

Crosby and Deming.   Both of these approaches are holistic and do not invite a piecemeal implementation strategy. That said, however, the Crosby model does lend itself more to prudent modifications to suit the host organization. Deming, on the other hand, calls for an almost instantaneous belief and total adoption of a new way of organizational life— one filled with radical value shifts.

Juran.   A danger, perhaps, in the Juran model is the apparent ease with which his methodology could be targeted at parts of the organization only. A manager attempting a piecemeal implementation of Juran's methods might forget that, in the end, the entire organization must subscribe to the same deep commitment to quality. While Juran selectively picks his subunits for application of the quality improvement process, he still requires an organization-wide commitment.

How Well Does Each Approach Handle Resistance?

Crosby and Juran. Resistance to change is inevitable, but it need not be a barrier. Crosby's learning-based model is perhaps best suited to accommodating resistance by allowing the individual to acknowledge his or her doubts and, then, to satisfy them through education and training. Juran also accommodates resistance by insisting that changes be justified through analysis and team-building processes.

Deming. On the surface, one can easily conclude that Deming's approach is dogmatic and uncompromising, and in many respects Deming himself cultivates this image. Yet his statistical methods are, in effect, learning tools that not only objectively structure problems in ways that make them easily understood, but also objectively disarm critics of change by depending on facts, not gospel.

WHERE TO FROM HERE?

Adopting a Total Quality Management program is a big decision and one that should be made with care and after consultation with others in your organization. Consider the advice given to Alice by the Cheshire Cat when, during her adventures in Wonderland, she could not decide which of two paths to take:

> "Cheshire Puss," Alice began, rather timidly . . . "Would you tell me please, which way ought I go from here?"
> "That depends a good deal on where you want to get to," said the Cat.
> "I don't much care where—" said Alice.
> "Then it doesn't matter which way you go," said the Cat.
> "—so long as I get somewhere," Alice added as an explanation.
> "Oh, you're sure to do that," said the Cat, "if you only walk long enough."
>
> (Lewis Carroll, *Alice's Adventures in Wonderland*)

If, like Alice, you really don't care where you and your company are going, then it really doesn't matter what you do regarding Total Quality

Management. But if you do care, then which way you go will make all the difference in the world.

JUST PICK ONE

In his book *Thriving on Chaos* Tom Peters notes:

> You should have a system. There's a lot of controversy here: Should you follow W. Edwards Deming, father of the Japanese quality revolution via statistical process control? Or Phil Crosby, author of *Quality Is Free,* and so prominent that GM bought a 10 percent stake in his firm? . . . Or Joseph Juran? Or invent a system of your own? Eventually you will develop your own scheme if you are successful.

During the mid-1980s, when quality management was first gaining some acceptance in the United States, it really didn't matter which approach—Crosby, Deming, or Juran—was adopted. Simply by being among the leaders, the early adopting firms were easily well ahead of competitors still operating under traditional management practices. Those days are over. In the 1990s, as more and more firms turn to Total Quality Management strategies out of necessity—just to maintain their competitive positions nationally and internationally—there will be a growing need to carefully compare approaches and to adopt the quality initiatives that best fit a company's situation.

The Situational Approach

Perhaps the single most crucial step for a CEO preparing to adopt and implement a Total Quality Management program is an honest and frank appraisal of the current status of the organization. For starters, the following questions should be carefully answered:

- How will the organization react to change?
- Who are the potential champions of the change?
- What are realistic expectations for the organization?
- How much time is available to make changes?
- Will it be an organization-wide effort, or will you target a single subunit?
- How will you measure results?

During your situational assessment, keep good notes. It will be to your advantage to construct your own version of an "As Is/To Be" table that summarizes and compares your organization's current quality situation to your vision of it in the future. Table 4–8 can be used a prototype.

Picking a Strategy

This chapter has been designed to first introduce you to, and then compare, the ideas of a few of the leading quality gurus. Once you have a feel for your organization's current needs and the depth of your initial step toward Total Quality Management, you can begin to consider how the strategies of Crosby, Deming, and Juran apply specifically to your situation.

As discussed earlier, each approach has a number of common elements. The decision to adopt elements of one approach over another,

TABLE 4–8
Where to from Here?

"As Is" State	*"To Be" State*
From an environment that . . .	*To one that . . .*
Has many different and often conflicting goals among its divisions and departments	Has a common vision shared by everyone
Punishes mistakes, hides or rationalizes problems	Openly discusses problems and sees defects as opportunities for improvement
Rewards following established policies	Rewards risk taking and creative thinking
Lets short-term problems drive and dominate work activity	Focuses on long-term continuous process improvement
Relies on inspection to catch mistakes before the customer receives the product	Improves work processes to prevent mistakes from occurring
Gives management full authority for top-down decisions for change	Trusts and empowers employees to contribute to decision making
Tolerates turf battles as inevitable	Facilitates and rewards cross-functional cooperation
Makes decisions arbitrarily	Bases all decisions on objective data
Has a negative or indifferent self-image	Feels like a winner, with achievements creating good morale

Source: David Carr and Ian Littman, *Excellence in Government* (Coopers & Lybrand, 1990).

therefore, will probably hinge on the appeal you find in a unique aspect present in one approach but absent in the others. For example, a highly technical firm employing many engineers may find Juran far more appealing than the idealistic approach favored by Deming. A firm with a history of organizational development may find Crosby's organizational stage model culturally more comfortable.

Table 4–9 is a comparison of Crosby's fourteen steps, Deming's fourteen points, and Juran's seven-point breakthrough sequence. Each of the steps and/or points was allotted to one of eight generic Total Quality Management implementation tasks. Four of the task categories deal with people-oriented tasks, and four are more technical in nature. The resulting table will help you compare the relative weight given by the quality gurus to each of the eight Total Quality Management categories. With an idea of the strengths and weaknesses of your current organization in

TABLE 4–9
Comparative Assessment Matrix: Quality Management Tasks

	Crosby's 14 Steps (Table 4–2)*	Deming's 14 Points (Table 4–4)	Juran's 7 Points (Table 4–5)
People-Oriented Tasks			
Build top management commitment	1	1	1
Teamwork	2, 10, 13	9, 4	3, 5, 6
Improve quality awareness	5, 7, 9, 12	2, 3, 8, 10, 11, 12	5
Expand training	8	6, 7, 13	5
Technically Oriented Tasks			
Measure quality	3	3, 4	4
Quality of cost recognition	4	4, 3	2
Take corrective action	6, 11	14	6, 7
Continuous improvement process	14	5	7

*Refer to table noted for detailed description of each step/point delineated in quality leader's philosophy.

mind, try to decide which of the eight categories will be your greatest challenge in beginning your Total Quality Management program.

If, for example, you anticipate that building an awareness of quality in your organization will be a particularly difficult challenge, you may want to take a closer look at Crosby and Deming since their approaches have a strong awareness-building focus.

QUALITY DEMYSTIFIED

This chapter has been both a historical and an intellectual introduction to the central ideas behind the Total Quality Management movement. As with all innovations that challenge a long-held set of beliefs and practices, Total Quality Management has not been quickly accepted in the business community. While the ideas of Deming are as American as apple pie, they were first exported in the 1950s to Japan, where they ripened, and only recently were they imported back into the United States.

Having surveyed a range of definitions of "quality" and a variety of well-known approaches to implanting Total Quality Management in an organization, you are ready to seriously consider the development of a specific Total Quality Management methodology for your firm. Challenging the organizational status quo does involve some risks; however, I hope you have gained a solid appreciation for the enormous benefits the introduction of Total Quality Management offers your business.

It is hoped that this chapter has also helped "demystify" the aura that often surrounds the quality management gurus. Crosby, Deming, and Juran do, indeed, offer new insights into a leader's role in the management process. But there is no magic hidden behind their ideas. With determination, every business executive can learn to achieve a higher level of quality. What the gurus cannot do, however, is supply that precious ingredient: the will to act. That drive comes from within, and it is developed bit by bit. By the time you have finished this book, you should have acquired both the tools and the desire to put Total Quality Management into practice.

The final message contained in this chapter is this: There is no one best way. A situational approach, where business leaders must carefully match their unique organizational environment to a customized Total Quality Management program, is the recommended route to achieving world-class quality products and services in the 1990s.

CHAPTER 5

ASSESS YOUR QUALITY

SELF-ASSESSMENT APPROACH

This chapter provides a method for assessing the current practices, policies, procedures, and attitudes throughout your own organization as they relate to quality enhancement, and provides the opportunity to assess the effects of any changes as they relate to quality enhancement. It also provides an opportunity to check your progress by occasionally reevaluating your performance. This self-assessment asks questions concerning:

- *Climate.* People's perceptions about their organization and/or work units.
- *Processes.* The organization's or work unit's policies, practices, and procedures.
- *Management tools.* The specific techniques used to promote quality improvements throughout the organization or work units.
- *Outcomes.* Mission accomplishment.

The self-assessment questions are divided into four groups: climate, processes, tools, and outcomes. Some of the questions ask you to consider the entire *organization* in your response, and others ask you to think only about your immediate *work unit*. The definitions of these two terms need to be clear in your mind prior to the use of this self-assessment so that you are referring to the organization and work unit in the same way as the self-assessment.

Decide which organization and work unit you wish to examine and enter the names below. For example, you may be in charge of a corporation. The corporation may contain three divisions. The divisions, in turn, may be composed of several departments. Depending on your interest, the corporation may be designated as the organization, and one of the three divisions as the work unit.

Name of organization = _____

Work unit = _____

Another term you will encounter is *customer,* defined as anyone who receives the work that your work unit(s) or your organization performs. Note that customers can be another organization, another work unit, or any organization member. The traditional notion of "customer" as someone outside your immediate organization or work unit that uses or buys your product or service can also apply. In all cases, consider that your customer relies on and judges the quality of the work that you do.

The source of this evaluation structure is the *Quality and Productivity Self-Assessment Guide,* a public domain federal report. You may reproduce this chapter to aid you or your team in using this self-assessment tool.

To conduct this Total Quality Management self-assessment, complete the following worksheets for each self-assessment element (climate, processes, tools, outcomes). There are 215 self-assessment questions, which can be answered in approximately 15 minutes. The scoring rationale follows the questions.

ASSESSMENT OF ORGANIZATION CLIMATE

The list of statements that begins on the next page is presented for your evaluation and ranking. There are no wrong answers. Circle the number that you feel best indicates your extent of agreement with the statement. The legend for the questionnaire is (1) strongly disagree, (2) disagree, (3) somewhat disagree, (4) somewhat agree, (5) agree, and (6) strongly agree.

	Strongly Disagree				Strongly Agree
1. People in this organization are aware of its overall mission.	1	2	3	4	5	6
2. In general, this organization's customers believe that we care about what they think.	1	2	3	4	5	6
3. People in this organization are aware of its overall mission.	1	2	3	4	5	6
4. It's in everyone's best interests that this organization be successful.	1	2	3	4	5	6
5. People in this organization are aware of how the organization's mission contributes to higher-level missions and objectives.	1	2	3	4	5	6
6. In general, this organization's customers would not "go elsewhere" even if it were possible.	1	2	3	4	5	6

People in this organization:

7. Try to plan ahead for changes (such as in policy) that might impact our mission performance.	1	2	3	4	5	6
8. Try to plan ahead for technological changes (such as new development in computer software) that might impact our mission performance.	1	2	3	4	5	6
9. Regularly work together to plan for the future.	1	2	3	4	5	6
10. See continuing improvement as essential.	1	2	3	4	5	6
11. Care about what will happen to the organization after they are reassigned.	1	2	3	4	5	6

12. Creativity is actively encouraged in this organization.	1	2	3	4	5	6
13. Innovators are the people who get ahead in this organization.	1	2	3	4	5	6

14. The quality of our work is second only to mission accomplishment as the overriding focus of this organization.	1	2	3	4	5	6

Legend: (1) strongly disagree, (2) disagree, (3) somewhat disagree, (4) somewhat agree, (5) agree, (6) strongly agree.

	Strongly Disagree				*Strongly Agree*	
15. Every member of this organization is concerned with the need for quality.	1	2	3	4	5	6
16. Continuous quality improvements within this organization can lead to more productive use of our resources.	1	2	3	4	5	6
17. People in this organization know how to define the quality of what we do.	1	2	3	4	5	6
18. Every member of this organization needs to contribute to quality improvement.	1	2	3	4	5	6

People in this organization:

19. Live up to high ethical standards.	1	2	3	4	5	6
20. Like to do a good job.	1	2	3	4	5	6
21. Emphasize doing things right the first time.	1	2	3	4	5	6

The leader(s) in this organization (people at the highest level):

22. Are committed to providing top quality services/products/work.	1	2	3	4	5	6
23. Regularly review the quality of work produced.	1	2	3	4	5	6
24. Ask people about ways to improve the work produced.	1	2	3	4	5	6
25. Follow-up suggestions for improvement.	1	2	3	4	5	6

The leader(s) in this organization (people at the highest level):

26. Set examples of quality performance in their day-to-day activities.	1	2	3	4	5	6
27. Regularly review progress toward meeting goals and objectives.	1	2	3	4	5	6
28. Attempt to find out why the organization may not be meeting a particular goal/objective.	1	2	3	4	5	6

People in my work unit:

29. Turn to their supervisors for advice about how to improve their work.	1	2	3	4	5	6

Legend: (1) strongly disagree, (2) disagree, (3) somewhat disagree, (4) somewhat agree, (5) agree, (6) strongly agree.

		Strongly Disagree				*Strongly Agree*	
30.	Know how their supervisors will help them find answers to problems they may be having.	1	2	3	4	5	6
31.	Are challenged by their supervisors to find ways to improve the system.	1	2	3	4	5	6

The supervisors in my work unit:

32.	Make the continuous improvement of our work top priority.	1	2	3	4	5	6
33.	Regularly ask our customers about the quality of work they receive.	1	2	3	4	5	6
34.	The structure of our organization makes it easy to focus on quality.	1	2	3	4	5	6
35.	The way we do things in this organization is consistent with quality.	1	2	3	4	5	6
36.	People in my work unit understand how a quality emphasis leads to more productive use of resources.	1	2	3	4	5	6
37.	People in my work unit can describe the organization's quality and productivity policy.	1	2	3	4	5	6
38.	People in my work unit believe that quality and productivity improvement is their responsibility.	1	2	3	4	5	6
39.	People in my work unit take pride in their work.	1	2	3	4	5	6
40.	People in my work unit share responsibility for the success or failure of our services/products.	1	2	3	4	5	6
41.	People in my work unit believe that their work is important to the success of the overall organization.	1	2	3	4	5	6
42.	We have good relationships between departments in this organization.	1	2	3	4	5	6
43.	Co-workers in this organization cooperate with each other to get the job done.	1	2	3	4	5	6
44.	A spirit of cooperation and teamwork exists in this organization.	1	2	3	4	5	6

	Strongly Disagree					Strongly Agree
45. We have good relationships with other organizations that we work with.	1	2	3	4	5	6
46. Supervisors in my work unit request employee opinions and data.	1	2	3	4	5	6
47. People in my work unit are involved in improving our services/products/work.	1	2	3	4	5	6
48. We have the appropriate personnel in my work unit to get the job done properly.	1	2	3	4	5	6
49. The work goals or standards in my work unit are generally fair.	1	2	3	4	5	6
50. The supervisors in my work unit do a good job of setting work expectations.	1	2	3	4	5	6
51. People in my work unit are friendly with one another.	1	2	3	4	5	6
52. People in my work unit enjoy their co-workers.	1	2	3	4	5	6
53. We have the right tools, equipment, and materials in my work unit to get the job done.	1	2	3	4	5	6
54. The materials and supplies we need in my work unit are delivered on time as ordered.	1	2	3	4	5	6
55. The distribution of work among the people in my work unit is well-balanced.	1	2	3	4	5	6
56. In my work unit, we have enough time to perform our jobs in a professional manner.	1	2	3	4	5	6
57. My work unit is structured properly to get the job done.	1	2	3	4	5	6
58. People in my work unit are rewarded for good work.	1	2	3	4	5	6
59. People in my work unit are paid fairly for the work that they do.	1	2	3	4	5	6

Legend: (1) strongly disagree, (2) disagree, (3) somewhat disagree, (4) somewhat agree, (5) agree, (6) strongly agree.

	Strongly Disagree					Strongly Agree
60. Attempts are made to promote the people in my work unit who do good work.	1	2	3	4	5	6
61. People in my work unit receive promotions because they earned them.	1	2	3	4	5	6
62. Supervisors in my work unit give credit to people when they do a good job.	1	2	3	4	5	6
63. There are penalties for people in my work unit.	1	2	3	4	5	6
64. There is quick recognition for people in my work unit for outstanding performance by an individual or team.	1	2	3	4	5	6
65. People in my work unit know who their customers are.	1	2	3	4	5	6
66. People in my work unit care about our customers.	1	2	3	4	5	6
67. There are effective communication channels between departments in this organization.	1	2	3	4	5	6
68. People in my work unit do not have to rely on "the grapevine" or rumors for information.	1	2	3	4	5	6
69. People in my work unit have ample opportunity to exchange information with their supervisors.	1	2	3	4	5	6
70. People in my work unit get the facts and the information they need to do a good job.	1	2	3	4	5	6

ASSESSMENT OF PROCESSES

The statements in the following sections are varied in format. In each case, circle the response number to the right of each statement that most closely represents the extent of your perception about your organization.

	Yes	No	Not Sure
This organization has:			
71. Used surveys of some/all of its members in order to determine whether improvements in quality are needed.	2	1	1
72. Used formal interviews with some/all of its members in order to determine whether improvement in quality are needed.	2	1	1
73. Informally asked some/all of its members for their opinions about whether improvements in quality are needed.	2	1	1
74. Asked senior management people for their opinions about whether improvements in quality are needed.	2	1	1
75. Analyzed data concerning goal/objective accomplishments in order to determine whether improvements in quality are needed.	2	1	1
76. Relied on "higher order" directives in order to determine whether improvements in quality are needed.	2	1	1
77. Asked established team members to report periodically.	2	1	1
This organization is (or might become) committed to quality improvement because:			
78. We are mandated to do so by a higher authority.	2	1	1
79. The people at the top level of this organization are/were dissatisfied with the quality being achieved.	2	1	1
80. We want to improve an already acceptable quality record.	2	1	1
81. We want to maintain a specified level of service in the face of budget reductions.	2	1	1
82. The people we serve deserve our best efforts.	2	1	1

	Yes	No	Don't Have Policy
This organization has a quality improvement policy that:			
83. Is written.	2	1	1
84. Has specific goals and objectives.	2	1	1
85. Everyone in the organization has seen.	2	1	1
86. Is taken seriously by people.	2	1	1
87. Holds people accountable for success/failure.	2	1	1

	Yes	No	Does Not Apply
Responsibility for quality performance improvement:			
88. Is accepted by senior management.	2	1	1
89. Is accepted by middle management.	2	1	1
90. Is accepted by almost all organizational members.	2	1	1
91. This organization has a separately identified office that oversees its quality improvement efforts.	2	1	1
92. Quality improvement concerns are discussed/monitored at least on a quarterly basis.	2	1	1
93. Managers at all levels have clearly defined roles in our quality improvement process.	2	1	1
94. This organization uses teams to monitor quality improvement projects.	2	1	1
95. Managers at all levels are responsible for the success or failure of our quality improvement efforts.	2	1	1
96. The organization has a database or tracking system for relevant quality information.	2	1	1

	Yes	No	Not Sure
In order to determine what our customers think about our products/services/work, we:			
97. Conduct surveys on a regular basis.	2	1	1
98. Ask them informally.	2	1	1

	Yes	No	Not Sure
99. Monitor complaints.	2	1	1
100. Ask our employees who have contact with our customers.	2	1	1

The leaders at the top level in this organization:

	Yes	No	Not Sure
101. Have agreed upon a definition of quality improvement.	2	1	1
102. Have set long-term goals concerning quality improvement.	2	1	1
103. Have set short-term objectives concerning quality improvement.	2	1	1
104. Have defined performance measures to monitor progress toward reaching objectives and goals.	2	1	1

How many work units within this organization:

	Almost None					Almost All
105. Know how the organization defines quality improvement?	1	2	3	4	5	6
106. Have set long-term goals concerning quality improvement?	1	2	3	4	5	6
107. Have set short-term objectives concerning quality improvement?	1	2	3	4	5	6
108. Have defined performance measures to monitor progress toward reaching their objectives and goals?	1	2	3	4	5	6

How many organizational members:

	Almost None					Almost All
109. Can specify, if asked, what goals or objectives they are working toward?	1	2	3	4	5	6
110. Were invited to participate in setting goals or objectives related to their work?	1	2	3	4	5	6
111. Know how the goals/objectives they are working toward relate to their work unit's mission?	1	2	3	4	5	6
112. Know how performance measures relate to monitoring their accomplishment of goals and objectives?	1	2	3	4	5	6

Legend: (1) almost none, (2) very few, (3) some, (4) quite a few, (5) most, (6) almost all.

	Yes	No	Not Sure
Long-range planning in this organization includes:			
113. Integration of quality improvement planning into general business planning.	2	1	1
114. Prioritizing quality improvement issues.	2	1	1
115. Customer input.	2	1	1
116. Employee input.	2	1	1
117. Quality improvement implementation strategies for all work units.	2	1	1
118. A means for monitoring quality improvement effectiveness over time.	2	1	1
In terms of setting organizational improvement priorities, we have considered or evaluated:			
119. Changing our business strategy.	2	1	1
120. Improving our work methods or procedures.	2	1	1
121. Bettering our employee utilization.	2	1	1
122. Revising or instituting training programs.	2	1	1
123. Acquiring recent technological improvements (equipment, materials).	2	1	1

	Strongly Disagree					Strongly Agree
124. The structure of this organization supports its efforts to carry out its mission.	1	2	3	4	5	6
125. Organizational members have the information they need to do their work.	1	2	3	4	5	6
126. This organization has a realistic schedule for replacing outdated equipment.	1	2	3	4	5	6

Legend: (1) strongly disagree, (2) disagree, (3) somewhat disagree, (4) somewhat agree, (5) agree, (6) strongly agree.

	Strongly Disagree					Strongly Agree
127. Organizational members have been adequately trained to use the equipment they have.	1	2	3	4	5	6
128. Before equipment is bought by or issued to this organization, plans have been made concerning how it will be used and who will use it.	1	2	3	4	5	6
129. Efforts are made to update work methods in this organization (e.g., the way work is organized and the tools or materials used to accomplish it).	1	2	3	4	5	6
130. People in charge of similar work units frequently share information about their work methods and practices.	1	2	3	4	5	6
131. Updating work methods can be key to quality improvement.	1	2	3	4	5	6
Organization members with good ideas are likely to:						
132. Formally submit them through a suggestion system.	1	2	3	4	5	6
133. Tell their supervisors.	1	2	3	4	5	6
134. Be asked periodically what they think.	1	2	3	4	5	6

Legend: (1) strongly disagree, (2) disagree, (3) somewhat disagree, (4) somewhat agree, (5) agree, (6) strongly agree.

	Yes	No	Not Sure
135. This organization has a suggestion program.	2	1	1
136. This organization has conducted brainstorming sessions that included lower-level organizational members.	2	1	1
137. This organization has used teams to gather information or solve problems.	2	1	1

	Strongly Disagree				Strongly Agree	
138. Creative thinking is rewarded in this organization.	1	2	3	4	5	6
139. Taking risks is rewarded in this organization.	1	2	3	4	5	6
140. Managers at all levels have the authority to try a promising new approach.	1	2	3	4	5	6
141. A promising new approach is likely to be approved quickly for a trial.	1	2	3	4	5	6
142. The future strength of this organization is dependent on the continuing growth of its members through appropriate training.	1	2	3	4	5	6

Legend: (1) strongly disagree, (2) disagree, (3) somewhat disagree, (4) somewhat agree, (5) agree, (6) strongly agree.

143. Circle the response number next to the *one* statement that best represents your organization.

Most nonsupervisory members have direct input in setting goals or expectations for their work.   6

Most nonsupervisory members have indirect input through representatives in setting goals or expectations for their work.   4

Most nonsupervisory members can negotiate with management after they are assigned goals or expectations for their work.   3

Most nonsupervisory members have no input about goals or expectations for their work.   1

144. Circle the response number next to the *one* statement that best represents your organization.

Most organizational members attend mandatory in-house training programs to learn about quality improvement techniques.   6

Most organizational members attend in-house training programs on a voluntary basis to learn about quality improvement techniques.   5

Most organizational members attend outside seminars to learn about quality improvement techniques.   4

Most organizational members review resources (books, tapes) that are available in-house to learn about quality improvement techniques.   3

None of the above.   1

	Yes	No	Not Sure
In order to tell how well we are doing as an organization, we monitor data about:			
145. Our efficiency.	2	1	1
146. Our effectiveness.	2	1	1
147. Our productivity.	2	1	1
148. The quality of our services/products/work.	2	1	1
149. The timeliness of our work.	2	1	1
150. Our innovativeness.	2	1	1
151. The quality of working life for our members.	2	1	1
152. Our finances.	2	1	1

	Yes	No	Don't Collect Data
The performance data that this organization collects:			
153. Are tracked over time.	2	1	1
154. Are compared with goals, standards, or objectives.	2	1	1
155. Are compared with other similar organizations.	2	1	1
The performance data that this organization collects:			
156. Are evaluated at least quarterly.	2	1	1
157. Are used to identify problems/barriers.	2	1	1
158. Are evaluated by a team or task force.	2	1	1
159. Are used to identify opportunities for quality improvement.	2	1	1

	Yes	No	Not Sure
160. Organizational members are informed about how this work unit stands in relation to goals, objectives, or standards.	2	1	1
Top-performing managers at all levels in this organization:			
161. Can expect a monetary bonus or award.	2	1	1
162. Can expect an award.	2	1	1

	Yes	No	Not Sure
163. Can expect to be recognized by leaders at the top level.	2	1	1
164. Can expect to be told they are doing a great job.	2	1	1
165. Can expect increased responsibility.	2	1	1
Top-performing organizational members:			
166. Can expect a monetary bonus or award.	2	1	1
167. Can expect an award.	2	1	1
168. Can expect to be recognized by leaders at the top level.	2	1	1
169. Can expect to be told they are doing a great job.	2	1	1
170. Can expect increased responsibility.	2	1	1
171. The performance appraisals (non-Deming organizations) of managers at all levels include quality improvement criteria.	2	1	1
172. The performance appraisals (non-Deming organizations) of organizational members include quality improvement criteria.	2	1	1

MANAGEMENT TOOLS ASSESSMENT

	Yes	No	Not Sure
This organization has:			
173. Used surveys to assess employee opinion about the organization's practices or policies.	2	1	1
174. Used surveys to gather information about what in the organization needs improving.	2	1	1
175. Used surveys to assess the outcomes of its work.	2	1	1
176. Used surveys to assess quality of its work.	2	1	1
177. Used surveys to assess employee opinions about the goals/objectives they are working toward.	2	1	1

	Yes	*No*	*Not Sure*
178. Called groups of individuals together to define or clarify the organization's mission and/or work.	2	1	1
179. Called groups of individuals together to define long-term organizational-level goals and/or long-term work unit–level goals.	2	1	1
180. Called groups of individuals together to define short-term organizational objectives and/or short-term work unit objectives.	2	1	1
181. Called groups of individuals together to identify obstacles to goal/objective accomplishment.	2	1	1
182. Called groups of individuals together to define performance measures to track progress toward goal attainment.	2	1	1
183. The organization uses statistical process control charts or graphs to track data over time.	2	1	1
184. This organization uses diagrams or flowcharts to highlight potential causes of problems.	2	1	1
185. This organization has evaluated its office and work space design.	2	1	1
186. This organization has a high-quality information resource library.	2	1	1
187. This organization has arranged workshops to promote quality awareness among its members.	2	1	1
188. This organization has published newsletters containing quality improvement information.	2	1	1
189. This organization has posted information on bulletin boards about quality improvement.	2	1	1
190. This organization has held contests to reward the "most improved" work units.	2	1	1
191. This organization has attempted to inform and involve everyone in quality improvement.	2	1	1

	Yes	No	Not Sure
192. This organization has used team building (techniques to improve group member relationships).	2	1	1
193. This organization has established improvement teams (groups of individuals who come together to solve quality-related problems).	2	1	1

ORGANIZATIONAL ASSESSMENT

	Strongly Disagree					Strongly Agree
194. Work delays are uncommon in this organization.	1	2	3	4	5	6
195. Once a job or project gets started, it's usually finished without undue delay.	1	2	3	4	5	6
196. There is little wastage of materials and supplies.	1	2	3	4	5	6
197. People make efforts to reuse or salvage excess materials and supplies whenever possible.	1	2	3	4	5	6
198. Tools and/or equipment are maintained and operated at peak efficiency.	1	2	3	4	5	6
199. Our tools and/or equipment rarely require repair.	1	2	3	4	5	6
200. This organization has sufficient personnel to accomplish its mission.	1	2	3	4	5	6
201. The personnel turnover rate is low.	1	2	3	4	5	6
202. Working conditions (noise, heat, light, dirt) in this organization are excellent.	1	2	3	4	5	6
203. Work facilities (bathrooms, cafeterias, conference rooms, etc.) are excellent.	1	2	3	4	5	6

Legend: (1) strongly disagree, (2) disagree, (3) somewhat disagree, (4) somewhat agree, (5) agree, (6) strongly agree.

	Strongly Disagree					Strongly Agree
204. Organizational members are well-trained.	1	2	3	4	5	6
205. Organizational members receive the guidance and assistance they need to accomplish their work.	1	2	3	4	5	6
206. This organization's materials and supplies are well accounted for without unexplained losses.	1	2	3	4	5	6
207. This organization's materials and supplies meet quality specifications.	1	2	3	4	5	6
Organizational members rarely need to:						
208. Shift work priorities in order to get jobs done.	1	2	3	4	5	6
209. Redo a job or task.	1	2	3	4	5	6
The organization's customers:						
210. Are satisfied with the quality of our work.	1	2	3	4	5	6
211. Seldom complain.	1	2	3	4	5	6
The organization's customers:						
212. Are satisfied with the quantity of our work.	1	2	3	4	5	6
213. Are satisfied with the timeliness of our work.	1	2	3	4	5	6
The organization's customers:						
214. Find minimal errors in our work.	1	2	3	4	5	6
215. Find our work consistent.	1	2	3	4	5	6

Legend: (1) strongly disagree, (2) disagree, (3) somewhat disagree, (4) somewhat agree, (5) agree, (6) strongly agree.

SCORING SELF-ASSESSMENT

The following scoring worksheets provide a way to evaluate your self-assessment. Transfer the value of your responses to the questions or sets of questions as indicated by the worksheet groupings, and then divide the number shown on the form. Carry out the division to two decimal points. For example, say you responded "6", "5," "4," "3," "2," and "1" to Climate questions 1 through 6, respectively. On the Climate Scoring Worksheet you would write "21" in the blank for Awareness of Strategic Challenge, divide 21 by 6 (the value indicated), then write "3.50" in the blank in the Your Score column. A scoring summary table, which shows the target score for each category, follows each worksheet. Transfer the worksheet scores to the corresponding category in the table. In our example, you would write "3.50" in the Your Score column next to the Awareness of Strategic Challenge category.

By comparing your scores with the target scores, you can evaluate how you and your organization perceive quality. If your score is equal to or lower than a target score, you need to improve your approach to quality in that area. Review the Total Quality Management principles and practices described in Chapter 6 to discover ways you can significantly improve your quality.

Climate Scoring Worksheet

			Your Score
Awareness of Strategic Challenge	Add response numbers from questions 1–6 and place total in space at right.	_____ ÷ 6 =	_____
Vision for the Future	Add response numbers from questions 7–11 and place total in space at right.	_____ ÷ 5 =	_____
Innovation	Add response numbers from questions 12–13 and place total in space at right.	_____ ÷ 2 =	_____
Quality Policy/Philosophy	Add response numbers from questions 14–18 and place total in space at right.	_____ ÷ 5 =	_____
Value Systems/Ethics	Add response numbers from questions 19–21 and place total in space at right.	_____ ÷ 3 =	_____
Strategic Focus	Total of scores (questions 1–21).	_____ ÷ 21 =	_____
Top Management Involvement	Add response numbers from questions 22–25 and place total in space at right.	_____ ÷ 4 =	_____

*Your
Score*

Visible Commitment to Goals	Add response numbers from questions 26–28 and place total in space at right.	_____ ÷ 3 =	_____
Role in Quality Improvement Process	Add response numbers from questions 29–31 and place total in space at right.	_____ ÷ 3 =	_____
Concern for Improvement	Add response numbers from questions 32–33 and place total in spaces at right.	_____ ÷ 2 =	_____
Systems/Structure for Quality Improvement	Add response numbers from questions 34–35 and place total in space at right.	_____ ÷ 2 =	_____
Leadership and Management	Total of scores (questions 22–35).	_____ ÷ 14 =	_____

Awareness of Productivity/Quality Issues	Add response numbers from questions 36–37 and place total in space at right.	_____ ÷ 2 =	_____
Attitudes/Morale	Add response numbers from questions 38–41 and place total in space at right.	_____ ÷ 4 =	_____
Cooperation	Add response numbers from questions 42–45 and place total in space at right.	_____ ÷ 4 =	_____
Involvement	Add response numbers from questions 46–47 and place total in space at right.	_____ ÷ 2 =	_____
Perceptions of Work Environment	Add response numbers from questions 48–50 and place total in space at right.	_____ ÷ 3 =	_____
Social Interactions	Add response numbers from questions 51–52 and place total in space at right.	_____ ÷ 2 =	_____
Task Characteristics	Add response numbers from questions 53–57 and place total in space at right.	_____ ÷ 5 =	_____
Consequential Constraints	Add response numbers from questions 58–64 and place total in space at right.	_____ ÷ 7 =	_____
Work Force	Total of scores (questions 36–64).	_____ ÷ 29 =	_____

			Your Score

Customer Orientation	Add response numbers from questions 65–66 and place total in space at right.	_____ ÷ 2 =	_____
Communications	Add response numbers from questions 67–70 and place total in space at right.	_____ ÷ 4 =	_____

Copy the result for each category from your Climate Scoring Worksheet to the corresponding space in Table 5–1, Summary of Climate Scores. If any score is *lower* than the target score it means that some practices typically considered helpful for quality may be absent in your organization.

TABLE 5-1
Summary of Climate Scores

Category	Your Score*	Target Score
Awareness of Strategic Challenge	_____	3.50
Vision for the Future	_____	3.50
Innovation	_____	3.50
Quality Policy/Philosophy	_____	3.50
Value Systems/Ethics	_____	3.50
Top Management Involvement	_____	3.50
Visible Commitment to Goals	_____	3.50
Role in Quality Improvement Process	_____	3.50
Concern for Improvement	_____	3.50
Systems/Structure for Quality Improvement	_____	3.50
Awareness of Productivity/Quality Issues	_____	3.50
Attitudes/Morale	_____	3.50
Cooperation	_____	3.50
Involvement	_____	3.50
Perceptions of Work Environment	_____	3.50
Social Interactions	_____	3.50
Task Characteristics	_____	3.50
Consequential Constraints	_____	3.50
Customer Orientation	_____	3.50
Communications	═══════	3.50
Total (Average your score by adding the values in this column and dividing by 20.)	_____	3.50

*From the Climate Scoring Worksheet.

Process Scoring Worksheet

				Your Score
Job Analysis	Add response numbers from questions 71–77 and place total in space at right.	_____	÷ 7 =	_____
Higher Authority	Add response numbers from questions 78–82 and place total in space at right.	_____	÷ 5 =	_____

Your
Score

Quality Emphasis	Add response numbers from questions 83–87 and place total in space at right.	_____ ÷ 5 =	_____
Top Management Leadership	Add response numbers from questions 88–96 and place total in space at right.	_____ ÷ 9 =	_____
Customer/Service Activities	Add response numbers from questions 97–100 and place total in space at right.	_____ ÷ 4 =	_____
Define Improvement	Add response numbers from questions 101–104 and place total in space at right.	_____ ÷ 4 =	_____
Unit Goals	Add response numbers from questions 105–108 and place total in space at right.	_____ ÷ 4 =	_____
Organization Goals	Add response numbers from questions 109–112 and place total in space at right.	_____ ÷ 4 =	_____
Quality Planning	Add response numbers from questions 113–118 and place total in space at right.	_____ ÷ 6 =	_____
Planning Strategy	Add response numbers from questions 119–123 and place total in space at right.	_____ ÷ 5 =	_____
Organizational Streamlining	Add response numbers from questions 124–125 and place total in space at right.	_____ ÷ 2 =	_____
Investment/Appropriate Technology	Add response numbers from questions 126–128 and place total in space at right.	_____ ÷ 3 =	_____
Methods/Process Improvement	Add response numbers from questions 129–131 and place total in space at right.	_____ ÷ 3 =	_____
New Ideas	Add response numbers from questions 132–134 and place total in space at right.	_____ ÷ 3 =	_____
People-Oriented Input	Add response numbers from questions 135–137 and place total in space at right.	_____ ÷ 3 =	_____
Track Progress	Add response numbers from questions 138–144 and place total in space at right.	_____ ÷ 7 =	_____

			Your Score
Measurement	Add response numbers from questions 145–152 and place total in space at right.	_____ ÷ 8 =	_____
Feedback	Add response numbers from questions 153–155 and place total in space at right.	_____ ÷ 3 =	_____
Evaluation	Add response numbers from questions 156–159 and place total in space at right.	_____ ÷ 4 =	_____
Results	Place response number from question 160 in space at right.	_____ =	_____
Awards	Add response numbers from questions 161–170 and place total in space at right.	_____ ÷ 10 =	_____
Personnel Evaluations	Add response numbers from questions 171–172 and place total in space at right.	_____ ÷ 2 =	_____

Copy the result for each processes category from this Process Scoring Worksheet to the corresponding space in Table 5–2, Summary of Process Scores. After you have placed your scores in the appropriate spaces, please refer to the adjacent column for score interpretation. Next to each category, if your score is *lower* than or equal to the target score, you need to review your quality program.

TABLE 5–2
Summary of Process Scores

Category	Your Score*	Target Score
Job Analysis	————	1.50
Higher Authority	————	1.50
Quality Emphasis	————	1.70
Top Management Leadership	————	1.55
Customer/Service Activities	————	1.60
Define Improvement	————	1.60
Unit Goals	————	3.50
Organization Goals	————	3.50
Quality Planning	————	1.50
Planning Strategy	————	1.50
Organizational Streamlining	————	3.50
Investment/Appropriate Technology	————	3.50
Methods/Process Improvement	————	3.50
New Ideas	————	3.50
People-Oriented Input	————	1.40
Track Progress	————	3.50
Measurement	————	1.50
Feedback	————	1.40
Evaluation	————	1.50
Results	————	1.00
Awards	————	1.50
Personnel Evaluations	————	<u>1.50</u>
Total (Average your score by adding the values in this column and dividing by 22.)	————	2.12

*From the Process Scoring Worksheet.

Management Tools Scoring Worksheet

			Your Score
Assessments	Add response numbers from questions 173–177 and place total in space at right.	_____ ÷ 5 =	_____
Definition of Tools	Add response numbers from questions 178–182 and place total in space at right.	_____ ÷ 5 =	_____
Measurement/Process Analysis	Add response numbers from questions 183–185 and place total in space at right.	_____ ÷ 3 =	_____
Awareness/ Communication	Add response numbers from questions 186–190 and place total in space at right.	_____ ÷ 5 =	_____
Organizational Development	Add response numbers from questions 191–193 and place total in space at right.	_____ ÷ 3 =	_____

Copy the result for each management tools category from this worksheet to the corresponding space in Table 5–3, Summary of Management Tools Scores. After you have placed your scores in the appropriate spaces, refer to the adjacent column for score interpretation. If your score is *lower* than or equal to the target score, you may want to review your quality program.

TABLE 5–3
Summary of Management Tools Scores

Category	Your Score*	Target Score
Assessments	_____	1.30
Definition of Tools	_____	1.50
Measurement/Process Analysis	_____	1.50
Awareness/Communication	_____	1.50
Organizational Development	_____	1.50
Total (Average your score by adding the values in this column and dividing by 5.)	_____	1.46

*From the Management Tools Scoring Worksheet.

Organizational Outcomes Scoring Worksheet

			Your Score
Work Flow/Delays	Add response numbers from questions 194–195 and place total in space at right.	_____ ÷ 2 =	_____
Waste	Add response numbers from questions 196–197 and place total in space at right.	_____ ÷ 2 =	_____
Tools/Equipment	Add response numbers from questions 198–199 and place total in space at right.	_____ ÷ 2 =	_____
Staffing	Add response numbers from questions 200–201 and place total in space at right.	_____ ÷ 2 =	_____
Facilities	Add response numbers from questions 202–203 and place total in space at right.	_____ ÷ 2 =	_____
Training	Add response numbers from questions 204–205 and place total in space at right.	_____ ÷ 2 =	_____
Supplies/Parts	Add response numbers from questions 206–207 and place total in space at right.	_____ ÷ 2 =	_____
Organization/Group Structure	Add response numbers from questions 208–209 and place total in space at right.	_____ ÷ 2 =	_____
Customer Quality Survey	Add response numbers from questions 210–211 and place total in space at right.	_____ ÷ 2 =	_____
Quantity	Add response numbers from questions 212–213 and place total in space at right.	_____ ÷ 2 =	_____
Reliability	Add response numbers from questions 214–215 and place total in space at right.	_____ ÷ 2 =	_____

Copy the result for each organizational outcome category to the corresponding space in the Summary in Table 5–4. If any score is *lower* than or equal to 3.50, you need to review your Total Quality Management approach.

TABLE 5-4
Summary of Organizational Outcomes Scores

Category	Your Score*	Target Score
Work Flow/Delays	_____	3.50
Waste	_____	3.50
Tools/Equipment	_____	3.50
Staffing	_____	3.50
Facilities	_____	3.50
Training	_____	3.50
Supplies/Parts	_____	3.50
Organization/Group Structure	_____	3.50
Customer Quality Survey	_____	3.50
Quantity	_____	3.50
Reliability	_____	3.50
Total (Average your score by adding the values in this column and dividing by 11.)	_____	3.50

*From the Organizational Outcomes Scoring Worksheet.

COMPUTERIZED ANALYSIS

Again, this chapter is an edited version of the *Quality and Productivity Self-Assessment Guide*. If you want to have more members of your company conduct this type of self-examination and compare your impressions of your perceived level of quality, you might consider purchasing an automated version of the analysis, available for use on IBM PC–compatible equipment. The software can be obtained from DPPO, Two Skyline Place, Room 1404, 5203 Leesburg Pike, Falls Church, Virginia, 22041, (703) 756-2346. Contact Lee Wexel for price and availability of the latest version of the software.

ASSESSMENT LEADS TO ACTION

In this chapter you have taken an "armchair" approach to your organization's perceived level of quality. This self-assessment guide has provided a scoring methodology that alerts you to the strengths and weaknesses in your quality efforts. The total scores are really not important.

But *how* you responded to each category and the impression you now have about the potential to improve your quality, your service, and your profitability is very important.

Chapter 6 briefly describes the key Total Quality Management principles and practices that you can apply to your business to significantly improve your quality.

CHAPTER 6

HOW TO SIGNIFICANTLY
IMPROVE YOUR QUALITY

ADOPT TOTAL QUALITY MANAGEMENT STRATEGY

Total Quality Management means that you are meeting your customer requirements by doing the right things right the first time. To provide high-quality products and services, management must believe that an obsession for quality and perfection must pervade all facets of a business, from customer input to product design and engineering, production, service support, and human resource management. The driving force behind Total Quality Management is customer satisfaction.

Total Quality Management begins with a strategic decision, a decision that must be made and fully supported by top management. That decision, simply put, is the decision to compete as a world-class company. Total Quality Management concentrates on quality performance—in every facet of a business—as the primary strategy for achieving and maintaining a competitive advantage. It requires taking a systematic view of an organization and looking at how each part interrelates with the whole process. In addition, it demands continuous improvement as a way of life.

The Total Quality Management methodology is based on four concepts. These concepts simply state that an organization must have (1) quality management systems, (2) quality products, services, and technology, and (3) quality people; and that (4) the combined energies of its management, products, and people must be focused on customer satisfaction.

Total Quality Management provides a framework for your application of its concepts, principles, and practices in terms of your specific needs. Total Quality Management is the integration and synergy of leading quality initiatives developed by Crosby, Deming, and Juran.

TOTAL QUALITY MANAGEMENT ACTIVITIES

Getting started with improvement would be easy if we didn't have so much work to do! But we have so much work to do precisely because we have not recognized the importance of Total Quality Management and the benefits of continuously improving every system and process. We must get our systems under control and eliminate the sources of unnecessary and unproductive work.

Getting started and sustaining the early quality improvement initiative is the most difficult task in Total Quality Management. It requires us to make time in our already tight schedules to do something that we perceive to be an additional task. We must modify many of our long-held notions about what good management is all about in exchange for the promise of improvement. You might be surprised that anyone is willing to take these first steps; however, many have already done so and are being richly rewarded. By ultimately gaining real control over our work processes instead of permitting them to control us, we will make large gains.

Those who have blazed the trail toward continuous improvement have left us a legacy of many lessons learned. Many have had false starts, traveled down dead-end roads, and had to start over. If there is one consistent lesson from those who have led this effort, it is that there is no universal strategy for success. The road to continuous improvement is and must be an appropriately tailored, optimized, and personal one. A general behavior and set of actions, however, characterize most successful efforts. That behavior and those actions are presented here as a suggested general strategy for starting your Total Quality Management journey.

While this section speaks to you directly, most behavior and many actions apply equally to your organization as a whole. The elements of this general strategy are listed roughly in order of recommended implementation. The experience of many organizations is that focused application of specific improvement techniques and tools promotes continuous improvement. In this chapter, the earlier elements provide a foundation that is essential for successful process improvement efforts and for creating a culture of continuous improvement that will have long-term success and ultimately be self-sustaining. Some elements are necessary only during the initial phases, but most are periodic or continuous activities that should become routine, ongoing behavior by the organization or individual.

The basic elements of Total Quality Management fall into 12 areas of activity: (1) demonstrate leadership; (2) build awareness; (3) improve communication; (4) continue to present your vision; (5) focus on the customer; (6) demonstrate success; (7) develop teamwork; (8) provide support, training, and education; (9) build trust and respect; (10) create a Total Quality Management environment in which continuous improvement is a way of life; (11) continuously improve all processes; and (12) apply your quality improvement process to your suppliers. Each of these areas encompasses a number of actions.

Demonstrate Leadership.   Total Quality Management depends on people more than anything else, and people lead or are led—they are not managed. Total Quality Management depends on effective leadership, and you must provide that leadership. By taking the initiative, providing an example, and showing the way, you can lead your subordinates and inspire your peers to follow your example. Top leadership is essential, but Total Quality Management leaders are needed at all organizational levels. Effective leadership does not necessarily depend on your place in the organization, but rather on your enthusiasm and your visible commitment to the process of continuous improvement.

Build Awareness.   Building awareness—understanding what Total Quality Management is and why it is important to you and your organization—is one of the first and perhaps most important steps in implementing Total Quality Management. Every person in the organization must become aware of the need to improve, of the promise offered by Total Quality Management, of the various methodologies, and of the tools and techniques available for improvement efforts. Awareness is the key that opens the door to Total Quality Management's potential.

Improve Communication.   As you work on building awareness throughout your organization, begin to establish lines of communication both horizontally and vertically. Honest, open communication is probably the single most important factor in successfully creating a Total Quality Management environment. Fostering such communication will take time, but it can lead to trust and mutual respect, and can sometimes be the only thing that keeps the effort alive. If people keep talking to one another, they can work through problems, overcome barriers, and find encouragement and support from others involved in quality efforts.

Continue to Present Your Vision. Constancy of purpose establishes a common direction for all organizational elements and ensures that efforts at all levels contribute to achieving broad objectives relevant to the entire organization. Communicating your vision of the organization's goals and objectives throughout the organization is essential to focusing improvement efforts for the common benefit. Your behavior and attitudes must reinforce this constancy of purpose, and you must be conscious of the unspoken signals you send your subordinates.

Focus on the Customer. Every process in your organization has a customer, and without a customer a process has no purpose. The customer is the recipient of the process's products or services and defines the quality of those products and services. It is only through focusing on your customers that you can truly optimize your processes, because it is only through your customers that you may effectively define your goals and objectives for improvement. You must focus on both your organization's external customers and your internal customers, who are other members of your organization that depend on your products or services for their own processes.

Demonstrate Success. The success or failure of your initial Total Quality Management efforts and projects can greatly affect how easily you can get your organization to adopt Total Quality Management ideas. It pays to choose these early efforts carefully, looking for opportunities that (1) have a good chance of success; (2) are visible throughout the company and, preferably, to important external customers; and (3) can significantly improve the lives of workers and managers alike. The trick is to find something that is neither so large that you are doomed to failure nor so small that no one will notice if improvements are made.

Develop Teamwork. Teamwork is the engine that drives many improvement efforts. Creating teams allows you to apply diverse skills and experience to your processes and problem solving. Teams provide an underlying basis of experience and history for your improvement effort and are a vehicle through which you allow all individuals to participate in that effort. Not only must individuals cooperate within teams, the teams must cooperate together throughout the organization. An atmosphere of teamwork should permeate your organization, affecting not only formal team efforts but also each individual's interaction in the organization.

Encouraging teamwork often involves teaching people who already work together to consciously act as a team. These natural work groups exist as permanent teams whose objective is the continuous improvement of the processes they own.

Provide Support, Training, and Education.   If you expect to implement Total Quality Management yourself and expect your subordinates to follow suit, you must ensure that adequate time and training resources are available to support your effort. Total Quality Management does not depend on additional people or money; rather, it relies on the availability of time for individuals and groups to pursue improvement efforts and on the availability of training and education to develop needed skills and experience in Total Quality Management improvement tools and techniques. You must make those time and training resources available for yourself and your people; doing so is one way for you to demonstrate your commitment to the improvement effort.

While awareness is the way you get your Total Quality Management effort moving, education and training help accelerate it dramatically. Provided in the right place at the right time, education and training allow you and your subordinates to develop skills and experience in the techniques necessary to implement Total Quality Management. That experience is the first step to making Total Quality Management a part of your day-to-day work life. And, of course, technical training and education are essential to improving each employee's specific job skills. Education and training are comprehensive, intensive, and unending. Quality improvement efforts begin and continue with lifelong education and training.

Build Trust and Respect.   Employees who trust their managers and who are trusted and respected in turn can provide the edge that organizations need to provide superior services or products. Workers have the best, most up-to-date knowledge about how well processes are working, what problems have arisen, and how things could be better. If workers know their opinions are respected, they will share their knowledge and creativity with management—the only way to ensure continuous improvement.

Trust and respect are essential for individual participation. Without such an atmosphere, people will not take actions or make recommendations they perceive to be risky to themselves. Total Quality Management is a process that depends on every person being unafraid to take chances and unworried about risking self-esteem. You must be open and honest with your people and establish channels of communication that are reliable and accessible to everyone in the organization. If people broach ideas, they should be praised; if they identify problems in the process or system, they should be thanked; when they contribute, they should be recognized; when they fail, they should be supported; and when they succeed, they should be rewarded. As their leader, you are responsible for creating an atmosphere of trust and support, and you are responsible for maintaining each individual's sense of self-worth and self-esteem.

Create a Total Quality Management Environment in Which Continuous Improvement Is a Way of Life. By making continuous improvement a part of your daily routine, you will integrate it into all aspects of your work. Continuous improvement only approaches maturity when it is applied routinely to all of your organization's work. Routine application entails using the process improvement cycle in all areas, collecting data and using those data to assess process suitability, removing roadblocks to your improvement efforts and those of others, and continuously improving your knowledge and expertise in process improvement. Ideally, continuous improvement should be your normal approach to doing your work; it must become your way of life.

Continuously Improve All Processes. Continuous process improvement, as the basis of Total Quality Management, is a never-ending effort. Perfection is an ultimate, unattainable goal, but its ideal is the basis for continuous improvement efforts. You must view everything your organization does in terms of interrelated processes. Process improvement should become your organization's way of life. Goals and objectives are realized through process improvement. Your own focus should be to improve all the processes you own and remove all those barriers under your control that hinder others from improving their own processes. The only true measure of your performance over time is the degree of process improvement you effect.

Process standardization is a means of defining a process and ensuring that everyone understands and employs it in a consistent manner. It is difficult to improve something that is not well-defined. Process standards communicate the current, best-known way of performing a process and ensure consistent process performance by a variety of individuals. With an established standard, people have a way to know that they are doing their jobs correctly, and you have a means of assessing their performance objectively. Process standards provide the baseline from which to continuously improve the process. The people doing the work should maintain and update standards as they improve their processes so that the standards always reflect the current, best-known means of doing the work.

Apply Your Quality Improvement Process to Your Suppliers. Your organization's ability to improve its processes depends in part on the inputs to those processes. To the extent that you procure materials and services from other organizations, your continuous improvement effort depends on those suppliers. Expanding your improvement culture to all your suppliers will help ensure that the quality of your process inputs is sufficient to meet your own improvement objectives. You can expand your culture of continuous improvement by working more closely with your suppliers, by helping them get their own improvement efforts underway, by building mutual trust and respect, and generally by becoming a better customer yourself.

IMPROVE YOUR QUALITY

This chapter has described the concepts and principles involved in implementing the Total Quality Management methodology. By tailoring these concepts and principles to your unique operation, you can significantly improve your quality, increase productivity, improve your world-class competitive position, and make more money than by doing business as usual.

CHAPTER 7

TOOLS AND TECHNIQUES

THE RIGHT TOOL

This chapter provides the manager with a primer on Total Quality Management tools, techniques, and methods. These generic tools are representative of those that can be used to improve any process and are presented to provide an awareness of what they are, why they are used, and how to use them. Not all of the tools are appropriate for use in all applications.

Tools and techniques are essential for implementing the Total Quality Management improvement process. *Tools* make it possible for you to accomplish work; make meaningful measurements; and analyze, visualize, and understand information. *Techniques* help you to organize and accomplish quality analysis in a structured and systematic manner.

GRAPHIC TOOLS

As a Chinese proverb says, a picture is worth many words *and* numbers. Graphic displays allow you to create a logical storyboard that most people can understand at a glance.

A number of factors can lead to the decision to use a particular graphic tool, including the unique application and an individual's or team's experience and preferences. Most graphic tools are oriented toward a certain type of activity, and each tool has its strengths and weaknesses. This section summarizes some of the common graphic tools used to implement the Total Quality Management methodology. Table 7–1 shows when you need to use particular graphic tools.

TABLE 7–1
Use of Graphic Tools

Graphic Tool	Use When You Need to . . .
Bar chart	Compare quantity of data among different categories to help visualize differences.
Cause-and-effect (fishbone) diagram	Systematically analyze cause-and-effect relationships and identify potential root causes of a problem.
Checksheet	Gather a variety of data in a systematic fashion for a clear and objective picture of the facts.
Control chart	Monitor the performance of a process with frequent outputs to determine if its performance is meeting customer requirements or if it can be improved to meet or exceed them.
Flowchart	Describe an existing process, develop modifications, or design an entirely new process.
Histogram	Display the dispersion or spread of the data under consideration.
Pareto chart	Identify major factors in a subject being analyzed and highlight "the vital few" in contrast to "the trivial many."
Scatter diagram	Show the relationship between two variables.
Time line chart	Visually display complex and quantifiable data. These charts often show changes in quantity over time.

Each of these graphic tools is briefly described to enhance the manager's understanding of its use under the Total Quality Management methodology.

Bar Chart

Bar charts show a comparison of quantities by the length of the bars that represent them (such as frequencies of events in different locations, cost of different types of breakdowns, and so on). Bars may be horizontal or vertical.

Along with time line charts, bar charts are among the most common of data displays; however, two differences between them are worth noting. The obvious difference is that a bar chart uses height columns, while the time chart connects data points with a line. Visually, then, the bar chart emphasizes differences (or similarities) between and among the columns of various heights. The time chart emphasizes the direction of change over time. The second difference is that the divisions along the horizontal line of the time chart are time (quantitative) intervals. The divisions along the horizontal axis of the bar chart are nominal categories.

Figure 7–1 is an example of a bar chart. It shows the number of household appliances sold to some measured group (such as "within households with annual earnings of more than $50,000 per year"). From the bar chart, we can conclude that TVs continue to be the item most frequently purchased and that microwaves are increasing in popularity, but that ranges and refrigerators are purchased relatively infrequently. This particular bar chart is really two bar charts superimposed: one for 1980 and one for 1990.

As with all graphic displays of data, the bar chart tells its story at a glance. The more data you have to analyze, the more important the use of graphics becomes. Bar charts make graphic comparisons of quantity easy to see. To construct a bar chart, proceed as follows:

FIGURE 7–1
Example of Bar Chart

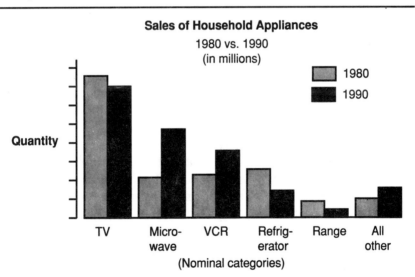

Source: *A Guide to Benchmarking in Xerox.*

- Collect the raw data on a checksheet, if necessary.
- List the categories (usually words rather than numbers) across the horizontal scale at the bottom. You may set them in any sequence, such as in descending order or any other way that makes sense. Label all categories.
- To set the vertical scale to the left, find both the largest and smallest value from the data and make sure the scale is broad enough to include both. Label both the scale and the intervals.
- Determine the quantity of each category, and draw the bar accordingly. Generally speaking, bars should not touch or overlap.
- Bar charts can show and compare double or triple bars for different years or different populations (for example, households with earnings under $50,000).
- Give your bar chart a descriptive title. Include any legends that show what different patterns or colors represent.

Cause-and-Effect (Fishbone) Diagram

The cause-and-effect diagram is a graphic representation of the relationships between an effect (problem) and its potential causes. This tool is useful in brainstorming, examining processes, and planning activities. The process of constructing a cause-and-effect diagram helps stimulate thinking about an issue, helps organize thoughts into a rational whole, and generates discussion and the airing of viewpoints. The cause-and-effect diagram documents the level of understanding about an issue and provides a framework from which to begin expanding that understanding.

Cause-and-effect diagrams can be used to explore a wide variety of topics and relationships, including those between an existing problem and the factors that might bear on it; a desired future outcome and the factors that relate to it; or any event past, present, or future and its causal factors.

Cause-and-effect diagrams go by several names: fishbone diagram, which describes how it looks, and Ishikawa diagram, for its "inventor," Kaoru Ishikawa, a Japanese quality leader.

The problem—or effect—appears in a box to the right (the "head" of the fish) as shown in Figure 7–2. To the left are the "bones" of the fish on which causes are organized and displayed as categories. The entries are words or nominal data. In this example, the problem or effect is that

FIGURE 7–2
Example of Cause-and-Effect (Fishbone) Diagram

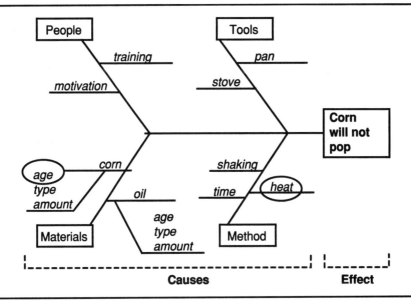

the corn will not pop. The four factors that may be causing this are people, tools for popping corn, materials, and the method or process used. These are the four main "bones" for this example, but a different problem would suggest different major bones. For example, if our problem were "poor sales of the X3 portable," we might select salespeople, product, price, promotion, and/or environment as the major bones of the diagram.

The fishbone diagram ensures that quality analysis groups thoroughly examine all possible causes or categories. More importantly, it provides a process for groups to follow. And because the fishbone is a graphic display, it serves to focus the attention of the group on something more concrete that everyone sees and interprets in a more or less consistent manner.

Here's how to develop a cause-and-effect diagram:

- Define the effect or current situation as clearly as possible. You can always go back and refine it later as you collect new data. Write the effect in the head of the fish.

- Many groups prefer to begin by brainstorming causes, and listing them on a flip chart in no particular order. When the group runs dry of ideas, they look for categories and similarities suggested by the list. These major categories or themes become the big bones.
- To encourage lots of ideas, ask *why, why, why.* When the answers begin to sound silly, you can stop.
- Draw the major bones and label them. You may decide on three, four, or more major themes. Use generic branches (people, methods, materials, machines) if helpful.
- Place the causes from the brainstorm list as small bones under the appropriate big bone.
- The organization of the brainstormed causes will no doubt stimulate other ideas for causes. The group should be encouraged to add as many potential causes as they can think of. For each cause identified, ask, What caused this?
- The group can then highlight the cause(s) they believe to be contributing to the effect. In the popcorn example (Figure 7–2), the group has circled "age of corn" and "amount of heat" as the most likely causes.
- To verify causes, you will need to collect information to either accept or reject the cause(s).
- Work on most important causes (e.g., use design of experiments).
- Desensitize, eliminate, or control causes.

Checksheet

A checksheet provides a list of check-off items that permit data to be collected quickly and easily in a simple standardized format that lends itself to quantitative analysis. Checksheets are frequently used to collect data on numbers of defective items, defect locations, and defect causes. Figure 7–3 is a simple example of a checksheet.

Make a checksheet by laying out the categories of information and data about the items onto a standardized form or grid. Determine the categories by asking such fact-finding questions as:

- What happens?
- Who does it, receives it, is responsible for it?
- Where—place?

FIGURE 7–3
Simple Example of a Checksheet

CHECKSHEET

Product: TRC Receiver unit   Date: 9/09/93

Name: Hunt
Lot: 51

Total examined: 200

Defect type	Defect count	Subtotal
Chipped	ЦНt +Ht ЦНt	15
Off-color	ЛНt ЖТ ЛНt НН II	22
Bent	НН	5
	Grand total: 42	

- When—time of day, month, how often?
- How does it happen, how much, how long, and so on?

Do not ask *why*. This will lead you to search for causes while still trying to determine if a problem exists and what it looks like. The checksheet should be designed to facilitate the collection of as many different kinds of data as are useful. The team can brainstorm items and then refine the list through multivoting. It is also helpful to gather a little data before designing your checksheet. You may determine the appropriate categories from this smaller sample. The checksheet should also clearly indicate who collected the data and where, when, and how it was collected. In a sample, the total population from which the data were gathered should also be indicated.

Control Chart

A control chart is used to monitor the performance of a process with frequent outputs. It provides a pictorial representation of an ongoing process and is based on four concepts:

- All processes fluctuate with time.
- Individual points are unpredictable.
- A stable process fluctuates randomly, and groups of points from a stable process tend to fall within predictable bounds.
- An unstable process does not fluctuate randomly, and these fluctuations are generally out of the range of normal operations.

The control chart, shown in Figure 7–4, is a graph that displays data taken over time and also shows computed variations of those data. Control charts are used to show the variation on a variety of variables including average ($\bar{X}$) and range (R), and also the number of defects (PN), percent defective (P), defects per variable unit (U), and defects per fixed

FIGURE 7–4
Example of Control Chart

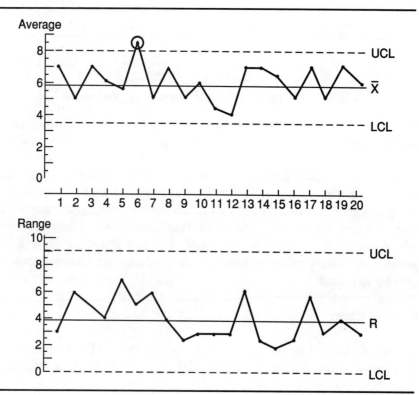

unit (C). *A Guide to Quality Control* by Ishikawa provides excellent guidance on using control charts. The control chart allows you to distinguish between measurements that are predictably within the inherent capability of the process (common causes of variation) and measurements that are unpredictable and produced by special causes.

The upper and lower control limits (UCL and LCL, respectively) must not be confused with specification limits. Control limit averages can describe the natural variation of the process such that points within the limits are generally indicative of normal and expected variation. Points outside the limits signal that something has occurred that requires special attention because it may be outside the built-in systematic cause of variation in the process. Each individual point out of the limits should be explained, however.

These charts help you understand the inherent capability of your processes, bring your processes under control by eliminating the special causes of variation, reduce tampering with processes that are under statistical control, and monitor the effects of process changes aimed at improvement.

To construct a control chart, follow these basic steps:

- Determine the control limits, which are a function of sample size, to describe the expected variation of a process.
- Collect data.
- Plot data on the control chart to assess performance and identify points outside established control limits.
- Determine causes of points outside control limits.
- Identify ways to eliminate special causes and reduce normal variation.

After constructing your control chart, examine it to see where the data points are located. If your process is fairly consistent and stable, most of the data points should fall within the established limits. Control charts illustrate fluctuations within the process that occur in a nonrandom pattern. Points that fall outside one of the control limits should be reported or investigated.

Once you've created your control chart, you can continue to use it to determine whether your operations are staying within the operating limits you've established. As you add points, examine the chart for favorable or unfavorable out-of-control points, and look for special or assignable causes.

There are many types of control charts. The one you use depends on the type of data collected. Because choosing and developing control charts are rather complex processes, it is suggested that your quality specialist be asked for assistance when a control chart is deemed necessary.

Flowchart

A flowchart is a pictorial representation of the steps in a process. It is a useful tool for determining how a process really works. By examining how various steps in a process relate to one another, you can often uncover potential sources of trouble. Flowcharts can be applied to anything from the flow of materials to the steps in making a sale or servicing a product.

Flowcharts permit you to examine and understand relationships in a process or project. They provide a step-by-step schema or picture that serves to create a common language, ensure common understanding about sequence, and focus collective attention on shared concerns.

Several different types of flowcharts are particularly useful in the continuous improvement process. Three frequently used charts are the top-down flowchart, the detailed flowchart, and the work-flow diagram. The top-down flowchart (Figure 7–5) presents only the major or most fundamental steps in a process or project. It helps you and your team to easily visualize the process in a single, simple flow diagram. Key value-added actions associated with each major activity are listed below their respective flow diagram steps. You can construct a top-down flowchart

FIGURE 7–5
Example of Top-Down Flowchart

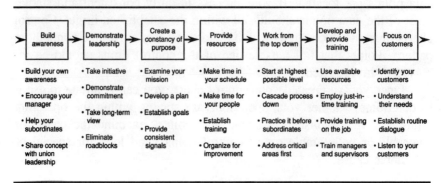

FIGURE 7-6
Sample Detailed Flowchart

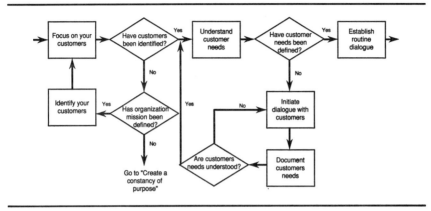

fairly quickly and easily. You generally do so before attempting to produce detailed flowcharts for a process. By limiting the top-down flowchart to significant value-added activity, you reduce the likelihood of becoming bogged down in the detail.

The detailed flowchart (Figure 7-6) provides very specific information about process flow. At its most detailed level, every decision point, feedback loop, and process step is represented. Detailed flowcharts should be used only when the level of detail provided by the top-down or other simpler flowcharts is insufficient to support understanding, analysis, and improvement activity. The detailed flowchart may also be useful and appropriate for critical processes, where precisely following a specific procedure is essential. The work-flow diagram is a graphic representation or picture of how work actually flows through a physical space or facility. It is very useful for analyzing flow processes, illustrating flow inefficiency, and planning process-flow improvement.

Histogram

A histogram is a visual representation of the spread or dispersion of variable data (e.g., the number of defects per lot). In histograms of natural data, many items tend to fall toward the center of the distribution (central tendency), with progressively fewer items as you move from the center. This information is represented by a series of rectangles or bars proportional in height to the frequency of the group or class represented, as shown in Figure 7-7. Because class intervals (but not numbers) will

FIGURE 7–7
Example of a Histogram

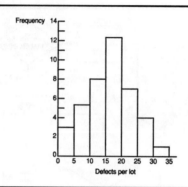

be equal in size, the rectangles are of equal width. The heights of the rectangles relative to one another indicate the proportion of data points in each class.

Histograms help to identify changes or shifts in processes as changes are made. They show how variable measurements of a process or product can be, and they help in the establishment of standards. Once standards have been set, measurements can be compared to these standards.

To construct a histogram, proceed as follows:

- Collect the data you plan to chart, and count the total number of data points.
- Determine the range of your data by subtracting the smallest data point from the largest.
- Keep the number of data bars in your graph to between six and twelve. To determine the width of each class interval (bar), divide the range (above) by the desired number of bars.
- Place your class intervals (groupings of data) on the horizontal axis.
- Place your frequency or number scale on the vertical axis.
- Arrange the data points in ascending order.
- Draw the height of each bar to represent the number of frequency of its class interval using the scale on the vertical axis; each bar should be the same width with all data points included.

Pareto Chart

A Pareto chart is used when you need to discover or display the relative importance of data or variables (problems, causes, or conditions). It helps highlight the *"vital few"* in contrast to the *"trivial many."* It may be used to examine the how, what, when, where, and why of a suspected problem cause. It also helps teams identify which problems, causes, or conditions are the most significant or frequent so they can work on these first.

Like most charts and graphs, the Pareto chart is an illustration of your data as of a specific time and date. Once your team has addressed the most significant problem, cause, or condition in your Pareto chart, you can redraw it with new data and pick another area to improve.

In the late 1800s, Vilfredo Pareto, an Italian economist, found that typically 80 percent of the wealth in a region was concentrated in less than 20 percent of the population. Later, Joseph Juran formulated what he called the Pareto Principle of problems: Only a vital few elements (20 percent) account for the majority (80 percent) of the problems. For example, only 20 percent of your equipment problems account for 80 percent of your downtime. Because this Pareto Principle has proven to be valid in numerous situations, it points to how useful it is for organizations to examine their data carefully to identify the vital few items that most deserve attention.

The Pareto chart shown in Figure 7–8 is a bar chart in which the data are arranged in descending order of their importance, generally by magnitude of frequency, cost, time, or a similar parameter. The chart is really two charts in one: part bar chart and part pie chart. The bars are easy to see, but the ascending line that plots the cumulative height of the bars is really a pie chart "unrolled."

To create a Pareto chart, proceed as follows:

- Select the most likely causes of a problem (from the cause/effect diagram).
- Collect the data on causes (using a checksheet, perhaps).
- Summarize the numbers of observations and calculate the percentages of each cause.
- The right vertical scale is always set from zero to 100 percent.
- The left vertical scale is the same height as the right scale; it begins with 0 at the bottom and ends with the number of observations at the top, directly across from 100 percent.

FIGURE 7–8
Example of a Pareto Chart

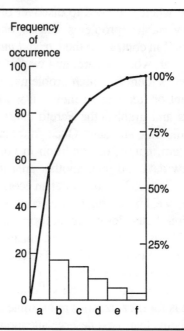

- Draw the columns, using the left scale.
- Plot the first point at the upper-right corner of the first column.
- Calculate and add together the percentages of cause 1 and cause 2. Place the second point, corresponding to the sum, across from the right scale directly over the second column or bar. For the third point, add the percentage of cause 3 to the total of 1 and 2, and plot accordingly. The total of all the columns added together should be 100 percent, and the last point will be at the 100 percent point.
- Join the dots with a line.

Scatter Diagram

Scatter diagrams (Figure 7–9) and their related correlation analysis permit you to examine two factors at one time and to determine the relationship that may exist between them. The graphic display can help lead

FIGURE 7–9
Examples of Scatter Diagram Correlation

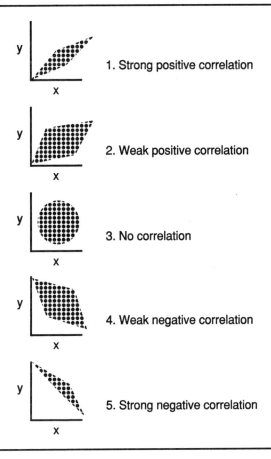

1. Strong positive correlation

2. Weak positive correlation

3. No correlation

4. Weak negative correlation

5. Strong negative correlation

Source: U.S. Government, *Total Quality Management Introduction.*

you to the possible causes of problems, even when the linkage between the factors is counterintuitive. The pattern or distribution of data points in a scatter diagram describes the strength of the relationship between the factors being examined. However, even a strong correlation does not imply a cause-and-effect relationship between the factors. Additional work may be required to uncover the nature of the indicated relationship.

The scatter diagram shows plotted points against two measures: one displayed on the vertical (*y*) axis, the other on the horizontal (*x*) axis. The visual pattern of the plotted points gives quick information about the presence of a relationship or correlation.

If there is a correlation (either positive or negative) between two measures, you can assume that if you can change the incidence of one measure, the other will move as well. For example, if telephone call duration is positively correlated to customer satisfaction, then changing telephone call duration will produce a change in customer satisfaction.

To prepare a scatter diagram proceed as follows:

- Collect the two selected measures for each occurrence.
- Draw the horizontal and vertical scales.
- Assign the horizontal (x) axis to the independent variable. The independent variable is the one you can have an effect on, such as call duration. The dependent variable is the other variable that depends on the first. The dependent variable is assigned to the vertical (y) axis. Establish the interval scales for both and label.
- Plot each data point on the grid.
- To interpret the relationship, you can "eyeball" it, but a statistician can perform some quantitative tests on the data to give you a more accurate numeric indication of correlation.

Time Line Chart

The time line chart as shown in Figure 7–10 is a graphic display of changes over some period of time. The left scale is a quantity: percentages or simple counts of frequency. The horizontal line is divided into time intervals such as "days of the week," "months," or even an ordinal sequence such as "first job," "second job," and so on.

The line that joins the plot marks gives a visual "moving picture" of the fluctuations over time. Defect rates are reported on time lines in order to spot trends. To prepare a time line chart, proceed as follows:

- Collect the raw data on a checksheet, if necessary.
- Develop time intervals (usually hour, day, week, etc.) across the horizontal axis at the bottom. The intervals should be evenly spaced. Label each interval.
- Draw a line to connect the quantities observed on each successive interval.
- Connect the points with a line.

FIGURE 7-10
Example of Time Line Chart

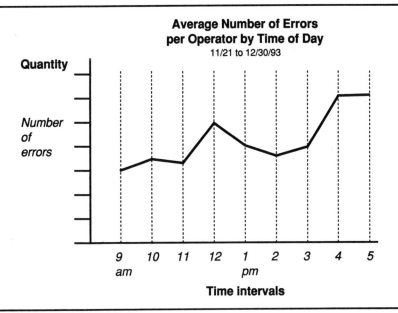

- Add horizontal and vertical grid lines if the points are difficult to read, as shown in the figure.
- Title the chart to define the period of time over which the data were collected.

TECHNIQUES

This section summarizes some of the basic techniques used to implement the Total Quality Management methodology. Table 7-2 shows when you need to use particular techniques. Each of these techniques is briefly described to enhance the manager's understanding of their use under the Total Quality Management methodology.

Action Plan

The Total Quality Management team's action plan is a catalog of things that must be done to ensure a smooth and objective trial and implemen-

TABLE 7–2
Use of Total Quality Management Techniques

Quality Technique	Use When You Need to . . .
Action plan	Explain implementation plans to management and workers, and ensure an organized, objective implementation.
Barriers and aids	Analyze a situation and make use of available aids and/or overcome barriers that prevent implementation of a solution.
Benchmarking	Measure your processes/performance against your competitors.
Brainstorming	Generate, clarify, and evaluate a sizable list of ideas, problems, or issues.
Concurrent engineering (CE)	Shorten the design-to-development life cycle of a product.
Cost estimation	Determine the dollar impact when prioritizing and selecting improvement opportunities.
Cost of quality	Understand the hidden costs of a product or service.
Customer needs analysis	Identify what customers expect of you, their requirements, and what you have jointly agreed to provide.
Customer/supplier model	Identify the total customer/supplier relationship, and analyze and/or improve your work process.
Customer/supplier questionnaire	Assess your relations with your customers and suppliers.
Deming/Shewhart cycle	Implement a continuous improvement process.
Design of experiments	Reduce costs, stabilize production processes, and desensitize production variables.
Interviewing	Broaden the team's foundation of knowledge, and identify other people who are not on the team but who are sources of needed information.
Multivoting	Accomplish list reduction and prioritization quickly and with a high degree of group agreement.
Nominal group technique (NGT)	Reach consensus within a structured situation.
Problem selection matrix	Prioritize improvement opportunities.
Problem statement matrix	State specifically the improvement opportunity that the team is addressing.
Quality function deployment (QFD)	Transform customer wants and needs into quantitative terms.
Solutions selection matrix	Select those potential solutions that best address the root causes of the problem.
Statistical process control (SPC)	Improve process performance.

tation of the solution. Although the action plan may have different formats, it should answer who, what, when, where, and how, and it should consider the barriers and aids for success. Figure 7–11 is a typical example of an action plan. To develop an action plan, proceed as follows:

- Have the team analyze the proposed improvement or solution.
- Break it down into steps.
- Consider the materials and numbers of people involved at each level.
- Brainstorm, if necessary, for other items of possible significance.
- Add items to the list until you think the list is complete.

Barriers and Aids

Barriers-and-aids analysis is a technique for pinpointing and analyzing elements that resist change (barriers) or push for change (aids). This focused brainstorming technique helps a team meet its objectives by planning to overcome barriers and making maximum use of available aids. Factors to consider in the analysis are (1) people, (2) environment, (3) hardware, and (4) dollars.

To construct a barriers-and-aids analysis, like the example shown in Figure 7–12, proceed as follows:

FIGURE 7–11
Typical Example of an Action Plan

NO.	TASK/PROJECT	PRIORITY/ DUE DATE	ASSIGNED TO	DATE ASSIGNED	STATUS/REMARKS

Action Plan
Prepared By _____ Date _____ Page ___ of ___
TASK ASSIGNMENT RECORD   Loc'n/Proj. _____ Period _____

Source: *AT&T Quality Improvement Process Guidebook.*

FIGURE 7-12
Example of Elements of a Barriers-and-Aids Analysis

Barriers and Aids

Forces Pushing Against Quality Improvement	Forces Pushing For Quality Improvement
Lack of dollars	Team
People shortage	Personal commitment
Vested interest/old attitude	Management support
Would the team stay together?	Support of line manager
Other priorities	Communications
• Time	• Within team
• Maintain work flow	• Outside team
• Complicated techniques	New techniques
	Increasing cost of failure
	Good planning
	Specific goals

- Identify the solution, task, change, or concern.
- Brainstorm a list of barriers (forces pushing against change).
- Brainstorm a list of aids (forces pushing for change). It is not necessary to come up with an aid for every barrier.
- Rank listed items by level of significance: high, medium, or low.
- Match aids that balance or overcome barriers.
- List matching barriers and aids on a chart.
- List nonmatching barriers and aids, and brainstorm any offsetting factors.
- Use your rankings to identify items needing team action.
- Develop an action plan.

Benchmarking

Benchmarking is a significant element of the Total Quality Management methodology. Benchmarking (Figure 7-13) provides a method for measuring your processes against those of recognized leaders. It helps you to establish priorities and targets leading to process improvement. Bench-

FIGURE 7-13
Illustration of Comparative Benchmarking

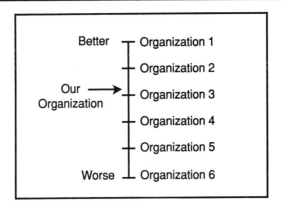

marking is conducted when you want to know where you stand with respect to your local competitors or other world-class competitors. The basic elements of benchmarking include these steps:

- Identify processes to benchmark and their key characteristics.
- Determine what to benchmark: companies, organizations, or processes.
- Determine benchmarks by collecting and analyzing data from direct contact, surveys, interviews, technical journals, and advertisements.
- From each benchmark item identified, determine the "best of class" target.
- Evaluate your process in terms of the benchmarks, and set improvement goals.

Brainstorming

Brainstorming is a way of using a group of people to quickly generate, clarify, and evaluate a sizable list of ideas, problems, issues, and the like. In this case, the emphasis is on *quantity* of ideas, not quality. It can be an excellent technique for tapping the creative thinking of a team.

There are three phases of Brainstorming. First, during the *generation phase,* the leader reviews the rules for brainstorming, and the team members generate a list of items. Next, during the *clarification phase,* the team goes over the list to make sure that everyone understands all the items; discussion will take place later. Finally, during the *evaluation phase,* the team reviews the list to eliminate duplications, irrelevancies, or issues that are off limits.

Keep in mind that brainstorming is a subjective technique that must later be substantiated by data. To conduct a brainstorming session, proceed as follows:

- State purpose clearly.
- Allow each person to take a turn in sequence, or suggest that ideas be expressed spontaneously.
- Offer one thought at a time.
- Don't criticize ideas.
- Don't discuss ideas.
- Build on other's ideas.
- Record ideas where visible to team members.

Techniques such as multivoting or normal group techniques (NGT) will generally be used next to select those items that the team should pursue.

Simultaneous (Concurrent) Engineering

Simultaneous (concurrent) engineering is an approach where design alternatives, manufacturing process alternatives, and manufacturing technology alternatives are dealt with in parallel and interactively beginning with the initial design trade-off studies.

Traditionally, analysis of quality and producibility has been an after-the-fact review of designs to assess the impact of proposed design features on manufacturing cost and to identify alternatives for the major production cost drivers. With simultaneous (concurrent) engineering, the focus is on both product and process definition simultaneously. This approach can be used to shorten the design-to-development life cycle and reduce costs by examining the interaction of functional disciplines from the perspective of a cross-functional process.

Apply the basic elements involved in simultaneous (concurrent) engineering as follows:

- Use cross-functional teams, including design, quality, marketing, manufacturing, and support.

- Identify and reduce variability in production and use through carefully selected design parameters.
- Extend traditional design approach to include such techniques as enterprise integration, design for assembly, robust design, computer-aided design, design for manufacture, group technology, electronic data interchange, and value analysis.
- See also the description of the following tools: design of experiments, quality function deployment (QFD), and team building.

Cost Estimation

Cost estimation helps you select improvement opportunities. Total Quality Management teams can determine problems with the largest dollar impact by estimating costs using the bottom-up approach and top-down approach. To use the *bottom-up approach,* proceed as follows:

- Estimate how many times the problem occurs per unit. (Example: three times per week.)
- Estimate time and cost per unit to fix. (Example: 2 people × 3 hours × $17 per hour = $102.)
- Calculate annual cost (without overhead expenses) by multiplying above factors by weeks worked. (Example: 3 people per week × $102 × 50 weeks per year = $15,300 per year.)

To use the *top-down approach,* follow these two steps:

- Estimate percent of total labor or other expenditure.
- Multiply estimate by budgeted annual cost to calculate amount spent on the problem. (Example: 13 percent × $18,000 per year budgeted = $2,340 per year.)

Cost of Quality

Cost of quality consists of all the costs associated with maintaining acceptable quality plus the costs incurred as a result of failure to achieve this quality. The cost of quality technique provides managers with cost details often hidden from them. Cost of quality analysis should be performed to highlight costs savings by doing the job right the first time.

Here's how to conduct a cost of quality review:

- Identify quality costs. These are cost of nonconformance and cost of conformance, as shown in Figure 7–14.
- Develop method for collecting data and reporting on cost of quality.
- Identify the most significant costs.
- Identify the cause of these major costs.
- Identify the solutions to reduce or eliminate causes.
- Implement solutions.

Customer Needs Analysis

Customer Needs Analysis is a technique for determining the key measurable characteristics that are important to your customer. Customer Needs Analysis is a Total Quality Management team effort between you and your customers to answer the following questions:

- What are the *major outputs* of our process?
- Who are the *customers* (both immediate and downstream) for each of these outputs?
- What do our customers say are the *key quality characteristics* that they need in our outputs?
- How can we *measure* our performance on these key characteristics?
- What *goal* would our customers like to see us achieve on these measures?

Possible key quality characteristics are:

FIGURE 7–14
Example of Cost of Quality Impact on Nonconformance

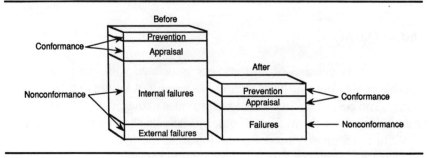

- Accuracy.
- Completeness.
- Flexibility.
- Timeliness.
- Uniformity.

- Understandability.
- Relevance.
- Consistency.
- Reliability.

Potential measurements are:

- Physical parameters.
- Time.
- Cost.

- Customer satisfaction.
- Defects and rework.
- Work output.

Customer/Supplier Model

The customer/supplier model is a representation of the customer/supplier relationship depicted by three triangles, shown in Figure 7–15, in which the center triangle represents the work you do—that is, your value-added tasks. The left triangle represents your supplier(s)—the people or organizations who provide you with the input(s) you need to perform your job. The right triangle represents your customer(s)—the people or organization(s) who receive your output or the result of your work.

Additional components of the customer/supplier model are requirements and feedback. Requirements are the most critical characteristics of

FIGURE 7–15
Illustration of Customer/Supplier Model

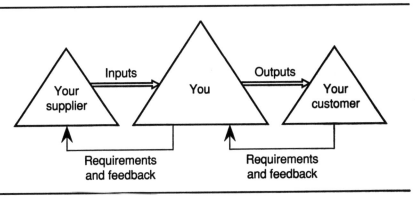

Source: *AT&T Quality Improvement Process Guidebook.*

your outputs as defined by your customer. Customer feedback communicates the degree to which your output conforms to the negotiated requirements.

Analysis of your organization's customer/supplier model is an effective technique to appraise the total impact of quality.

Customer/Supplier Questionnaire

Use this questionnaire as a technique to assess your relations with your customers and suppliers.

Ask yourself these questions about your relationship with your customers:

- What are your primary outputs as a supplier—information, products, and/or services?
- Who are your customers—the primary, direct users or recipients of your outputs?
- What are your customers' requirements for your outputs?
- How do you determine their requirements?
- What are the characteristics of your output that can be measured to determine whether your customers' requirements are met?
- What are the major quality problems that prevent you from meeting your customers' requirements?
- What obstacles stand in your way of resolving these problems?
- What would it take to resolve these problems?

Ask yourself these questions about your relationship with your suppliers:

- Who are your suppliers? Who do you depend on for input—information, products, and/or services—to fulfill your requirements as one who adds value to their inputs?
- What primary inputs do you receive from them?
- What are your requirements for those inputs?
- How do you communicate your requirements to your suppliers?
- How do you provide feedback to suppliers regarding how they are performing?

Deming/Shewhart (PDCA) Cycle

The Shewhart cycle, also known as the Deming or Plan-Do-Check-Act (PDCA) cycle (see Figure 7–16), represents a cyclic continuous improve-

FIGURE 7–16
Illustration of Shewhart (PDCA) Cycle

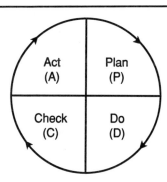

ment process for planning and testing improvement activities. When an improvement idea is identified, it is often wise to test it on a small scale prior to full implementation to validate its benefit. Additionally, by introducing a change on a small scale, employees have time to accept it and are more likely to support it.

The basic elements of the Deming/Shewhart cycle are the Plan (P), Do (D), Check (C), and Act (A) steps often referred to as the PDCA cycle. To implement this technique, proceed as noted below:

- Plan (P) a change or test.
- Do (D) the change or test, preferably on a small scale.
- Check (C) the effects of the change or test.
- Act (A) on what was learned.
- Repeat the Plan step, with new knowledge.
- Repeat the Do step, and continue onward with continuous process improvement.

Design of Experiments

Design-of-experiments analysis is a technique where the analyst chooses factors for study, deliberately varies those factors in a predetermined way, and then studies the effect of these actions. This technique improves the design-to-production transition by quickly optimizing product and process design. It also reduces costs, stabilizes production processes, and desensitizes production variables.

The applications for the design-of-experiments analysis are many. You can use the technique to compare two machines or methods, to study the relative effects of various process variables, to determine the optimal values for process variables, to evaluate measurement system error, or to determine design tolerances.

Here's how to implement the design of experiments technique:

- Identify the important variables, whether they are product or process parameters, material or components from suppliers, environmental or measuring equipment factors.
- Separate these important variables—generally no more than one to four.
- Reduce the variation on the important variables (including the tight control of interaction effects) through redesign, close tolerancing design, supplier process improvement, and so on.
- Open up the tolerances on the unimportant variables to reduce costs.

Interviewing

Interviewing is a data-gathering process to help Total Quality Management teams gain the benefit of others' experience and specialized knowledge. Prepare for the interview as follows:

- Gather background information on the topic and interviewee.
- Outline the areas to be covered and major questions to be asked.
- Tell the interviewee the purpose and proposed length of the interview.
- Plan to meet in a comfortable setting.

During the interview, make sure you do the following:

- Help the interviewee feel comfortable.
- Remain analytical and objective.
- Take notes.
- Ask open-ended questions to encourage ideas.
- Ask who, what, where, when, why, and how.
- Summarize what you learned.

After the interview, don't forget to thank the interviewee. Try to review and interpret the data you've collected as soon as possible, while still fresh in your mind.

Multivoting

Multivoting is a structured series of votes by a Total Quality Management team used to help reduce and prioritize a list containing a large number of items to a manageable few (usually three to five). Multivoting may be used throughout the process after a team discusses the various items on a brainstorm list that is too lengthy for the items to be addressed at once.

Multivoting steps are as follows:

- First vote: Each person votes for as many items as desired, but only once per item. Circle the items receiving a relatively higher number of votes than the other items. (Example: For a team with ten members, items receiving five or more votes are circled.)
- Second and subsequent votes: Each person votes the number of times equal to one-half the number of circled items. (Example: If six items received five or more votes during the first vote, then each person gets to vote three times during the second vote.)
- Continue multivoting until the list is reduced to three to five items, which can be further analyzed. Never multivote down to only one.

Nominal Group Technique (NGT)

Nominal group technique (NGT) is another method for reaching consensus. It is a group decision-making process used when priority or rank order must be established. NGT is similar to brainstorming; however, it is a structured approach to generate ideas and survey the opinions of a small (10 to 15 persons) group. NGT is very effective in producing many new ideas or solutions in a short time. It is structured to focus on problems, not people; to open lines of communication; to ensure participation; and to tolerate conflicting ideas. NGT helps build consensus and commitment to the final result.

These are the basic steps involved with using nominal group technique:

- Present issue, instructions.
- Generate ideas during five to ten minutes of quiet time, with no discussion.
- Gather ideas round-robin, one idea at a time, written on a flip chart without discussing them.

- Process or clarify ideas by eliminating duplicates and combining like ideas. Discuss the ideas as a group, but only to clarify their meaning, not to argue about them.
- Set priorities silently.
- Vote to establish the priority or rank of each item.
- Tabulate votes.
- Develop an action plan.

Quality Function Deployment (QFD)

Quality function deployment (QFD) is a conceptual map that provides the means for cross-functional planning and communication. It is a method for transforming customer wants and needs into quantitative terms.

Developed in Japan, quality function deployment is a proven technique for ensuring that quality is designed into products and services in an efficient and effective manner. QFD helps organizations design higher-quality, more competitive, lower-cost products more easily and quickly, and is aimed primarily at the development of new products. It starts early in new product design efforts and translates customer requirements into design and product characteristics, communicating them in a structured way to influence upstream design decisions and actions. Traditional design organizations have focused more on meeting specifications or technical requirements than on satisfying customer expectations. QFD links customer expectations to the technical considerations of the designer and manufacturer, and to the concept of value in a manner that connections and relationships can be understood and addressed.

Quality function deployment helps ensure quality products and processes by detecting and solving problems early. Downstream problems may occur and product quality may suffer when those who work on components and parts have little knowledge of customer requirements or the specifics of the final product and manufacturing processes. The QFD process forces management to analyze broad customer needs and expectations (such as ease of use or comfort) and relate them directly to product characteristics such as weight, strength, speed, and temperature. Those characteristics in turn are related to the processes involved in achieving the technical requirements. Specific techniques and tools are employed in the course of quality function deployment. One of the principal quality function deployment tools is the "house of quality" matrix shown in Figure 7–17.

FIGURE 7–17
House of Quality Matrix

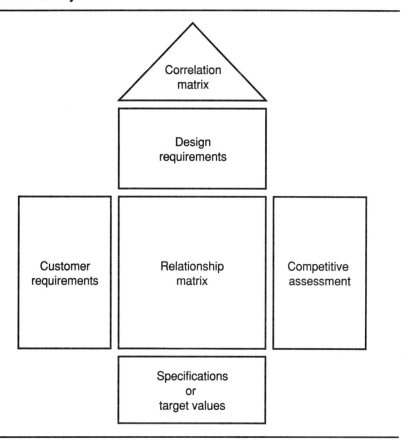

The matrix identifies specific customer-required characteristics, assigns priorities to them, and converts them to product attributes and design characteristics through cross-functional team activity. The matrix relates customer needs and expectations to specific product characteristics, such as thickness, strength, and weight, and links those characteristics to the product-related functional area processes. It communicates product-specific requirements, standards, and specifications in a coordinated and consistent way across all the functions that have responsibilities affecting the product. The generation and distribution of quality matrices force early identification of conflicting objectives and potential bottlenecks. Early cross-functional communication should be centered on quality—resolving many potential problems before major investments of time and money have been made.

Products should be designed to meet customer wants and needs so that customers will buy products and services and continue to buy them. Marketing people, design engineers, manufacturing engineers, and procurement specialists work closely together from the time a product or service is first conceived so they may better meet customer requirements. Quality function deployment provides a framework within which the cross-functional teams can work.

To begin the QFD process, ask these questions:

- What do customers want (attributes)?
- Are all preferences equally important?
- Will delivering perceived needs yield a competitive advantage?
- What are the characteristics that match customers' attributes?
- How does each characteristic affect each customer attribute?
- How does one change affect other characteristics?

Statistical Process Control (SPC)

Statistical process control (SPC) is an effective tool for improving performance of any process. It helps identify problems quickly and accurately. It also provides quantifiable data for analysis, provides a reference baseline, and promotes participation and decision making by people doing the job.

Statistical process control is an excellent technique for determining the cause of variation based on a statistical analysis of the problem. It uses probability theory to control and improve processes, and it is a major technique used in implementing Total Quality Management. Refer to one of the fundamental statistical publications noted in Appendix A, Additional Reading, for substantial "how to" information. The basic steps involved in statistical process control are these:

- Identify problems or performance improvement areas. Identify common and special causes. Common causes are random in nature, often minor. Special causes result from an abnormality in the system that prevents the process from becoming stable.
- Do a cause-and-effects analysis.

- Collect data.
- Apply statistical techniques (may need a quality statistical specialist).
- Analyze variations.
- Take corrective action.

THE OPTIONS

This chapter has briefly described the tools and techniques that you may use to improve your quality. It has provided a basic vocabulary and delineation of the application options for each of the Total Quality Management tools and techniques.

CHAPTER 8

THE QUALITY AWARDS

This chapter describes the three major quality awards, which are the Malcolm Baldrige National Quality Award in the United States, the Deming Prize awarded in Japan, and the European Quality Award.

THE MALCOLM BALDRIGE NATIONAL QUALITY AWARD

The quality of goods and services is central to a country's trade balance, competitiveness improvement, and standard of living. Some firms are rising to the challenge of the quality imperative. They are working hard to meet the ever-increasing requirements of customers who now have broader market choices. More businesses must join in quality improvement efforts to help themselves—and the nation—in the quest for excellence.

On August 20, 1987, President Reagan signed the Malcolm Baldrige National Quality Improvement Act, establishing an annual National Quality Award. The purposes of the award are to promote quality awareness, recognize quality achievements of U.S. companies, and publicize successful quality strategies.

The award program is managed by the National Institute of Standards and Technology, United States Department of Commerce. It is administered by the Malcolm Baldrige National Quality Award Consortium, a joint effort of the American Society for Quality Control and the American Productivity and Quality Center. All funding for the program is from private contributions.

The Malcolm Baldrige National Quality award criteria are the basis for making awards and providing feedback to applicants. In addition, they have three other important purposes: (1) to help elevate quality standards and expectations; (2) to facilitate communication and sharing among and within organizations of all types based upon common understanding of key quality requirement; and (3) to serve as a working tool for planning, training, assessment, and other uses.

The award criteria are directed toward dual results-oriented goals: To project key requirements for delivering ever-improving value to customers while at the same time maximizing the overall productivity and effectiveness of the delivering organization. To achieve these results-oriented goals, the criteria need to be built upon a set of values that together address and integrate the overall customer and company performance requirements.

The three categories of businesses eligible to apply for the award are manufacturing companies, service companies, and small businesses. Up to two awards may be given in each category each year. In addition to publicizing the receipt of the award, recipients are expected to share with other U.S. organizations information about their successful quality strategies.

Companies participating in the award process submit applications that include completion of the award examination. The award examination is based on quality excellence criteria created through the public/private partnership. In responding to these criteria, applicants are expected to provide information and data on their quality processes and quality improvement. Information and data submitted must be adequate to demonstrate that the applicant's approaches could be replicated or adapted by other companies.

The award examination is designed not only to serve as a reliable basis for making awards, but also to permit a diagnosis of the applicant's overall quality management. All award applicants receive feedback reports prepared by teams of U.S. quality experts.

The November–December 1991 issue of the *Harvard Business Review* presents an excellent evaluation of the award in "How the Baldrige Award Really Works," by David A. Garvin. If you are interested in applying for the Baldrige Award, read the Garvin article and the follow-up letters to the editor in the *Harvard Business Review*.

Should You Apply?

The question is often asked of Malcolm Baldrige Award–winning companies if one should apply for the award. Newt Hardie, vice president of quality for Milliken & Company, says he is often asked by companies if they "should go for the Baldrige." His response is, "What is your objective? If your objective is to win an award, don't do it. But if you want to improve your company, you cannot afford not to apply."

In summary, after dozens of interviews I could not find a company that was not enhanced by participation in the Malcolm Baldrige award process. Make the investment now. See how good you really are!

Description of the Malcolm Baldrige Examination

The Malcolm Baldrige Award examination[1] is based on criteria designed to set the quality excellence standard for organizations seeking the highest levels of overall quality performance and competitiveness. The examination addresses all key requirements to achieve quality excellence as well as the important interrelationships among these key requirements. By focusing not only on results but also on the conditions and processes that lead to results, the examination offers a framework that can be used by organizations to tailor their systems and processes toward ever-improving quality performance. Moreover, the mechanisms for tailoring are themselves included in the examination.

Core Values and Concepts

The award criteria are built on these core values and concepts:

- Customer-driven quality.
- Leadership.
- Continuous improvement.
- Full participation.
- Fast response.
- Design quality and prevention.
- Long-range outlook.
- Management by fact.
- Partnership development.
- Public responsibility.

Brief descriptions of the core values and concepts follow.

---

[1] This section is based on the 1992 Application Guidelines for the Malcolm Baldrige National Quality Award.

Customer-Driven Quality. Quality is judged by the customer. All product and service attributes that are of value to the customer and lead to customer satisfaction and preference must be addressed appropriately in quality systems. Value, satisfaction, and preference may be influenced by many factors throughout the customer's overall purchase, ownership, and service experiences. This experience centers on the relationship between the company and customers — the trust and confidence in products and services — that leads to loyalty and preference. This concept of quality reaches beyond the product and service attributes that meet basic requirements to emphasize those attributes that *enhance* the products and services and *differentiate* them from competing offerings. Such enhancement and differentiation may include new offerings, as well as unique product-product, service-service, or product-service combinations.

Customer-driven quality is thus a strategic concept. It is directed toward market share gain and customer retention. It demands constant sensitivity to emerging customer and market requirements, and measurement of the factors that drive customer satisfaction. It also demands awareness of developments in technology, and rapid and flexible response to customer and market requirements. Such requirements extend well beyond merely reducing defects and errors, meeting specifications, or reducing complaints. Nevertheless, defect and error reduction and elimination of causes of dissatisfaction contribute significantly to the customers' view of quality and are thus also important parts of customer-driven quality. In addition, the company's approach to recovering from defects and errors is crucial to its improving both quality and relationships with customer.

Leadership. A company's senior leaders must create clear and visible quality values and high expectations, and, accordingly, they must reinforce these values and expectations through substantial personal commitment and involvement. The leaders must take part in the creation of strategies, systems, and methods for achieving excellence. These systems and methods need to guide all activities and decisions of the company and encourage participation and creativity by all employees. Through their regular personal involvement in visible activities — such as planning, reviewing company quality performance, and recognizing employees for quality achievement — the senior leaders serve as role models for reinforcing the values and encouraging leadership in all levels of management.

Continuous Improvement.   Achieving the highest levels of quality and competitiveness requires a well-defined and well-executed approach to continuous improvement. Such improvement needs to be part of all operations and of all work unit activities of a company. Improvements may be of several types: (1) enhancing value to the customer through new and improved products and services; (2) reducing errors, defects, and waste; (3) improving responsiveness and cycle time performance; and (4) improving productivity and effectiveness in the use of all resources. Thus, improvement is driven not only by the objective to provide better quality, but also by the need to be responsive and efficient—both which confer additional marketplace advantages. To meet all of these objectives, the process of continuous improvement must contain regular cycles of planning, execution, and evaluation. This requires a basis—preferably a quantitative basis—for assessing progress and for deriving information for future cycles of improvement.

Full Participation.   If a company is to meet its quality and performance objectives, it must have a fully committed, well-trained, and involved work force. Reward and recognition systems need to reinforce full participation in company quality objectives. Factors bearing on the safety, health, well-being, and morale of employees must be considered in the continuous improvement objectives and activities of the company. Employees need education and training in quality skills related to performing their work and to understanding and solving quality-related problems. Training should be reinforced through on-the-job applications of learning, involvement, and empowerment. Training and participation increasingly need to be tailored to a more diverse work force.

Fast Response.   Success in competitive markets continues to demand ever-shorter product and service introduction cycles and more rapid response to customers. Indeed, fast response itself is often a major quality attribute. Reduction in cycle times and rapid response to customers can occur when work processes are designed to meet both quality and response goals. Accordingly, response time improvement should be included as a major focus with all quality improvement processes of work units. This goal requires that all designs, objectives, and work unit activities include measurement of cycle time and responsiveness. Major improvements in response time may require work processes and paths to be simplified and shortened. Response time improvements often drive simultaneous improvements in quality and productivity. Hence, a company might find it highly beneficial to consider response time, quality, and productivity objectives together.

Design Quality and Prevention. Quality systems should place strong emphasis on design quality, or problem prevention achieved through building quality into products and services and into the processes through which they are produced. Excellent design quality may lead to major reductions in "downstream" waste, problems, and associated costs. Design quality includes the creation of fault-tolerant (robust) processes and products. A major design issue is the design-to-introduction cycle time. To meet the constant demands of rapidly changing markets, companies need to focus more and more on shorter product and service introduction times. Consistent with the theme of design quality and prevention, continuous improvement and corrective actions need to emphasize interventions "upstream"—at the earliest stages in processes. This approach yields the maximum overall benefits of improvements and corrections. Such upstream intervention also needs to take into account the company's suppliers.

Long-Range Outlook. Achieving quality and market leadership requires a future orientation and long-term commitments to customers, employees, stockholders, and suppliers. Strategies, plans, and resource allocations need to reflect these commitments and address training, employee development, supplier development, technology evolution, and other factors that bear upon quality. A key part of the long-term commitment is regular review and assessment of progress relative to long-term plans.

Management by Fact. Meeting company quality and performance goals requires that process management be based on reliable information, data, and analysis. Quality assessment and quality improvement rely on facts and data of many types, including data about the customer, supplier, product and service performance, operations, market, and competitive comparisons, as well as employee-related and cost and financial information. Analysis is the process of extracting larger meaning from data to support evaluation and decision making at various levels within the company. Such analysis may entail using data individually or in combination to reveal information—such as trends, projections, and cause and effect—that might not be evident without analysis. Facts, data, and analysis support a variety of company efforts, such as planning, reviewing company performance, improving operations, and comparing company quality performance with competitors' quality performance.

A major consideration relating to the use of data and analysis for improving competitive performance involves the creation and use of performance indicators. Performance indicators are measurable characteristics of products, services, processes, and operations the company uses to evaluate performance and to track progress. The indicators should be selected to best represent the factors that determine customer satisfaction and operational performance. A system of indicators tied to customer and/or company performance requirements represents a clear and objective basis for aligning all activities of the company toward common goals. Through the analysis of data obtained in the tracking processes, the indicators themselves may be evaluated and changed. For example, indicators selected to measure product and service quality may be judged by how well they correlate with customer satisfaction.

Partnership Development.   Companies should seek to build internal and external partnerships, which serve mutual and larger community interests. These partnerships might include those that promote labor-management cooperation—such as agreements with unions, cooperation with suppliers and customers, and linkages with education organizations. Partnerships should consider longer-term objectives as well as short-term needs, thereby creating a basis for mutual investments. The building of partnerships should address means of regular communication, approaches to evaluating progress, means for modifying objectives, and methods for accommodating to changing conditions.

Public Responsibility.   A company's customer requirements and quality system objectives should address areas of corporate citizenship and responsibility. These responsibilities include business ethics, public health and safety, environment, and sharing of quality-related information in the company's business and geographic communities. Health, safety, and environmental considerations need to take into account the life cycle of products and services and include factors such as waste generation. Quality planning in such cases should address adverse contingencies that may arise throughout the life cycle of production, distribution, and use of products. Plans should consider problem avoidance and company response if avoidance fails, such as how to maintain public trust and confidence. Inclusion of public responsibility areas within a quality system means not only meeting all local, state, and federal legal and regulatory requirements, but also treating these and related requirements as areas for continuous improvement. In addition, companies should support—within reasonable limits of their resources—national, industry, trade, and community activities to share nonproprietary quality-related information.

Criteria Framework

The core values and concepts that drive the award criteria are embodied in seven categories:

1.0 Leadership.
2.0 Information and Analysis.
3.0 Strategic Quality Planning.
4.0 Human Resource Development and Management.
5.0 Management of Process Quality.
6.0 Quality and Operational Results.
7.0 Customer Focus and Satisfaction.

The framework connecting and integrating the categories, depicted in Figure 8–1, consists of four basic elements, which are defined here.

Driver. Senior executive leadership creates the values, goals, and systems, and guides the sustained pursuit of quality and performance objectives.

System. The system is the set of well-defined and well-designed processes for meeting the company's quality and performance requirements.

Measures of Progress. Measures of progress provide a results-oriented basis for channeling actions to the delivery of ever-improving customer value and company performance.

Goal. The basic aim of the Total Quality Management process is the delivery of ever-improving value to customers.

The seven criteria categories shown in Figure 8–1 are further subdivided into examination items and areas to address. These are described in the pages that follow.

FIGURE 8–1
Baldrige Award Criteria Framework: Dynamic Relationships

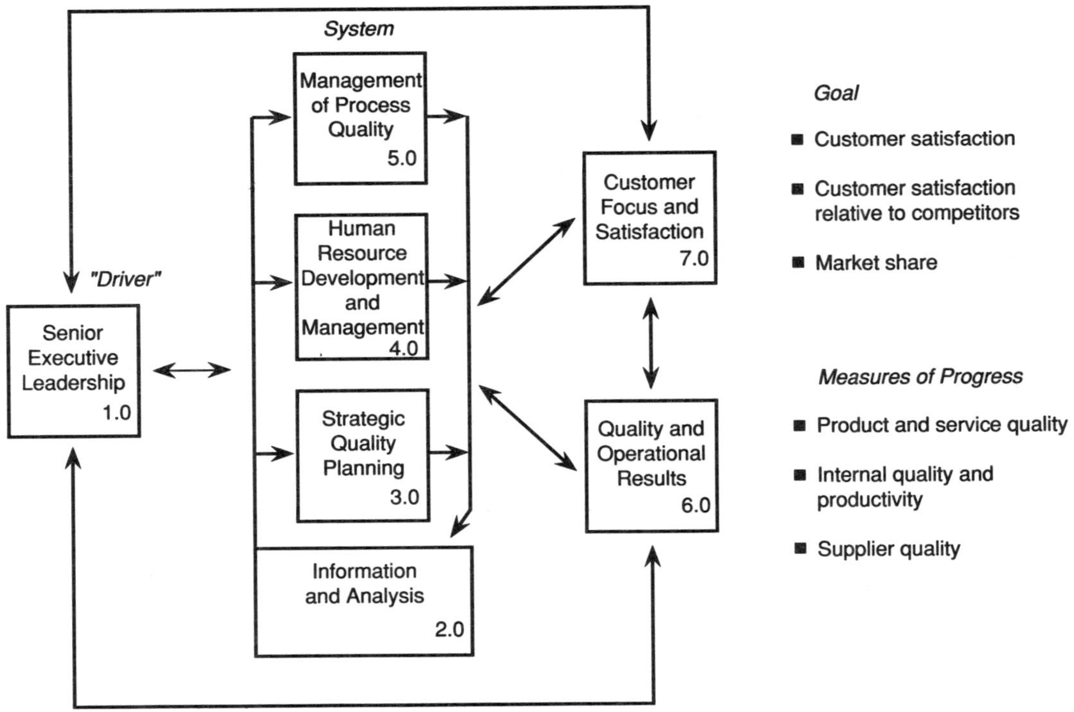

Goal
- Customer satisfaction
- Customer satisfaction relative to competitors
- Market share

Measures of Progress
- Product and service quality
- Internal quality and productivity
- Supplier quality

System

Customer Focus and Satisfaction 7.0

Quality and Operational Results 6.0

Management of Process Quality 5.0

Human Resource Development and Management 4.0

Strategic Quality Planning 3.0

Information and Analysis 2.0

"Driver"

Senior Executive Leadership 1.0

Examination Items.   In all, there are 28 examination items among the seven examination categories. Examination categories each contain two or more examination items. Each item focuses on a major element of an effective quality system. All information submitted by applicants is in response to the specific requirements given within these items. Each item is assigned an examination point value.

Areas to Address.   Each examination item includes a set of areas to address (areas). The areas serve to illustrate and clarify the intent of the items and to place limits on the types and amounts of information the applicant should provide. Areas are not assigned individual point values, because their relative importance depends on factors such as the applicant's type and size of business and quality system.

The Pivotal Role of the Quality and Operational Results Category

The Quality and Operational Results category (6.0) plays a central role in the award criteria. This category provides a focus and purpose for all quality system actions. In addition, it represents the bridge between the quality system and the customer. Through this focus, the dual purpose of quality—superior value of offerings as viewed by the customer and the marketplace, and superior company performance as determined through productivity and effectiveness indicators—is maintained. The other major purpose of this category is to provide key information (measures of progress) for evaluation and improvement of quality system processes and practices.

The Quality and Operational Results category consists of four items, which are discussed here.

Product and Service Quality Results.   This item calls for reporting quality levels and improvements for key product and service attributes— attributes that truly matter to the customer and to the marketplace. These attributes are derived from customer-related items ("listening posts"), which make up category 7.0. If the attributes have been properly selected, improvements in them should show a strong positive correlation with customer and marketplace improvement indicators. The correlation between quality and customer indicators is a critical management tool. It is a device for focusing on key attributes. In addition, the correlation may reveal emerging or changing market segments or changing importance of attributes.

Company Operation Results.   This item calls for reporting performance and improvements in quality and productivity of the company. Such attributes are of two types: (1) generic, or common to all companies, and (2) business-specific. Generic attributes include cycle time, internal quality, and those attributes that relate to productivity as reflected in use of labor, materials, energy, capital, and assets. Indicators of productivity, cycle time, or internal quality should reflect overall company performance. Business- or company-specific effectiveness indicators vary greatly and may include indicators such as rates of invention, environmental quality, export levels, new markets, and percent of sales from recently introduced products or services.

Business Process and Support Service Results.   This item calls for reporting performance and improvements in quality, productivity, and effectiveness of the business processes and support services that support the principal product and service production activities. This item permits a company to demonstrate how its support units link to and contribute to overall improvement in quality and overall improvement in company operational performance. Thus, a company will find this item to be a useful device for aligning support activities with the company's overall principal quality, productivity, and business objectives. Through this item, special requirements—which differ from work unit to work unit and define work-unit effectiveness—can be set, tracked, and linked to one another.

Supplier Quality Results.   This item calls for reporting quality levels and improvements in key indicators of supplier quality. The term *supplier* refers to external providers of products and services, upstream and/or downstream from the company. The focus should be on the most critical quality attributes from the point of view of the company, the buyer of the products and services. Trends and levels of quality should reflect results by whatever means they occur—via improvements by suppliers within the supply base, through changes in selection of suppliers, or both.

Key Characteristics of the Award Criteria

1. *The criteria are directed toward producing results.* The values outlined above are directed toward the results-oriented goals of the criteria. Results, as used in the criteria, are a composite of key performance areas:

- Customer satisfaction.
- Customer satisfaction relative to competitors.
- Market share.
- Customer indicators such as complaints and customer retention.
- Market responsiveness and cycle time.
- Product and service quality.
- Internal quality, productivity, waste reduction, and asset utilization.
- Company-specific effectiveness indicators such as new markets, new technology, and new products.
- Supplier quality and supplier development.
- Environmental quality, occupational safety and health, and regulatory compliance.
- Employee development, well-being, and satisfaction.
- Contributions to national and community well-being.

Assessment of these results is based on one or more of three factors: (1) improvement trends, (2) current levels, and (3) benchmarks, evaluations, and other comparisons that establish levels and trends relative to the performance of others, especially appropriately selected leaders.

2. *The criteria are nonprescriptive.* The criteria represent an integrated set of requirements incorporating the 10 core values described above. However, the criteria do not prescribe how the core values are to be implemented in a particular company. Specifically, they do not prescribe the following:

- Company organization.
- Quality organization, if any. (The seven categories of the criteria do not necessarily correspond to departments or company units.)
- Specific quality techniques.
- Type of quality system.
- Method of quality system implementation.
- Technologies to be used.

The criteria are nonprescriptive for two important reasons. First, organizations, techniques, and technologies vary greatly among businesses, depending on business size, type, and other factors. Second, by focusing on requirements, companies are encouraged to develop unique, creative, or adaptive overall approaches to achieving the goals of the criteria.

3. *The criteria link process to results.* The award criteria provide a link between processes and results, as described above in the section about the pivotal role of the Quality and Operational Results category. Integration in the criteria is achieved through many direct and indirect relationships and linkages among the requirements. In addition, many parts of the criteria call for aggregation and assessment of unit-level and company-level performance, thus encouraging an integrated view of all activities.

4. *The criteria are part of a diagnostic system.* The criteria and the scoring system make up a two-part diagnostic system. The criteria focus on requirements. The scoring system focuses on the factors that should be used in assessing strengths and areas for improvement. Together the two parts of the diagnostic system direct attention to activities that contribute to reaching the goals of the criteria.

5. *The criteria are comprehensive.* The requirements contained in the criteria cover all operations, processes, and work units of the company. In addition, the criteria support business strategy and business decisions and pertain to all transactions, including those related to fulfilling public responsibilities.

6. *The criteria include key learning cycles.* The arrows in Figure 8–1 denote linkage and dynamic relationships and feedback among the framework elements. The primary dynamic characteristic of the criteria is their inclusion of cycles of continuous improvement. These cycles of learning, adaptation, and improvement are explicit and implicit in every part of the criteria. The cycles have four clearly defined stages:

(1) Planning, design of processes, selection of indicators, and deployment of requirements.

(2) Execution of plans.

(3) Assessment of progress, taking into account internal and external indicators.

(4) Revision of plans—taking into account progress, learning, and new information.

7. *The criteria emphasize quality system alignment.* The criteria call for improvement cycles to occur at all levels and in all parts of the company. In order to ensure that improvement cycles carried out in different parts of the organization do not operate at counter purposes, overall aims need to be consistent or aligned. Alignment in the award criteria is achieved by interconnecting and mutually reinforcing key indicators, which are derived from overall company requirements. The latter relate directly to delivery of customer value, improvement of organizational performance, or both. The use of key indicators channels activities toward agreed-upon goals. At the same time, use of indicators avoids detailed procedural prescriptions or unnecessary centralization of process management. Key indicators provide a basis for deploying customer and company performance requirements to all work units. Such alignment ensures consistency and at the same time challenges work units to consider new approaches to superior performance.

Linkage of the Award Criteria to Quality-Related Corporate Issues

Incremental and Breakthrough Improvement. Nonprescriptive, results-oriented criteria and key indicators are used so companies will focus on what needs to be improved. This approach helps to ensure that improvements throughout the organization contribute to the organization's overall purposes. In addition to supporting creativity in approach and organization, results-oriented criteria and key indicators encourage "breakthrough thinking"—openness to the possibility for major improvements as well as incremental ones. Conversely, breakthrough changes may be discouraged if key indicators are tied too directly to existing work methods, processes, and organizations. For this reason, analysis of operations, processes, and progress should focus on the selection of the value of the indicators themselves. This will help to ensure that indicator selection does not unwittingly contribute to stifling creativity and preventing beneficial changes in organization.

Benchmarks also may serve a useful purpose in stimulating breakthrough thinking. Benchmarks offer the opportunity to achieve significant improvements based on adoption or adaptation of current best practice. In addition, they help encourage creativity through exposure to alternative approaches and results. Benchmarks also represent a clear challenge to beat the best, thus encouraging major improvements—rather than only incremental refinements—of existing approaches. As with key indicators, benchmark selection is critical, and benchmarks should be reviewed periodically for appropriateness.

Financial Performance. The award criteria address financial performance via three major avenues: (1) emphasis on quality factors and management actions that lead to better market performance, market share gain, and customer retention; (2) emphasis on improved productivity, asset utilization, and lower overall operating costs; and (3) support for business strategy development and business decisions.

The focus on superior offerings and lower costs of operation means that the criteria's principal route to improved financial performance is through requirements that seek to channel activities toward producing superior overall value. Delivering superior value—an important part of business strategy—also supports other business strategies such as pricing. For example, superior value offers the possibility of price premiums or competing through lower prices, which may enhance market share and asset utilization, and thus may contribute to improved financial performance.

Business strategy usually addresses factors in addition to quality and value. For example, strategy may address market niche, facilities location, diversification, acquisition, export development, research, technology leadership, and rapid product turnover. A basic premise of the award criteria is that quality principles support the development and evaluation of business decisions and strategies, even though many factors other than product and service quality must be considered. Here are some examples of applications of the criteria to business decisions and strategies:

- Quality management of the information used in business decisions and strategy—scope, validity, and analysis.
- Quality requirements of niches, new businesses, export target markets.
- Analysis of factors—societal, regulatory, economic, competitive, and risk—that may bear on the success or failure of strategy.
- Development of scenarios built around possible outcomes of strategy or decisions, including risks of failures, probable consequences of failures, and management of failure.
- Lessons learned from previous strategy developments, within the company or available through research.

Business Factors Considered in the Evaluation of Applications

The award examination is designed to permit evaluation of any quality system for manufacturing and service companies of any size, type of business, or scope of market. The 28 items and 89 areas to address have been selected because of their importance to virtually all businesses. Nevertheless, the importance of the items and areas to address may not be equally applicable to all businesses, even to businesses of comparable size in the same industry. Specific business factors that may bear on the evaluation are considered at every stage of evaluation. Following is an outline of the key business factors considered in the award examination.

- Size and resources of the applicant.
- Number and types of employees.
- Nature of the applicant's business: products, services, and technologies used.
- Special requirements of customers or markets.
- Scope of the applicant's market: local, regional, national, or international.
- Regulatory environment within which the applicant operates.
- Importance of suppliers, dealers, and other external businesses to the applicant and the degree of influence the applicant has over its suppliers.

Application Overview. Applicants need to submit a four-page overview that addresses key business factors that must be considered in the award evaluation process. The overview is intended to set the stage for the examiners who conduct the evaluation, and should contain the following information:

- Types of major products and services.
- Key quality requirements for products and services.
- Nature of major markets (local, regional, national, or international).
- Description of principal customers (consumers, other businesses, government).
- Competitive environment.
- Applicant's position in the industry.
- Major equipment and facilities used.
- Types of technologies used.
- General description of the applicant's employee base, including number, type, and education level.
- Importance of and types of suppliers of goods and services.
- Occupational health and safety, environmental, and other regulatory considerations.
- Other factors important to the applicant.

If the applicant is a subsidiary, a description of the organizational structure and management links to the parent company should be presented. Subsidiaries should also include information that shows key relationships to the parent company: (1) percent of employees, (2) percent of sales, and (3) types of products and services.

Assessment of these results is based on one or more of three factors: (1) improvement trends, (2) current levels, and (3) benchmarks, evaluations, and other comparisons that establish levels and trends relative to the performance of others, especially appropriately selected leaders.

Each examination item, such as 1.0 Leadership, includes a set of areas to address, as shown in Table 8–1. The areas serve to illustrate and clarify the intent of the items and, in doing so, place limits on the types and amounts of information the applicant should provide. Areas are not assigned individual point values, because their relative importance depends on factors such as the applicant's type and size of business and quality system.

1992 Examination

This section describes the basic examination based on the 1992 requirements. The discussion is keyed to the paragraph numbers used in the examination.

1.0 Leadership (90 points). The Leadership category examines how senior executives create and sustain clear and visible quality values and a management system for guiding all activities of the company toward quality excellence. Also considered are the senior executives' and company's quality leadership in the external community and how the company integrates its public responsibilities with its quality values and practices.

1.1 Senior Executive Leadership (45 points).
Describe the senior executives' leadership, personal involvement, and visibility in developing and maintaining a customer focus and an environment for quality excellence.

1.2 Management for Quality (25 points).
Describe how the company's customer focus and quality values are integrated into day-to-day leadership, management, and supervision of all company units.

TABLE 8–1
Examination Categories and Items

Examination Categories/Items		Maximum Points
1.0 Leadership		90
1.1 Senior Executive Leadership	45	
1.2 Management for Quality	25	
1.3 Public Responsibility	20	
2.0 Information and Analysis		80
2.1 Scope and Management of Quality and Performance Data and Information	15	
2.2 Competitive Comparisons and Benchmarks	25	
2.3 Analysis and Uses of Company-Level Data	40	
3.0 Strategic Quality Planning		60
3.1 Strategic Quality and Company Performance Planning Process	35	
3.2 Quality and Performance Plans	25	
4.0 Human Resource Development and Management		150
4.1 Human Resource Management	20	
4.2 Employee Involvement	40	
4.3 Quality Education and Training	40	
4.4 Employee Performance and Recognition	25	
4.5 Employee Well-Being and Morale	25	
5.0 Management of Process Quality		140
5.1 Design and Introduction of Quality Products and Services	40	
5.2 Process Management—Product and Service Production and Delivery Processes	35	
5.3 Process Management—Business Processes and Support Services	30	
5.4 Supplier Quality	20	
5.5 Quality Assessment	15	
6.0 Quality and Operational Results		180
6.1 Product and Service Quality Results	75	
6.2 Company Operational Results	45	
6.3 Business Process and Support Service Results	25	
6.4 Supplier Quality Results	35	
7.0 Customer Focus and Satisfaction		300
7.1 Customer Relationship Management	65	
7.2 Commitment to Customers	15	
7.3 Customer Satisfaction Determination	35	
7.4 Customer Satisfaction Results	75	
7.5 Customer Satisfaction Comparison	75	
7.6 Future Requirements and Expectations of Customers	35	
Total Points		**1000**

1.3 Public Responsibility (20 points).
Describe how the company includes its responsibilities to the public health, safety, environmental protection, and ethical business practices in its quality policies and improvement activities, and how it provides leadership in external groups.

2.0 Information and Analysis (80 points).   The Information and Analysis category examines the scope, validity, analysis, management, and use of data and information for driving quality excellence and improving competitive performance. Also scrutinized is the adequacy of the company's data, information, and analysis system to support improvement of the company's customer focus, products, services, and internal operations.

2.1 Scope and Management of Quality Performance Data and Information (15 points).
Describe the company's base of data and information used for planning, day-to-day management, and evaluation of quality. Describe also how data and information reliability, timeliness, and access are assured.

2.2 Competitive Comparisons and Benchmarks (25 points).
Describe the company's approach to selecting data and information for competitive comparisons and world-class benchmarks to support quality and performance planning, evaluation, and improvement.

2.3 Analysis and Uses of Company-Level Data (40 points).
Describe how quality- and performance-related data and information are analyzed and used to support the company's overall operational and planning objectives.

3.0 Strategic Quality Planning (60 points).   The Strategic Quality Planning category considers the company's planning process and how all key quality requirements are integrated into overall business planning. Also examined are the company's short- and longer-term plans and how quality and performance requirements are deployed to all work units.

3.1 Strategic Quality and Company Performance Planning Process (35 points).
Describe the company's strategic planning process for the short term (1–2 years) and longer term (3 years or more) for quality

leadership and customer satisfaction leadership. Include how this process integrates quality and company performance requirements and how plans are deployed.

3.2 Quality Performance Plans (25 points).
Summarize the company's quality and performance plans and goals for the short term (1–2 years) and the longer term (3 years or more).

4.0 Human Resource Development and Management (150 points). The Human Resource Development and Management category addresses the key elements of how the company develops and realizes the full potential of the work force in order to pursue the company's quality and performance objectives. Also examined are the company's efforts to build and maintain an environment for quality excellence conducive to full participation and personal and organizational growth.

4.1 Human Resource Management (20 points).
Describe how the company's overall human resource development and management plans and practices support its quality and company performance plans and address all categories and types of employees.

4.2 Employee Involvement (40 points).
Describe the means available for all employees to contribute effectively to meeting the company's quality and performance objectives; summarize trends in involvement.

4.3 Employee Education and Training (40 points).
Describe how the company determines what quality and related education and training is needed by employees and how the company utilizes the knowledge and skills acquired; summarize the types of quality and related education and training received by employees in all categories.

4.4 Employee Performance and Recognition (25 points).
Describe how the company's employee performance, recognition, promotion, compensation, reward, and feedback processes support the attainment of the company's quality and performance objectives.

4.5 Employee Well-Being and Morale (25 points).
Describe how the company maintains a work environment conducive to the well-being and growth of all employees; summarize trends and levels in key indicators of well-being and morale.

5.0 Management of Process Quality (140 points). The Management of Process Quality category considers the systematic approaches the company uses to pursue ever-higher quality and company performance. Examined are the key elements of process management, including design, management of process quality for all work units and suppliers, systematic quality improvement, and quality assessment.

5.1 Design and Introduction of Quality Products and Services (40 points).
Describe how new and/or improved products and services are designed and introduced and how processes are designed to meet key product and service quality requirements and company performance requirements.

5.2 Process Management—Product and Service Production and Delivery Processes (35 points).
Describe how the company's product and service production and delivery processes are managed so that current quality requirements are met and quality and performance are continuously improved.

5.3 Process Management—Business Processes and Support Services (30 points).
Describe how the company's business processes and support services are managed so that current requirements are met and quality and performance are continuously improved.

5.4 Supplier Quality (20 points).
Describe how the quality of materials, components, and services furnished by other businesses is assured and continuously improved.

5.5 Quality Assessment (15 points).
Describe how the company assesses the quality and performance of its systems, processes, and practices and the quality of its products and services.

6.0 Quality and Operational Results (180 points). The Quality and Operational Results category examines the company's quality levels and improvement trends in quality, company operational performance, and supplier quality. Also scrutinized are current quality and performance levels relative to those of competitors.

6.1 Product and Service Quality Results (75 points).
Summarize trends in quality and current quality levels for key product and service features; compare the company's current quality levels with those of competitors.

6.2 Company Operational Results (45 points).
Summarize trends and levels in overall company operational performance and provide a comparison of this performance with competitors and appropriate benchmarks.

6.3 Business Process and Support Service Results (25 points).
Summarize trends and current levels in quality and performance improvement for business processes and support services.

6.4 Supplier Quality Results (35 points).
Summarize trends in quality and current quality levels of suppliers; compare the company's supplier quality with that of competitors and with key benchmarks.

7.0 Customer Focus and Satisfaction (300 points).   The Customer Focus and Satisfaction category examines the company's relationships with customers and its knowledge of customer requirements and of the key quality factors that determine marketplace competitiveness. Also considered are the company's methods for determining customer satisfaction and current trends and levels of satisfaction, and for assessing these results relative to competitors.

7.1 Customer Relationship Management (65 points).
Describe how the company provides effective management of its relationships with its customers and uses information gained from customers to improve customer relationship management strategies and practices.

7.2 Commitment to Customers (15 points).
Describe the company's explicit and implicit commitments to customers regarding its products and services.

7.3 Customer Satisfaction Determination (35 points).
Describe the company's method for determining customer satisfaction and customer satisfaction relative to competitors; describe how these methods are evaluated and improved.

7.4 Customers Satisfaction Results (75 points).
Summarize trends in the company's customer satisfaction and trends in key indicators of dissatisfaction.

7.5 Customer Satisfaction Comparison (75 points).
Compare the company's customer satisfaction results with those of competitors.

7.6 Future Requirements and Expectations of Customers (35 points).
Describe how the company determines future requirements and expectations of customers.

How It's Scored

The system for scoring examination items is based on three evaluation dimensions: approach, deployment, and results. All examination items require applicants to furnish information relating to one or more of these dimensions. Scoring guidelines are outlined in Table 8–2.

THE DEMING PRIZE

In 1950, W. Edwards Deming was invited to Japan by the Union of Japanese Scientists and Engineers (JUSE) to lecture on the applicability of using quality control in manufacturing companies. The impact of Deming's teaching was widespread and swift to take root. In 1951, JUSE instituted the Deming Prize to honor Deming for his friendship and achievements in industrial quality control. Today, companies wishing to improve the level of quality within their organization compete for the Deming Prize, not only to achieve the honor and prestige of winning, but to realize the improvements that come from implementing his quality principles.

Categories of the Deming Prize

Under the Deming Prize guidelines, awards offered by the Deming Prize Committee include the Deming Prize for the Individual Person, the Deming Application Prizes, and the Quality Control Award for Factory.

The Deming Prize for Individual Person. This prize is for a person who shows excellent achievement in the theory or application of the statistical quality control, or a person who makes an outstanding contribution to the dissemination of statistical quality control.

TABLE 8–2
Scoring Guidelines

Score	Approach	Deployment	Results
0%	• Anecdotal, no system evident	• Anecdotal	• Anecdotal
10–40%	• Beginnings of systematic prevention basis	• Some to many major areas of business	• Some positive trends in the areas deployed
50%	• Sound, systematic prevention basis that includes evaluation/ improvement cycles	• Most major areas of business	• Positive trends in most major areas
	• Some evidence of integration	• Some support areas	• Some evidence that results are caused by approach
60–90%	• Sound systematic prevention basis with evidence of refinement through evaluation/ improvement cycles	• Major areas of business	• Good to excellent in major areas
	• Good integration	• From some to many support areas	• Positive trends—from some to many support areas
			• Evidence that results are caused by approach
100%	• Sound, systematic prevention basis refined through evaluation/ improvement cycles	• Major areas and support areas	• Excellent (world-class) results in major areas
	• Excellent integration	• All operations	• Good to excellent in support areas
			• Sustained results
			• Results clearly caused by approach

The Deming Application Prizes.   These prizes are for enterprises (including public institutions) or divisions that achieve the most distinctive improvement of performance through the implementation of company-wide quality control based on statistical quality control. Awarded especially to enterprises of medium or small size is the Deming Application Prize for Small Enterprise, while the prize awarded to corporate divisions is known as the Deming Application Prize for Division.

The Deming Application Prize to Overseas Companies.   Because its initial purpose was to encourage the development of quality control in Japan, the Deming Prize was originally restricted to Japanese companies. In recent years, however, strong interest in the Deming Application Prize has been shown by non-Japanese companies.

The Deming Prize Committee, therefore, has revised the basic regulations, establishing in 1984 the "Regulations Regarding the Management of the Deming Application Prize" to allow the acceptance of oversea companies as candidates. However, if the number of applicants exceeds the examination capability of the Deming Prize Committee because of scheduling limitations, some of the applications may be carried forward to the next year or later.

Examination Items

The prize committee examines and judges the manner in which each and every segment of the company conducts the activities that are essential for the proper control of product and service quality—activities such as investigation, research, development, design, purchase, production, inspection, and sales. Each of the 10 areas for examination (described in Table 8–3) are evaluated with regard to the method used to maintain effective control over costs, profits, appointed dates of deliveries, safety, inventories, manufacturing processes, equipment maintenance, instrumentation, personnel and labor relations, education and training, new product development, research, the relationship with subcontractors, associates, material suppliers and sales companies, the handling of complaints, the utilization of customers' opinions, the quality assurance and after-sale services to customers and the relationship with companies to which products are delivered. The term *quality control* as used in the Deming Prize examination denotes company-wide quality control (CWQC) based on statistical quality control techniques.

TABLE 8–3
Checklist for the Deming Application Prize

Item	Particulars
1. Policy	(1) Policies pursued for management, quality, and quality control (2) Method of establishing policies (3) Justifiability and consistency of policies (4) Utilization of statistical methods (5) Transmission and diffusion of policies (6) Review of policies and the results achieved (7) Relationship between policies and long- and short-term planning
2. Organization and its management	(1) Explicitness of the scopes of authority and responsibility (2) Appropriateness of delegations of authority (3) Interdivisional cooperation (4) Committees and their activities (5) Utilization of staff (6) Utilization of QC Circle activities (7) Quality control diagnosis
3. Education and dissemination	(1) Education programs and results (2) Quality- and control-consciousness, degrees of understanding of quality control (3) Teaching of statistical concepts and methods, and the extent of their dissemination (4) Grasp of the effectiveness of quality control (5) Education of related company (particularly those in the same group, subcontractors, consignees, and distributors) (6) QC Circle activities (7) System of suggesting ways of improvements and its actual conditions
4. Collection, dissemination and use of information on quality	(1) Collection of external information (2) Transmission of information between divisions (3) Speed of information transmission (use of computers) (4) Data processing, statistical analysis of information and utilization of the results
5. Analysis	(1) Selection of key problems and themes (2) Propriety of the analytical approach (3) Utilization of statistical methods (4) Linkage with proper technology (5) Quality analysis, process analysis (6) Utilization of analytical results (7) Assertiveness of improvement suggestions

Source: The Deming Prize Guide, 1989, Union of Japanese Scientists and Engineers.

TABLE 8–3 (concluded)

Item	Particulars
6. Standardization	(1) Systematization of standards (2) Method of establishing, revising, and abolishing standards (3) Outcome of the establishment, revision, or abolition of standards (4) Contents of the standards (5) Utilization of statistical methods (6) Accumulation of technology (7) Utilization of standards
7. Control	(1) Systems for the control of quality and such related matters as cost and quantity (2) Control items and control points (3) Utilization of such statistical control methods as control charts and other statistical concepts (4) Contribution to performance of QC Circle activities (5) Actual conditions of control activities (6) State of matters under control
8. Quality assurance	(1) Procedure for the development of new products and services (analysis and upgrading of quality, checking of design, reliability, and other properties) (2) Safety and immunity from product liability (3) Process design, process analysis, and process control and improvement (4) Process capability (5) Instrumentation, gauging, testing, and inspecting (6) Equipment maintenance, and control of subcontracting, purchasing, and services (7) Quality assurance system and its audit (8) Utilization of statistical methods (9) Evaluation and audit of quality (10) Actual state of quality assurance
9. Results	(1) Measurement of results (2) Substantive results in quality, services, delivery time, cost, profits, safety, environment, etc. (3) Intangible results (4) Measures for overcoming defects
10. Planning for the future	(1) Grasp of the present state of affairs and the concreteness of the plan (2) Measures for overcoming defects (3) Plans for further advances (4) Linkage with the long-term plans

1. *Company policy and planning.* How the policy for management, quality, and quality control is determined and transmitted throughout all sectors of the company is examined together with the results achieved. Whether the contents of the policy are appropriate and clearly presented is also considered.

2. *Organization and its management.* Whether the scope of responsibility and authority is clearly defined, how cooperation is promoted among all departments, and how the organization is managed for carrying out quality control are examined.

3. *Quality control education and dissemination.* How quality control is taught, as well as how employees are educated through training courses and routine work in the company concerned and the related companies, are evaluated. The extent to which the concept of quality control and statistical techniques are understood and utilized, and the activeness of quality circles, are examined.

4. *Collection, transmission, and utilization of information on quality.* How the collection and dissemination of information on quality within and outside the company are conducted by and among the head office, factories, branches, sales offices, and the organizational units are examined, together with the evaluation of the organization and the systems used, and how fast information is transmitted, sorted, analyzed, and utilized.

5. *Analysis.* Whether or not critical problems regarding quality are properly grasped and analyzed with respect to overall quality and the existing production process is scrutinized, as well as whether the results are being interpreted in the frame of the available technology. A check is also made on whether proper statistical methods are being used.

6. *Standardization.* The establishment, revision, and rescission of standards and the manner of their control and systematization are examined, together with the use of standards for the enhancement of company technology.

7. *Control ("Kanri").* How the procedures used for the maintenance and improvement of quality are reviewed from time to time as necessary is examined. Also scrutinized is how the responsibility for and the authority over these matters are defined, while a check is made on the use of control charts and other related statistical techniques.

8. *Quality Assurance.* New product development, quality analysis, design, production, inspection, equipment maintenance, purchasing, sales, services, and other activities at each stage of the operation that are essential for quality assurance—including reliability—are closely examined, together with the overall quality assurance management system.

9. *Effects.* The effects of the implementation of quality control on the quality of products and services are examined. Whether products of sufficiently good quality are being manufactured and sold is evaluated. Also examined is whether products have been improved with respect to quality, quantity, and cost, as well as whether the whole company has been improved, not only in the "numerical" sense of quality and profit, but also in the "scientific" sense—as a way of thinking by employers and employees and a heightened will to work.

10. *Future plans.* Whether the strong and weak points in the present situation are properly recognized and whether the promotion of quality control is planned in the future and is likely to continue will be examined.

THE EUROPEAN QUALITY AWARD

In the 1980s, European companies began to realize that their only way of surviving in business was to pay much greater attention to quality. In many markets, quality has already become the competitive edge.

Again, quality is not confined to the quality of a product or a service. It applies to delivery, administration, customer service, and every other aspect of a company's activities. Quality now encompasses all the ways in which a company meets the needs and expectations of its financial-stake holders, its customers, its people, and the community in which it operates.

Realizing this emerging requirement for Total Quality Management, many of the major companies in Europe have embarked on programs to improve their management and business processes. Evidence of significant benefits has already been seen—increased competitiveness, reduced costs, and greater satisfaction among all their interested parties.

In recognition of this potential, 14 leading Western European companies took the initiative of forming the European Foundation for Quality Management (EFQM) in 1988. As of January 1992, nearly 200 members from most Western European countries and most business sectors belonged to the EFQM.

EFQM has an important role to play: enhancing the position of Western European companies in the global market. This goal will be achieved in two ways: first, by accelerating the acceptance of quality as a strategy for global competitive advantage, and second, by stimulating and assisting the deployment of quality improvement activities.

Recognition of achievement is a feature of EFQM policy in line with these objectives. 1992 marked the inception of a major new European business quality award.

What Is the European Quality Award?

The European Quality Award consists of two parts: the *European Quality Prize,* which will be awarded to a number of companies that demonstrate excellence in the management of quality as their fundamental process for continuous improvement, and the *European Quality Award,* which is awarded to the most successful exponent of Total Quality Management in Western Europe. The trophy will be engraved and held nominally for one year by the recipient.

To receive the European Quality Prize (the Prize), applicants must demonstrate that their approach to Total Quality Management has contributed significantly to satisfying the expectations of customers, employees and others with an interest in the company for the past few years. A Prize-winning company is one that would be seen to excel in the European marketplace. It can be of any size or type; but, in its excellence through quality, it will be a model against which all companies can measure their own quality achievements and their own drive for continuous improvement.

Your company, organization, or business entity is invited to apply for the European Quality Award. Your application represents an opportunity to discover whether your European company rates as a European model of quality—and if not, the means by which your company can achieve that position.

Benefits

The first step in an application for the European Quality Award (the Award) is the collation of a body of quality management data from within your organization. This process is of significant value, even if your company is not successful in winning the Award. It will enable you to assess your own company's level of commitment to quality. It will also show you the extent to which that commitment is being deployed—vertically, through every level of the organization, and horizontally, in all areas of activity.

Furthermore, you will receive a feedback report that will concentrate on the strengths and the areas for improvement in your own approach to quality management.

The benefits for those companies receiving this prestigious award are many:

- Considerable status is attached to an award that is sponsored by the European Commission, the European Foundation for Quality Management, and the European Organization for Quality.
- The promotion of the Award, together with the opportunity to use the symbol of the European Quality Prize and the European Quality Award in corporate literature, will clearly establish that a company that has received an Award is a member of the most successful group of companies in Europe.
- The recognition of the winners' achievements in Total Quality Management will enable them to promote themselves as suppliers of established excellence.
- In the year following presentation of the Award, winners share their experience of Total Quality Management at EFQM seminars. These seminars offer an excellent platform for the promotion of their status as leaders in European Total Quality Management.

The intrinsic benefits of quality can be realized through its management. However, a winner of The European Quality Award can also reasonably expect to benefit from the emergence of new customers and new business opportunities.

Criteria

Winners of the European Quality Award will be leading European companies, subsidiaries, or divisions—models of quality for others to follow.

The principles of quality management apply equally across all sectors of business to companies of any size, in any Western European country. Application for the Award is open to all such companies, provided a small number of clear and relevant criteria are met.

First, because this is an award for Western Europe, all applicants must be able to demonstrate a history of significant commitment to Western Europe of at least five years. The definition of this commitment is that at least 50 percent of the applicant's business operations have been conducted within Western Europe for the past five years. The quality practices on which the application is based must be inspectable in Western Europe.

Second, if a company employs, on a permanent basis, less than five hundred people, the company as a whole must apply. If, however, the company employs more than five hundred people, a division or subsidiary can apply in its own right, providing that the parent company is not applying and that it is a clearly differentiated independent business entity within its parent company.

Finally, most businesses may apply:

- Publicly or privately owned.
- European and foreign owned.
- Joint ventures.
- Incorporated firms.
- Partnerships.
- Sole proprietorships.
- Holding companies.

Some, however, may not:

- Local, regional, national, and government agencies.
- Not-for-profit organizations.
- Trade associations.
- Professional societies.

Appraisal Process

When the application is received, it will be marked by a team of up to six evaluators, all of whom have undergone the same training course, thus maximizing consistency. The application is scored on the basis of the self-appraisal data you must supply with your application.

On the basis of this assessment, the Award jury will decide which applicants should be visited for further assessment. The visits involve the verification of the application and the inspection of the quality practices of the leading applicants.

After the jury's final review and decision, the European Quality Prize will be presented to the companies that demonstrate the highest standards of Total Quality Management. The Prizes will be presented at the EFQM's European Quality Management Forum. The forum will also be the venue for the presentation of the European Quality Award trophy to the most successful exponent of Total Quality Management in Western Europe.

Application for Award

An application submission should be formatted in the following way:

- No more than 75 pages in length.
- Loosely bound for ease of processing.
- Numbered on every page.
- Typed in English (although the applicant's own self-appraisal information may be submitted in the original language, provided it is clearly annotated and/or cross-referenced in English).

Twelve identical copies are required. Your application should be divided into the following sections:

Title Page.   Applicant's name (the applicant being the company or business entity), address and date of application.

Application Form.   This form must be signed by the applicant's chief executive officer. This signature indicates that all the information contained in the application is correct, that fees will be paid, and that all requirements of the submission have been met.

Table of Contents.

Overview.   This two-page summary provides information about the applicant and its business, including history, technology and raw materials, competitive environment, partnership arrangements, principal products and services, customer base, regulatory environment, and other important factors.

Self-Appraisal Material.   Self-appraisal material constitutes the vast majority of the application. Your organization probably has quality self-appraisal systems in place already. However, for the sake of consistency within the assessment process for the Award, information submitted must align with the award assessment model and requirements.

Fees. Payment of the initial application fee should accompany your application.

HOW TO OBTAIN AWARD INFORMATION

You can obtain a copy of the latest application guidelines for the Malcolm Baldrige National Quality Award by contacting:

Malcolm Baldrige National Quality Award
National Institute of Standards and Technology
Route 270 and Quince Orchard Road
Administration Building, Room A537
Gaithersburg, MD 20899
Phone: (301) 975–2036
Fax: (301) 948–3716

To obtain information concerning the Deming Prize, application can be obtained by contacting:

Mr. Junji Noguchi
Executive Director
Union of Japanese Scientists and Engineers
5–10–11 Sendagaya, Shibuya-Ku
Tokyo 151, Japan
Phone: (03) 5379–1227
Fax: (03) 225–1813

To obtain information concerning the European Quality Award, contact:

The European Foundation for Quality Management
Building "Reaal" Fellenoord 47A
5612 AA Eindhoven, The Netherlands
Phone: + 31 40 461075
Fax: + 31 40 432005

DOES YOUR COMPANY RANK AMONG THE BEST?

You can tell how you rank by reviewing the award requirements described in this chapter and evaluating your organization's quality status. You may wish to apply for these awards; but if you decide not to, consider reviewing these award requirements, ask your staff to review them, and determine by self-examination the areas in which you can improve your business.

Many companies use the application guidelines as standards of excellence, which they can use for self-assessment. In the European Community (EC), formal standards such as ISO 9000 have been promulgated as a baseline for designing products and receiving certification that products meets these quality standards. Appendix C provides a brief overview and update on the status of ISO 9000 and its U.S. and European application.

CHAPTER 9

BUSINESS SUCCESS STORIES

The Malcolm Baldrige National Quality Award, as described in Chapter 8, has been awarded to Solectron Corporation (1991 winner), ZYTEC Corporation (1991), Marlow Industries (1991), Cadillac Motor Car Company (1990), IBM Rochester (1990), Federal Express (1990), Wallace Company (1990), Milliken & Company (1989), Xerox Business Products (1989), Motorola Inc. (1988), Westinghouse Commercial Nuclear Fuel Division (1988), and Globe Metallurgical (1988). The efforts of several of these quality leaders are discussed briefly in this chapter. The corporate mission, objectives, and unique approach to quality are described to provide a reference point in determining how your business organization's quality efforts can be enhanced.

FEDERAL EXPRESS CORPORATION

The Federal Express Corporation was the Malcolm Baldrige Award's first winner in the service category. Seventeen years ago, Federal Express Corporation launched the air-express delivery industry. By constantly adhering to a management philosophy emphasizing people, service, and profit—in that order—the company achieved high levels of customer satisfaction and experienced rapid sales growth. Annual revenues topped $1 billion within 10 years of the company's founding, an exceptional achievement.

But past accomplishments do not ensure future success. That's why the management of Federal Express is setting ever-higher goals for quality performance and customer satisfaction, enhancing and expanding service, investing heavily in advanced technology, and building on its reputation as an excellent employer. Company leaders are increasingly stressing management by fact, analysis, and improvement.

Through a quality improvement process focusing on 12 service quality indicators (SQIs), which are all tied to customer expectations and articulated at all levels of its international service business, the Memphis-based firm continues to set higher standards for service and customer satisfaction. Measuring themselves against a 100 percent service standard, managers and employees strive to continuously improve all aspects of the way Federal Express does business.

Federal Express at a Glance

Conceived by chairman and chief executive officer Frederick W. Smith, Federal Express began operations in 1973. At that time a fleet of eight small aircraft was sufficient to handle demand. Five years later, the company employed 10,000 people, who handled a daily volume of 35,000 shipments. Today, approximately 90,000 Federal Express employees at more than 1,650 sites process 1.5 million shipments daily, all of which must be tracked in a central information system, sorted in a short time at facilities in Memphis, Indianapolis, Newark, Oakland, Los Angeles, Anchorage, and Brussels, and delivered by a highly decentralized distribution network. Federal Express's air cargo fleet is now the world's largest.

Federal Express revenues totaled $7 billion in fiscal year 1990. Domestic overnight and second-day deliveries accounted for nearly three-fourths of the total, with the remainder being international deliveries. The company's share of the domestic market in 1989 was 43 percent, compared with 26 percent for its nearest competitor.

People-Service-Profit

Federal Express's "people-service-profit" philosophy guides management policies and actions. The company has a well-developed and thoroughly deployed management evaluation system called Survey/Feedback/Action (SFA), which involves a survey of employees, analysis of each work group's results by the work group's manager, and a discussion between the manager and the work group to develop written action plans for the manager to improve and become more effective. Data from the SFA process are aggregated at all levels of the organization for use in policymaking.

Training of front-line personnel is a responsibility of managers, and "recurrency training" is a widely used instrument for improvement.

Teams regularly assess training needs, and a worldwide staff of training professionals devises programs to address those needs. To aid these efforts, Federal Express has developed an interactive video system for employee instruction. An internal television network, accessible throughout the company, also serves as an important avenue for employee education.

Consistently included in listings of the best U.S. companies to work for, Federal Express has a "no layoff" philosophy, and its "guaranteed fair treatment procedure" for handling employee grievances is used as a model by firms in many industries. Employees can participate in a program to qualify front-line workers for management positions. In addition, Federal Express has a well-developed recognition program for team and individual contributions to company performance. Over the last five years, at least 91 percent of employees responded that they were "proud to work for Federal Express."

Service Quality Indicators (SQI)

To spur progress toward its ultimate target of 100 percent customer satisfaction, Federal Express replaced its old measure of quality performance—percent of on-time deliveries—with an index that comprehensively describes how its performance is viewed by customers. Federal Express established the service quality indicators SQI to determine what the main areas of customer perception of service are and how Federal Express is meeting them. The purpose of the SQI is to *identify and eliminate causes*, not place blame.

The SQI has 12 components weighted to reflect the customers' view of their performance by placing greater weight on SQI categories that have the greatest impact on the customers' perception of service received. The number of average daily failure points for each component is calculated by multiplying the number of daily occurrences for that component by its assigned importance weight. Factors such as abandoned calls are included in order to measure internal performance that can significantly affect external customer service. SQI categories are expanded and adjusted as necessary.

The SQI is the sum of the average daily failure points for all 12 components and is tracked and reported on a weekly basis, with monthly summaries.

The service goal will always be 100 percent failure-free performance, with the emphasis on finding the root causes of failure and implementing solutions that *prevent* the failures rather than simply fix the consequences of failures. For example, if courier-mislabeled packages are a major cause of wrong day/late failures, the SQI team would focus on creating effective new solutions to prevent courier miscoding at the source, rather than perfecting the expensive expediting system. Effective quality improvement programs and teamwork such as this are essential to achieving the SQI goal. Knowing what makes a customer unhappy is important, but it is even more important to understand it and solve it through a concerted effort by several areas. Goal congruence, improved methods, contingency plans, and teamwork are vital parts of the total commitment to service.

To reach its aggressive quality goals, Federal Express has set up one cross-functional team for each service component in the SQI. A senior executive heads each team and assures the involvement of front-line employees, support personnel, and managers from all parts of the corporation when needed. Two of these corporate-wide teams have a network of more than 1,000 employees working on improvements.

The SQI measurements are directly linked to the corporate planning process, which begins with the chief executive and chief operating officers and an executive planning committee. SQIs form the basis on which corporative executives are evaluated. Individual performance objectives are established and monitored. Executive bonuses rest on the performance of the whole corporation in meeting performance improvement goals. And, in the annual employee survey, if employees do not rate management leadership at least as high as they rated them the year before, no executive receives a year-end bonus.

Quality Improvement at Federal Express

Although Federal Express is an acknowledged leader in the air freight industry, a formal quality improvement process (QIP) has been implemented throughout the entire corporation to continue meeting the needs of their customers. The objectives of the QIP are to (1) achieve a 100 percent service level, (2) increase profits, and (3) make Federal Express a better place to work by focusing everyone's attention on the quality policy of "Doing Right Things Right" and catching and fixing problems when they happen.

The corporate mission supports the philosophy that quality must be a part of the way they do business. Themes such as "Do it right the first time," "Make the first time you do it the only time anyone has to," "Fedexcellence," and "Q = P" (Quality = Productivity) have always been a part of the Federal Express culture. Even the people-service-profit philosophy is an expression of their commitment to quality. Now, in light of intense competition and expansion into global markets, quality becomes more than a slogan at Federal Express—it is the normal way of life.

Experts say that in an organization committed to quality as a way of life, three things happen:

- The level of customer satisfaction increases and satisfied customers bring more business, which ensures the financial health of the corporation and continued job security.
- Profits increase because time and money aren't wasted correcting mistakes.
- The quality of work life is improved because they have fewer customer complaints, less hassle, and less rework to deal with.

Quality improvement requires an ongoing commitment to continuous improvement, and it means meeting the needs of internal and external customers.

Continuous Improvement.   Quality improvement requires us to continuously develop ways to do better work. Continuous improvement means "Fix it now!" and "Prevent problems before they happen" and "Look for new ways to meet customer needs." The theory of "If it ain't broke, don't fix it" has no place in a quality organization. Instead, the approach needs to be "If it ain't broke, improve it."

Satisfying Internal and External Customers.   Quality begins and ends with the customer. The customer indicates what is the right thing to do, and then the company has to find the right way to do it. As the supplier of a service, Federal Express is famous for doing whatever it takes to satisfy the customer. Workers at all levels recognize who the ultimate customer is and know how important it is to meet customer needs. However, they also need to recognize and meet the needs of their internal customers— other Federal Express employees with whom they exchange information, products, and services every day. Just as one worker depends on services or products from others in order to do his or her job, so do others depend on that worker for products or services to do their jobs.

To make the work process flow smoothly and deliver a quality product to external customers, Federal Express builds positive working relationships with their internal customers. This can be accomplished by asking three questions:

- What do you need from me?
- What do you do with what I give you?
- Are there any gaps between what I give you and what you need?

The answers to these questions are the key to Doing Right Things Right.

Quality Action Teams

In a quality organization, everyone—not just management—must be committed to improving both quality and productivity. Everyone must share responsibility for achieving corporate goals. Quality Action Teams (QATs) involve employees in designing the work process for maximum quality at minimum cost. Teams generally are more effective than individuals in solving problems or improving the way things get done. When quality improvement actions are started, employees often ask, What's in it for me? Federal Express's experience has shown the following:

- Doing right things the first time makes your job easier.
- Quality of work life is improved because you have to deal with fewer customer complaints, less hassle, and less rework.
- Profits increase because the company doesn't waste time and money correcting mistakes.
- Quality work keeps Federal Express financially healthy and ensures job security.
- You have the opportunity to actively participate in problem solving.
- You are eligible to receive awards and recognition through various corporate programs.

Quality improvement activities are critical to the continued success of Federal Express. The competition will continue to get tougher, and the customer will continue to demand the best quality of service available for the prices they pay. Federal Express must meet all of these challenges, and they must do so better than anyone else. Constantly striving to improve the system and finding better ways of doing things will enable

Federal Express to keep its leadership position in the industry as it moves aggressively into the global marketplace.

GLOBE METALLURGICAL INC.

Globe Metallurgical Inc., a small business, is a major producer of silicon metal and ferrosilicon products, with plants located in Beverly, Ohio, and Selma, Alabama. The company, founded in 1873 as the Globe Iron Company in Jackson, Ohio, built the Beverly plant in 1955 and acquired the Selma plant in the mid-1960s. At the Beverly plant, Globe operates five submerged-arc electric furnaces, and has the capability to produce silicon metal and a full range of ferrosilicon products. The furnaces range in size from 10 to 20 megawatts. Once a specialist in the production of ferrochromium products, Globe abandoned the environmentally hazardous ferrochromium lines in 1985 to concentrate its ferrosilicon effort in the production of magnesium ferrosilicon products to serve the foundry industry. Magnesium ferrosilicon is used to convert gray iron to ductile iron in foundries, and ductile iron represents a growing segment of the iron castings market. The Selma plant contains two submerged-arc electric furnaces, and the plant specializes in the production of high-grade, low-impurity silicon metal. The furnaces at Selma are both in the 15 to 16 megawatt range. The silicon metal produced at Selma is devoted primarily to the chemical silicons industry and to applications requiring extremely low iron levels in the silicon metal, such as the electronic and solar cell industries.

Development of the Globe Quality System

In 1985, the Ford Motor Company approached its suppliers with its quality certification program, called Q-1. Because Globe supplied Ford with a number of alloys for its foundries, Globe management recognized that the criteria specified in the Q-1 program would have to be satisfied to sustain a long-term relationship with Ford. The first step to obtaining Q-1 certification was to undergo an extensive audit of the quality system by Ford personnel, called the Q-101 audit. If the supplier passes with a score of 140 or more out of 200, the supplier becomes eligible for an internal review of its performance history at all Ford locations using its products. If all the locations approve the supplier, the Q-1 Award is forthcoming.

Because the criteria are demanding, the Q-1 Award is recognized as a significant quality achievement in the U.S. auto industry.

The Ford Q-1 program has had the greatest initial impact on the development of the quality system at Globe. A self-assessment of the Q-101 criteria indicated to Globe management that the quality system in place was inadequate to satisfy the criteria, so a quality system was built around the criteria. The primary inadequacies of the system were that it was detection-based as opposed to prevention-based, and that it lacked implementation of statistical process control techniques, lacked quality planning, and lacked employee participation in the improvement process.

Because Globe was deficient in so many respects, the building of its quality system began simultaneously in three areas: (1) training the entire work force in statistical process control (SPC), (2) establishing a quality manual and the mechanics of the quality system, and (3) educating and training Globe's suppliers in the necessity of implementing statistical process control and a quality system.

Quality-Efficiency-Cost Committee

To establish the mechanics of a workable quality system, a Quality-Efficiency-Cost (QEC) committee was established at each plant, with a QEC steering committee overseeing the activities of the plant committees. The committees provide ideas for improvement in all three of the areas of quality, efficiency, and cost. The QEC steering committee comprises the top management of the company and is chaired by the president and chief executive officer. It meets monthly and discusses the broader issues of development and maintenance of the quality system, such as allocation of significant resources and planning. The plant QEC committees meet daily and are chaired by the plant manager. All department heads attend the meetings, and the discussion is much narrower in scope than in the steering committee meetings, concentrating on specific projects and implementation techniques. The plant manager, who also serves on the steering committee with upper management, serves as the conduit for bringing plant issues up to the steering-committee level, and for bringing steering committee issues down to the plant level for implementation. Initially, the Beverly plant QEC committee was given the task of examining each of the plant's processes and identifying the critical process variables that must be controlled through SPC or other techniques. This was done to assure that the final product will always be consistent with the customers' requirements without the need for 100 percent inspection of the final product. Thus, the emphasis was to build a quality system based on prevention techniques as opposed to the historical protection methodologies.

Globe Project Teams

Project teams are called on an ad hoc basis to address a particular problem or project. Unlike the other teams, salaried employees with particular expertise are invited onto project teams. This expertise includes Taguchi design of experiments, storyboarding, brainstorming techniques, and other statistical tools and techniques. Historically, the activities now undertaken by project teams were done solely by salaried employees, and the implementation of their ideas was dictated by management within a given department. In many instances, the hourly employees, whose ideas were not solicited in the development of the project, resented the implementation technique or felt that they knew of more effective techniques. Now that input is actively solicited from hourly employees, the hourly employees take a pride of ownership in the decision process and are much more likely to assist in implementation. Typically, there are seven departmental teams, three interdepartmental teams, two project teams, and two interplant teams in operation at any given time. More than 60 percent of the work force of both plants is involved in quality circle teams. An average of 70 ideas per week are generated to improve the quality, efficiency, and/or cost of the operation.

Quality Planning

Prior to 1986, quality was not given consideration in Globe's planning process. Today, the Continuous Improvement Plan is a vital document that is updated annually and distributed widely both internally and external to the company. The current plan is 20 pages, with 96 items for improvement identified. Each item in the plan fully supports items found in the company's Strategic Plan. Both plans cover a period of five years.

The structure of the Continuous Improvement Plan includes the goal of the improvement, the objective of the improvement item, individual projects that support the objectives, and assigned responsibilities and target dates. The QEC steering committee is responsible for developing the goals that are found in the plan, but the plant QEC committees are responsible for the much more specific activities of project determination and assignment of responsibilities. To ensure that the hourly employees have input and the ability to comment on the plan, copies are distributed, and hourly employees are invited to attend planning meetings. Many quality circle ideas that require large capital expenditures are incorporated into the plan each year. To track the progress of individual projects, an audit system has been established that requires the persons responsible to file update reports quarterly. The update reports are distributed by the quality manager, to whom they are returned. To assist the responsible parties in remembering their assignments, the projects have all been translated into a calendar format, which each employee receives to hang on the wall. As project deadlines approach, employees can readily ascertain their responsibilities by looking at the calendar. On due dates, the employee's name, project number, and a brief description of the specific project are printed on the calendar.

Quality Pays!

Because the QEC process, by definition, emphasizes quality, efficiency, and cost, many productivity improvements have been realized through the implementation of both quality- and productivity-enhancing techniques. In 1986, management became interested in the works of Shigeo Shingo, and began to apply many Shingo methods to the manufacturing process. It has been found that the Shingo techniques work in harmony with the techniques of Deming, Taguchi, and others. The productivity improved 36 percent company-wide in the period from 1986 through 1988. Documented savings of $10.3 million per year have been realized through the implementation of quality-related techniques.

MOTOROLA INC.

Motorola Inc. is one of the world's leading manufacturers of electronic equipment, systems, and components produced for both U.S. and international markets. Motorola products include two-way radios, pagers, and cellular radiotelephones, other forms of electronic communications systems, integrated circuits and discrete semiconductors, defense and aerospace electronics, data communications, and information processing and handling equipment. Ranked among the United States' 100 largest industrial companies, Motorola has about 102,000 employees worldwide. As a leader in its high-technology markets, Motorola is one of the few end-equipment manufacturers that can draw on expertise in both semiconductor technology and government electronics.

The company was founded in Chicago by Paul V. Galvin in 1928 as the Galvin Manufacturing Corporation. Its first product was a "battery eliminator," which allowed customers to operate radios directly from household current instead of the batteries supplied with early models. In the 1930s, the company successfully commercialized car radios under the brand name Motorola, a new word suggesting sound in motion. During this period, Motorola also established home radio and police radio departments, instituted pioneering personnel programs, and began national advertising. The name of the company was changed to Motorola Inc. in 1947 — a decade that also saw the company enter government work and open a research laboratory in Phoenix, Arizona, to explore solid-state electronics.

Motorola's attention to quality also has shown up on the bottom line, according to Richard Buetow, vice president and director of quality, who says that defects have been cut by 80 percent during the past few years, and the company has saved about $962 million in inspection and rework costs.

It wasn't always that way. Ten years ago, admits Motorola president Gary L. Tooker, the company faced the grim fact that many of its products and operations simply weren't making the grade. Top executives had a choice: Motorola could either continue losing its customers to Japan (as it had in consumer electronics during the late 1970s) or it could go back to basics.

Robert W. Galvin (then Motorola's chairman and head of the company's executive committee) chose the latter by personally visiting key customers around the world, then calling for a tenfold improvement in quality within five years. But even that wasn't tough enough, says Tooker; Galvin's goal eventually became one of "total customer satisfaction." Motorola now aims for a condition of six sigma— 3.4 defects per million opportunities—not just in manufacturing, but within every one of the company's operations by 1992. Buetow puts it another way; "We're striving for absolute perfection."

At Motorola, the quality culture is pervasive. Motorola top management formally restated their company objectives, beliefs, goals, and key initiatives in 1987, and quality remained as a central theme. Total customer satisfaction is Motorola's fundamental objective. It is the overriding responsibility of everyone in the company, and the focus of all of their efforts.

Motorola top management also reaffirmed two key beliefs that have been part of the Motorola culture since the company began in 1928: uncompromising integrity, and constant respect for people. The CEO has identified the following key goals for Motorola:

1. Increased global market share.
2. Best in class in terms of people, technology, marketing product, manufacturing, and service.
3. Superior financial results.

Quality and Productivity at Motorola

In an era of intense international competition, Motorola has maintained a position of leadership in the electronics industry through a combination of aggressive product innovation, strategic long-range planning, and a unique philosophy that allows each employee to contribute insights to the achievement of quality standards. This philosophy is translated into action through the teams, which together openly and effectively communicate ideas for improving processes and products. The Participative Management Program (PMP) assumes that under the right conditions, employees will suggest better ways to do their jobs. For many years, Motorola has sought the ideas of its employees. For about 10 years, a process of participative management has been in place. Each U.S. employee of the company who is not part of the Motorola Executive Incentive Program (MEIP) is a member of a PMP team. Teams are usually organized by function within an organization. Their purpose is to continually assess the process of performing their work, and to change it in ways that will reduce defects and reduce cycle time. The problem-solving efforts of these teams are directly analogous to quality circles. The quality and cycle-time improvement rates for these teams are the same as the corporate goal, thereby providing incentives that directly support the quality improvement process.

The Motorola Quality Improvement Process

Management of the quality improvement process is based on Motorola's practice of Management by Measurement. This style of management says that by establishing measurements that are correlated to the desired end result, and by regularly reviewing the actual measurements, the organization will focus on those actions necessary to achieve the required improvement.

In 1986, the communications sector adopted a uniform metric; total defects per unit. In addition, because all operations were using the same measurement, the goal for defect reduction was uniformly applied to all operations. The required percent reduction was the same, regardless of the absolute level. The improvement rate achieved by the communications sector was much greater than had been achieved in the five-year Ten Times program, and so the measurement was adopted by the entire corporation.

In January 1987, Motorola restated its corporate quality goal to be:

- Improve 10 times by 1989.
- Improve 100 times by 1991.
- Achieve six-sigma capability by 1992.

This goal is applied to all areas of the business, not just product quality.

Motorola's Quality Initiatives

The first of Motorola's five quality initiatives is achievement of *six-sigma quality*. Motorola intends that all products and services are to be at the six-sigma quality level (3.4 defects/million products) by 1992. This means designing products that will accept reasonable variation in component parts, and developing manufacturing processes that will produce minimum variation in the final output product. It also means analyzing all the services provided, breaking them down into their component parts, and designing systems that will achieve six-sigma performance. Motorola is taking statistical technologies and making them a part of each and every employee's job, regardless of assignment. Measuring this quality level begins by recording the defects found in every function of the business, then relating them to a product or process by the number of opportunities to fabricate the product or carry out the process. Motorola has converted their yield language to parts per million (ppm), and the six-sigma goal is 3.4 ppm defect levels across the company. Despite the wide variety of products and services, the corporate goal is the same six-sigma quality level by 1992.

Their second key initiative, *total cycle time reduction*, is closely related to six-sigma quality. Motorola defines cycle time as the elapsed time from the moment a customer places an order for an existing product to the time they deliver it. In the case of a new product, total cycle time is from the time they conceive of the product to the time it ships. Motorola examines the total system, including design, manufacturing, marketing, and administration.

The third initiative, *product and manufacturing leadership*, also emphasizes the need for product development and manufacturing disciplines to work together in an integrated world, applying principles of teamwork and simultaneous engineering.

Their fourth initiative, *profit improvement*, is a long-term, customer-driven approach that shows Motorola where to commit their resources to give customers what they need, thus improving long-term profits. It recognizes that investing in quality today will produce growth in the future.

The final initiative is *participative management* within, and *cooperation between organizations*. This teamwork approach is designed to achieve more synergy and greater efficiency and to improve quality.

WESTINGHOUSE COMMERCIAL NUCLEAR FUEL DIVISION

Westinghouse Electric Corporation is involved in many aspects of nuclear power plant design, manufacturing, and operation. The Commercial Nuclear Fuel Division (CNFD) is responsible for the engineering, manufacturing, and supply of pressurized water reactor (PWR) fuel assemblies for commercial nuclear power reactors. The fuel contained in these assemblies generates heat (through nuclear fission), which is converted to electricity.

CNFD is a division within the Energy Systems Business Unit of Westinghouse. It is a fully integrated fabricator of commercial PWR fuel comprised of the Western Zirconium Plant, near Ogden, Utah (which became part of CNFD in 1988), where zircalloy extrusions and other components are produced from zircon sands; the Specialty Metals Plant (SMP) in Blairsville, Pennsylvania, where nuclear-grade tubing is produced from the extrusions; the Fuel Manufacturing Plant in Columbia, South Carolina, where enriched uranium is converted into ceramic pellets and loaded into the fuel rod assemblies; and nuclear engineering, marketing, and administrative activities in Monroeville, Pennsylvania.

CNFD currently supplies 40 percent of the U.S. light-water reactor fuel market and 20 percent of the free-world market. This market leadership can be directly attributed to the quality of the division's products and services. Fuel produced at the Columbia Plant is responsible for more than 7 percent of the electricity produced in the United States.

Value Creation at Westinghouse

In the early 1980s, dramatic changes in the global marketplace caused Westinghouse corporate leadership to create a new management vision for Westinghouse. The corporation was becoming concerned about maturing market conditions and international competition. The new vision of Westinghouse was based on a management strategy independent of changes in technology or market conditions. It was based on the principle of "value creation."

As Westinghouse CEO John Marous has stated, the primary mission of both corporate- and division-level managers is to create value for the people who have a stake in the corporation—primarily its customers, stockholders, employees, and the community. Westinghouse believes that managing all of its businesses around the concept of Total Quality Management is the fundamental strategy for value creation.

The Westinghouse model for Total Quality Management is built on four imperatives: management leadership, product and process leadership, human resource excellence, and customer orientation. These imperatives, in turn, are broken down into conditions of excellence. Under the imperative of management leadership, there are four conditions required of management in a Total Quality Management environment. The first task of management is to create the right culture. The next task is planning, followed by communications, and, last, accountability.

Strategic Quality Planning

Westinghouse has discovered that the Total Quality Management concept must be viewed as an all-pervasive operating strategy for managing a business every day. Total Quality Management begins with a strategic decision—a decision that can only be made by top management—and that decision, simply put, is the decision to compete as a world-class company. Total Quality Management concentrates on quality performance, in every facet of a business, as the primary strategy for achieving and maintaining competitive advantage. It requires taking a systematic view of an organization—looking at how each part interrelates to the whole process. In addition, it demands continuous improvement as a way of life.

The Westinghouse Total Quality Management model is built on four imperatives. These imperatives simply state that an organization must have quality management systems, quality products and technology, and quality people—and that the combined energies of its management, products, and people must be focused on customer satisfaction.

Today, CNFD has programs in place to improve quality, on a continuous basis, in every segment of the organization. Management has discovered that Total Quality Management is not merely the sum of a lot of individual quality improvement programs. The power of Total Quality Management is much greater than that. Total Quality Management results from the synergy of all components of an organization working together.

Results Count

Total Quality Management has been the single most important factor in the division's overall business strategy. It has helped to reinforce CNFD's position as a world leader in the marketplace. But more importantly, it has given division personnel a totally new perspective and a new way of thinking. CNFD people constantly come up with new ideas for making things better.

The division is also living up to its commitment to deliver software—proposals, reports, documentation, and the like—to its customers, on time and devoid of errors. Accurate and timely data are crucial to customers, and the division rating is 98 percent on both scores.

In 1988, CNFD completed a record of 42 consecutive months of 100 percent on-time delivery of finished assemblies and related hardware.

Total Quality Management costs, which include internal and external failure costs as well as prevention and appraisal costs, have been reduced by 30 percent in four years, due mainly to reduced rework and scrap costs. CNFD has been able to increase its customer satisfaction rating, a relatively new measure, by about 6 percent in less than one year. That means customers are attaching greater value to the division's products and services than they did a year ago.

Lessons Learned

From its experience in quality improvement, Westinghouse CNFD has learned a number of lessons, which it believes can be applied with reasonable success to any business. First, an organization must have a common vision, and all people in that organization must embrace a common mission. Second, a framework for Total Quality Management is absolutely critical. This is the model or blueprint that keeps everyone focused on continuous improvement in all aspects of the business.

The third lesson can be summarized as, Measure, measure, measure. In addition, CNFD discovered that no quality improvement program can be successful unless both employees and customers are intimately involved in the process.

And finally, Total Quality Management requires a long-term commitment to continuous quality improvement. A Total Quality Management culture cannot be built overnight. Total Quality Management is not a short-term proposition. But neither are the rewards. The benefits of Total Quality Management are long-term for a company willing to make the commitment.

Long-term customer satisfaction and long-term industry leadership are what Total Quality Management is all about.

XEROX BUSINESS PRODUCTS AND SYSTEMS

For its first 15 years, Xerox was without equal—best in an industry whose products were synonymous with its name. But challenges came in the mid-1970s from foreign and U.S. competitors that surpassed Xerox reprographic products in both cost and quality.

Not even second best in some product categories, Xerox launched an ambitious quality improvement program in 1984 to arrest its decline in the world market it created. Today, the company can once again claim the title as the industry's best in nearly all copier-product markets. As a result, Xerox has not only halted loss of world market share, but also reversed it.

Xerox Business Products and Systems (BP & S), headquartered in Stamford, Connecticut, attributes the turnaround to its strategy of Leadership Through Quality. The company defines quality through the eyes of the customer. Xerox BP & S knows what customers want in products and services. Analyses of a wide variety of data, gathered with exhaustive collection efforts that include monthly surveys of 55,000 Xerox equipment owners, enable the company to identify customer requirements. The company uses this information to develop concrete business plans with measurable targets for achieving quality improvements necessary to meet customers' needs.

Xerox at a Glance

One of two Xerox Corporation businesses, Business Products and Systems employs 50,200 people at 83 U.S. locations. BP & S makes more than 250 types of document-processing equipment, generating $6 billion in 1988 U.S. sales, or 54 percent of the company's domestic revenues. Copiers and other duplicating equipment account for nearly 70 percent of BP & S revenues. The remainder is divided among sales of electronic printers and typing equipment, networks, work stations, and software products.

Leadership Through Quality

Customer satisfaction is the number one priority at Xerox. Their strategy for achieving that priority is Leadership Through Quality, the Xerox total quality initiative introduced in 1983 that pervades the entire organization. Personally driven by CEO David T. Kearns and his senior management team, Leadership Through Quality is guided by the simple but powerful Xerox quality policy:

> Xerox is a quality company. Quality is the basic business principle for Xerox. Quality means providing our external and internal customers with innovative products and services that fully satisfy their requirements. Quality improvement is the job of every Xerox employee.

At Xerox, quality is defined as "fully meeting customer requirements." To do this, Leadership Through Quality encompasses a wide range of initiatives. Key initiatives are *benchmarking* of Xerox performance against their competitors and industry leaders; *employee involvement* to fully realize all of their people's talents and capabilities for satisfying customers; and using the *quality tools and processes,* developed specifically for Xerox, for achieving continuous quality improvement. Among these processes are a six-step problem-solving process and a nine-step quality improvement process. The thrust of Leadership Through Quality is prevention; both processes are used at all levels of the organization to identify and correct potential difficulties, as well as to act on quality opportunities.

Leadership Through Quality has transformed the way Xerox does business. Establishing objectives with individual units, planning for future products, delivering current products, reviewing progress—all of these activities start with a focus on customer requirements, proceed through work processes built around quality, and are reviewed and evaluated against the original set of customer requirements. Decisions at every point are guided by Leadership Through Quality processes and based on factual data. Data for decision making in all these activities comes from more than 375 major information systems—of which 175 relate specifically to the management, evaluation, and planning of quality.

To support this massive quality effort, Xerox created an extensive training program. All Xerox employees have received at least the basic 28-hour Leadership Through Quality training; many have been trained in advanced quality techniques. Over the last four years, Xerox has invested four million man-hours and $125 million in Leadership Through Quality training.

Training and empowerment have furthered the basic Xerox strategy of employee involvement. Xerox estimates that at any given time, 75 percent of its employees are actively working on one or more of 7,000 quality improvement teams. The empowerment of field managers has been greatly enhanced by the creation of district partnerships, in which sales, service, and administration functions work closely to make customer-oriented decisions once made at higher organization levels. And on the front lines, the service organization's work-group strategy empowers customer service engineers to manage their workloads in ways that deliver better service to customers.

An important factor in Xerox's quality initiative is the Amalgamated Clothing and Textile Workers Union. Xerox and the union jointly encourage participation by union members in quality improvement processes, with such success that the partnership, unique in American industry, is considered a role model by other corporations. The recently ratified contract states that "every employee shall support the concept of continuous quality improvement while reducing quality costs through teamwork and the tools and processes of Leadership Through Quality.'' Union/management study teams have found ways to retain work inside the corporation—with resulting savings of $7 million annually and 250 jobs.

Xerox is proud of the results realized by Leadership Through Quality. Here are some of the results achieved over the last five years:

- A 78 percent improvement in the quality of Xerox machines.
- Year after year, Xerox copiers and printers continuously set new benchmarks for copy quality.
- More than 40 percent improvement in product reliability.
- The introduction of the industry's first three-year warranty, now offered on five Xerox copiers.
- A 73 percent reduction in production-line defective parts.

Xerox suppliers are made full partners with Xerox through continuous supplier involvement. Xerox supplier parts are process-qualified, which means a step-by-step procedure to analyze and qualify suppliers' production and control processes. Xerox provides training and follow-up in such areas as statistical process control, just-in-time, and total quality techniques.

But Xerox's proudest achievement is the response of their customers to Xerox's efforts to improve quality. They are actively soliciting their customers' requirements and reactions, surveying 55,000 of them monthly about performance in equipment, sales, service, and administrative support. Results have shown a 38 percent improvement in their customers' perceptions of Xerox's performance. Customers also show their satisfaction with Xerox in other ways: Their purchases of Xerox products enabled Xerox to reverse the erosion of their market share by Japanese firms—one of the very few American companies to have accomplished this. Customers also respond to Xerox quality through formal ratings.

In Xerox's continuous drive for quality improvement, they have set very demanding future targets. For example, their targets for 1993 include the following:

- Benchmark performance in their product development cycle schedule.
- A 50 percent reduction in unit manufacturing cost.
- A fourfold improvement in reliability.

Xerox is committed to continuous quality improvement because it is committed to customer satisfaction. Using Leadership Through Quality, the company is determined to constantly upgrade those processes and decisions that deliver world-class products to the most important members of Team Xerox: its customers.

Xerox Benchmarking System

In its quest to elevate its products and services to world-class status, Xerox BP & S devised a benchmarking system that has in itself become a model. The company measures its performance in about 240 key areas of product, service, and business performance. Derived from international studies, the ultimate target for each attribute is the level of performance achieved by the world leader, regardless of industry. Returns from the company's strategy for continuous quality improvement have materialized quickly, as noted below:

Customer Processes
- Highly satisfied customers have increased 38 percent and 39 percent for copier/duplicator and printing systems, respectively.
- Customer satisfactions within Xerox sales processes have improved 40 percent; service processes, 18 percent; and administrative processes, 21 percent.
- Billing quality has improved 35 percent.
- Service response time has improved 27 percent.
- Supply order returns have improved 38 percent.

Productivity
- Service visits per day have been increasing 4 percent a year.
- Product performance during the first 30 days of installation has increased 40 percent.
- Manufacturing lead times have been reduced 50 percent.
- Manufacturing labor and material overhead rates have been improved by 31 percent and 46 percent, respectively.
- Customer retention rate is 20 percent better than the U.S. industry average, and Xerox is gaining customers at a rate of more than four new customers for every three customers lost.

People
- 75 percent of all Xerox employees are actively involved with quality-improvement or problem-solving projects.
- 94 percent of Xerox employees acknowledge that customer satisfaction is their top priority.

- Employee turnover is 17 percent better than the average reported by the Bureau of National Affairs.

Safety

- Product safety has improved 70 percent with an associated 90 percent decrease in claims. Xerox has not had a product liability judgment in the last five years.
- Xerox employees are three times safer on the job than around the home. There has never been an industrial fatality or a major OSHA citation in Xerox.

These improvements have enabled Xerox BP & S to take additional steps to distinguish itself from the competition; for instance, it was the first in the industry to offer a three-year product warranty.

The thrust of Leadership Through Quality is ongoing with Xerox BP & S. The process of continuous quality improvement, directed toward greater customer satisfaction and enhanced business performance, is currently targeting a 50 percent reduction in unit manufacturing cost and fourfold improvement in reliability by 1993. Such goals illustrate the commitment concentrated in the Xerox quality policy, which states that "quality is the basic business principle at Xerox."

FOLLOW BY EXAMPLE!

This chapter has presented the approaches taken by major quality leaders who are world-class providers of products and/or services—from very large to small companies involved in diverse business, from Federal Express overnight package delivery to Xerox's turnaround of its copier business. Each of these companies has developed its own customized approach to improving quality. Each has recognized that quality is not a buzzword but a bedrock upon which these business leaders are now prospering.

CHAPTER 10

TOTAL QUALITY MANAGEMENT INTEGRATION

THE CIRM FRAMEWORK

An underlying assumption of the Amercian Production and Inventory Control Society's (APICS) Certified in Integrated Resource Management (CIRM) Program is that the world of manufacturing has fundamentally changed from what it was only 10 years ago. Whether or not a firm should improve its quality in order to bolster competitiveness is no longer a serious question. Today, firms that want to stay in business in the future *must* make the change—and the sooner the better.

The CIRM program is designed to provide the leadership, the framework, and the educational resources necessary to help the manufacturing industry meet the challenges of this new era. According to the *CIRM Study Guide,* the new era looks like this:

- Manufacturing must adopt a new mindset that promotes flexibility and encourages the principles that support efficient and profitable operations.
- The organization of tomorrow will require workers with breadth and skills that cut across a variety of functional management areas.
- The new management philosophy will stress integrated approaches to management and a dedicated, flexible work force.
- Personnel at all levels in the organization will require continuous education to master changing technologies.
- The CIRM program focuses on manufacturing organizations and a better understanding of how to integrate critical management and operating functions to attain a competitive advantage.

To achieve these goals, the CIRM program is divided into the following 13 cross-functional topic areas, as shown in Table 10–1.

In each of these areas, the CIRM program stresses both substantive basic knowledge and an appreciation for the ways in which each area interacts with the others. In other words, to know one or two parts of the manufacturing system is not enough. Managers must also be skilled at putting the pieces together in the most innovative way, in response to the needs of the customer. Japanese businesses implemented Total Quality Management methods for doing just that in the commercial sector. Now it's time for every business manager and manufacturing firm to learn how to integrate their operations using the Total Quality Management techniques discussed in this book. This chapter is designed to demonstrate how you can capture the competitive edge by integrating Total Quality Management in the other elements of your business.

The Integrated Resource Element/Total Quality Management Matrix (see Table 10–2) is our bridge between the CIRM program and Total Quality Management. Using this matrix as a cross-walk, the remainder of this chapter will show you how to integrate the functions of your manufacturing organization by incorporating the Total Quality Management principles, leadership roles, and practices and techniques discussed in

TABLE 10–1
CIRM Program Elements

I. Customers and Products
  A. Marketing and Sales
  B. Field Service
  C. Product Design and Development

II. Logistics
  A. Production and Inventory Control
  B. Procurement
  C. Distribution

III. Manufacturing Processes
  A. Industrial Facilities Management
  B. Process Design and Development
  C. Manufacturing

IV. Integration Support Functions
  A. Information Systems
  B. Human Resources
  C. Finance and Accounting
  D. Total Quality Management

TABLE 10-2

Integrated Resource Management/Total Quality Management Matrix

CIRM Integrated Resource Management Elements / Total Quality Management Elements	Demonstrate Leadership	Build Awareness	Improve Communication	Present Vision	Customer Focus	Demonstrate Success	Benchmarking	Develop Teamwork	Training	Build Trust	Create Quality Environment	Continuously Improve Processess	Extend to Suppliers
Integration Support Functions													
Total quality management	●	●	●	●	●	●	●	●	●	●	●	●	●
Human resources			●							0	0	●	
Information systems	0		0							0	0	●	
Finance and accounting				●	0						0	0	0
Customers and Products													
Marketing and Sales	0			0	●		0	0	0			●	
Field services	0			0	●	0	0	●	0	0	●	●	
Product design and development			0		●	0		●		0	0	●	●
Logistics													
Production and inventory control	0			0	●	0	0				0	●	●
Procurement	0			0	●	0	●				0	●	●
Distribution			●		●								●
Manufacturing Processes													
Industrial facilities management	●		0			0				0	●	●	
Process design and development	0		0		●	●	●	●		0	●	●	●
Manufacturing	0		0		●	●	0	●	0	0	●	●	●

Legend   ● Primary impact
        0 Secondary impact

previous chapters. Our discussion will cover the CIRM elements shown in Table 10–1. First, the scope of each topic area is outlined, based on its presentation in the CIRM *Guide*. This description is followed by a discussion of how managers can use Total Quality Management to knit these parts into a management system that matches the firm's operational requirements.

Customers and Products

Marketing and Sales. Mission: To develop and exploit markets and products, based on the company's distinct areas of competence, that meet the company's business objectives and satisfy customer needs.

The marketing function can be divided into market research, competitive analysis, market planning, demand forecasting, promotion and advertising, pricing, and distribution.

Market research involves the investigation of the needs of industrial and individual consumers to determine what products could be sold profitably. It is conducted using economic and demographic data, opinion surveys, and other information that indicates the location of the market and the buying power and preferences of potential buyers. These activities result in the identification of product characteristics.

Competitive analysis is the evaluation of the capabilities and direction of companies that offer products that could be chosen as alternatives. A direct competitor is one that offers the same type of product within the chosen geographic or industrial territory. An indirect competitor offers a product that can satisfy the consumer's need in a different way. A radio manufacturer has direct competition from other radio manufacturers, and indirect competition from television set and audiotape-player companies. Careful evaluation of a competitor's product portfolio is needed to determine the competitor's ability to provide products that are preferred by consumers. The economic viability and market strength of competitors must be analyzed carefully to avoid loss of market share. Manufacturing capability information about competitors can provide an understanding of their abilities to enter new markets or to expand in existing ones.

Market planning is the use of market research and competitive analysis for developing a strategy that will allow successful capture of a customer base. Product mix must be constituted in such a way that it offers solutions to consumer needs, is profitable, and provides a path for future sales to existing or new customers. Marketing objectives such as price, quality levels, service levels, and delivery performance expectations all affect the cost and revenue of a company. An effective market plan both ensures that considerations complement each other and assists the sales function in identifying potential customers.

Demand forecasting is a projection of volume, timing, and value of products that will be sold in future periods. Statistical or subjective methods can be employed to develop the forecast, which is used throughout the company: by marketing for directing sales efforts; by production and service for determining needed resources; and by finance for determining cash flow and potential profit.

Promotion and advertising are the tools used to create a favorable image of a product, to influence potential customers about how the product meets their needs, and to differentiate a product from its competition. The purpose of promotion and advertising is to improve sales.

Pricing is one of the most important responsibilities of marketing. The price sensitivity of a marketplace has great impact on the firm's ability to penetrate it profitably. Knowledge of acceptable price levels, awareness of the strategy of the competition, and an understanding of the cost of products are all important elements necessary to price a product properly.

Distribution channel selection and development is a responsibility of marketing. A direct-sales force, outside sales representatives, and commercial distributors are all examples of distribution channels. The nature of the product and the market determine the channels to be used.

Field Service.   Mission: To ensure that the customer receives full value from the product and to assist the customer in using the product to attain his or her objectives.

The field service function is planned within the corporate strategy. Through installation, maintenance and repair, customer training and other activities, field service ensures that the customer gets maximum value from the product. The field service function fits into the sales process as a technical resource. It influences a sale by demonstrating the level of service, quality, and commitment that a customer should expect after taking delivery.

Field service representatives are in frequent contact with customers. They can advise sales personnel when customers are ready for additional equipment. They also have opportunities to gather market intelligence.

Product design engineering and field service personnel have a need for direct communications. Field service personnel should be included in the product design team to ensure good performance of the product during its service life. Inclusion of field service at this point can produce a product with better repair characteristics, which will give greater utility to the customers. After product release, field service representatives provide feedback to design engineering so that opportunities for improvement to current and future products can be identified and implemented.

Product Design and Development.   Mission: To facilitate effective design of products that meet or exceed customer or market expectations and are consistent with objectives of the enterprise.

Product design and development generally begins either with a statement of need derived from market research and planning or from a product concept resulting from research and development activities. In either case, the goal of product design and development is an effective product that meets or exceeds customer or market expectations while satisfying the profit, quality, and other objectives of the enterprise.

Product acceptability is expressed in terms of how a product meets form, fit and function specifications. Form refers to the physical characteristics of the product. Fit refers to the dimensions of the product. Function refers to the ability of the product to satisfy a specific purpose.

Interdisciplinary design teams, which include manufacturing engineering, marketing, field service, cost accounting, and other interested parties, can be structured to improve the design, manufacturability, serviceability, and cost elements of a product. This concurrent engineering approach shortens product development cycles, improves quality, and results in a more cost-effective product.

Technological and social changes have presented an increased challenge to design engineers. Global market competition and shorter product life cycles have compressed the design time available. Tools available to the designers have also improved through technology, but they have not kept up with increased competitive pressure in all cases. Social changes have created greater government regulation and consumer awareness in the areas of safety, environment, and consumer rights. The design engineer must be aware of the laws and regulations that apply to the product and its use.

The competitive environment has created a greater emphasis on the concept of supplier partnerships. The supplier and customer work together more closely in product development efforts to bring the design closer to satisfying the objectives of both parties.

Of all the business relationship functions, the marketing and sales, field service, and product design and development functions have the most direct contact with customers. Their primary purpose is defining customer needs and satisfying those needs through excellence in design and service. To accomplish this goal, these functional areas must develop effective communication channels and have a close working relationship. There are common areas of responsibility between each function as well as areas in which all three share responsibility.

In developing new markets or products, information about the customer base and customers' experience with products currently in use is invaluable. Support during the selling process requires coordination to ensure that customer concerns and installation considerations are dealt with adequately. A broad base of information, developed around knowledge of customer desires (supplied by marketing), customer expansion requirements and satisfaction levels (provided by field service), and new product improvement possibilities (from product design and development), is used to provide the best product for the market.

Once the product has been purchased by a customer, the company has the obligation to provide a level of service high enough to earn repeat sales. Furthermore, continuous product improvement is needed in a competitive market for retaining and growing the customer base. The three functions in this mode have prime responsibility for keeping the company's product lines competitive through analyzing field performance, determining future customer needs, and employing technology improvements. This objective can only be accomplished through close communication and mutual participation. Formal and informal channels must be available for critical information to pass through the organization, so that decisions can be made that are consistent with service and profit objectives.

Logistics

Logistics represents the activities necessary for planning and procuring materials, controlling manufacturing, and planning and distributing products to customers. The production and inventory control function covers the planning and scheduling of the supply of materials to support manufacturing or conversion operations. Included are activities spanning receipt of deliveries from suppliers to delivery of finished goods to the customer. Management of resources, capacity, and inventory levels are essential to those activities.

Procurement refers to those activities involved in obtaining goods and services that meet quantity, quality, time, and price requirements. The distribution function represents those activities needed to receive, store, and transport materials and products for internal requirements and customers, including traffic management, warehousing, order processing, and management of finished goods.

Production and Inventory Control. Mission: To plan, schedule, coordinate, and control the supply of materials in order to support sales/marketing and distribution requirements.

Production and inventory control addresses the policies, strategies, and techniques required in planning and controlling a manufacturing operation. Proper inventory management is an important part of this process.

The main objective of this activity is to optimize customer service, inventory investment, manufacturing, purchasing, and distribution operations. How a firm chooses to manage these activities can have a significant impact on its profitability and world-class competitiveness. Evolving strategies, such as Just-in-Time (JIT) and Total Quality Management, are important contributors toward building a competitive advantage. Effective management of lead times helps an organization become more responsive to customer demand.

Effective production and inventory control requires a sound understanding of the fundamental elements of the discipline, including demand management, master planning, inventory management, capacity management, and scheduling. An understanding of the concepts and relationships that exist between these elements is stressed, rather than detailed knowledge of techniques themselves. New directions in production and inventory control, such as electronic interfaces with customers and suppliers, are also keys to world-class competitiveness.

Continuous improvements in production and inventory control are important competitiveness factors. Systemwide performance measurements—such as on-time deliveries, inventory turns, and supply lead times—are replacing more traditional indicators, which emphasized machine and labor efficiency.

Procurement. Mission: To procure quality goods and services in accordance with the business plan.

The goal of the procurement function is to procure quality goods and services using external resources, when required. The reasons for using external resources may reflect technological, economic, or strategic considerations. Despite widely varying organizational structures, a number of activities are common to any procurement function. Sourcing, negotiating, developing supplier relationships, order placement, order follow-up, and receipt of goods and services are common procurement transactions. Performance measures are changing to reflect these functions and evolving trends.

Procurement is evolving from management of purchase orders to co-ordination of supplier arrangements. This trend emphasizes the relationship between these functional activities in the context of an individual business, and it reduces the emphasis on traditional organizational structures.

Distribution.   Mission: To receive, store, and transport materials and products in order to meet customer requirements.

Distribution focuses on the processes of receiving, storing, and moving products, materials, and other resources to the point of need. The primary goal is to meet the customers' requirements. The term *customer* includes both the external purchaser of the finished goods and the internal persons performing logistics activities.

The activities performed as part of the distribution function should be integrated with the total business mission and strategic plans. Distribution focuses on the planning and management of finished goods, merchandizing, and transportation. Maximizing customer service and minimizing distribution costs are primary objectives. Issues such as owning versus contracting, structuring the distribution network, and effect on response time are considered in meeting those objectives. Global competition creates the need to examine advances that have an impact on the distribution function. These advances include employee involvement, continuous improvement, quality at the source, automated guided vehicle systems, and electronic data interchange.

Typical measurements of performance address reducing order cycle time, improving warehouse data accuracy, and eliminating damage and losses in transit.

Effective relationship interactions create the conditions for integrated flows along the entire supply chain. Planning for the resources to meet customer needs is rooted in distribution requirements (demand) and finished-good stock status (available supply), and passes from purchase requirements (for external supply) to procurement. Existing and future material plans may be modified by production and inventory control as a result of feedback from procurement about open orders, lead times, and supplier capabilities. Procurement and distribution interact with respect to receiving, transportation of materials, and evaluating supplier performance.

When decisions are made about issues such as warehousing and storage, shelf life, lot sizing, schedule changes, shipping schedules, and reporting and dealing with stock status exceptions, all three functions interact.

Manufacturing Processes

Manufacturing processes define the methods that companies use in designing, producing, and delivering goods and services required by the customer, and provide the execution component of the integrated manufacturing system. Manufacturing processes draw on three different but very interrelated subsystems: industrial facilities management, process design and development, and manufacturing.

Industrial facilities management is charged with the task of installing and maintaining the physical plant and its surroundings so that it is consistently operable, secure, safe, and in compliance with all relevant regulations. Process design and development is the counterpart of product design and development. It is the function charged with creating the most appropriate processes for providing the products required by the company in a timely and cost-effective manner. How the firm competes on the dimensions of cost, quality, lead time, and flexibility are often critically impacted by the actions and decisions made by personnel in this function as they commit resources (information, people, equipment, tooling, and investments) to meet customer requirements.

Industrial Facilities Management.   Mission: To install and maintain plant, equipment, and facility environments required to support the business objectives.

Industrial facilities management is not only a critical element of the manufacturing process; it is an integral and increasingly important element of corporate strategy. It focuses on the overall management, maintenance, and enhancement of the firm's physical plant. The term *physical plant* includes not only the machines and the shop floor, but also such areas as office space, parking lots, and grounds. Industrial facilities management is driven by several objectives. First, it increases resource availability, and it limits unplanned losses in capacity by implementing and operating an effective internal maintenance program. Second, it improves employee morale and productivity by creating and sustaining a safe, secure, and clean working environment. Third, it ensures that the firm's physical facilities are planned and maintained so as to comply with all applicable regulations. Finally, it is responsible for managing the interface with the community. All of these activities contribute directly to the ability of the firm to deliver its goods and services at the lowest cost.

The industrial facilities management function acts as a resource by keeping the manufacturing end current and aware of changes in regulations. It helps manufacturing assess the impact of these changes on its processes, operating procedures, resource requirements, and performance. It contributes to the efforts of manufacturing in maintaining productivity and efficiency through its maintenance and risk management plans. However, in a world characterized by the use of manufacturing systems such as JIT manufacturing and computer-integrated manufacturing, by the increased use of automation, and by greater demands for system predictability, managers are now recognizing the increased costs paid for neglecting the industrial facilities management function.

Process Design and Development.   Mission: To plan, specify, coordinate, and oversee the production methodology, equipment, tooling, and control devices for producing and delivering the firm's products in a manner consistent with the objectives of the enterprise.

Process design and development can best be described as a comprehensive activity aimed at developing and implementing an execution system for making a product or part in a way that is consistent with the objectives of the firm. The process design function must recognize that manufacturing is ultimately both strategic and tactical in nature. Once the process has been designed and installed, it defines the capabilities of the firm and determines how the firm will be able to compete. The capabilities of assembly lines are very different from those offered by job shops. As a result, the process design and development function must begin with an understanding of how the product to be manufactured in the new process is to compete in the marketplace. Once the basis of competition has been identified, this function must establish a process that is most consistent with, and supportive of, how the product is to compete. In short, there must be a strong fit between product and process.

The process design and development function is comprehensive in that it must address a variety of issues. At a macro level, the function must identify the most appropriate type of manufacturing process, layout, technology, and type of work force needed. At the micro level, it must deal with issues of equipment choice and location of this equipment on the shop floor. Process design and development generally begins with product design. Increasingly, the design of the process is done parallel with the design of the product. Process design and development requires interdisciplinary teams that include representatives from both inside and outside the firm. From inside the company, these teams should include representatives from manufacturing engineering, manufacturing, quality assurance, production and inventory control, facilities management, product engineering, cost accounting, operators, and others. In addition, suppliers often participate in these design teams. By involving the suppliers in the process design activities, a superior process can be developed.

As a result of the numerous technological and competitive changes occurring in the marketplace, the nature of process design and development is changing. Global market competition, shorter product and process life cycles, and the demand for greater variety in product offerings have affected this function in several ways. The lead time required to design and implement effective new processes must shrink. With the movement to smaller lot sizes and shorter lead times, the process must be characterized by simplicity and reduced setup times. Processes must be designed that are able to change quickly in response to market changes (e.g., the introduction and phase-out of products and models, and volume changes). Governmental regulations, employee expectations and demands, and increased consumer awareness call for resulting processes that are safe, environmentally sound, and allow for greater employee participation and involvement. In order to develop manufacturing processes that are consistent with the many demands now placed on them, the process design and development team must be aware of and draw on all available tools and technology.

Manufacturing. Mission: To plan and manage the effective use of resources (information, people, equipment, and investment) in order to produce goods that meet or exceed customer expectations for their delivery, quality, and cost.

The physical creation of the product or part is the responsibility of manufacturing. It is here that the products are created by drawing on the firm's resources and transforming them by means of a specific production process and physical facility. Manufacturing uses these resources and the production process to create goods that support corporate strategic objectives. Manufacturing embodies all of the planning and execution activities directly involved in this transformation process.

As a result of the same factors that are influencing process design and development, the nature of manufacturing is changing. Increased competition has forced manufacturing not only to think in terms of profit, loss, and cost, but also to focus on the transformation process as a value-adding activity. Activities that do not directly add value are becoming targets for elimination, revision, or combination with other activities. This procedure has become known as continuous process improvement. By focusing on value creation, the manufacturing function has begun to emphasize initiatives such as focused factories, reduction of variability, simplified work flows, and improved layouts. In addition, manufacturing has come to recognize that shop-floor personnel must now play a more active role in manufacturing activities.

This trend, together with the realization that the employees are often the people best suited to improve the effectiveness of current manufacturing practices, has led to the advent of self-managed, problem-solving teams and a cross-trained work force. In addition, the rapid proliferation of new manufacturing technologies has forced manufacturing to reexamine its needs. This reexamination often leads to a decision not to use technology that is state of the art, but rather to draw on the technology that is most appropriate to the needs of the firm and to its specific value-creation process.

Industrial facilities management, process design and development, and manufacturing are closely related and share one major objective: They must develop, implement, operate, maintain, and improve production systems that enable the firm to satisfy the needs of its customers at the lowest total cost. If the firm is to make a product or part within a process that performs well on the major dimensions of competition, the activities of these three areas must be coordinated, and cooperation between them must be established.

These activities are driven by the need to ensure that the manufacturing system is best able to support and service the customer. These functions can achieve this objective by sharing information. Knowledge of equipment reliability traits and appropriate regulations can influence process design. Process design can affect the staffing and skill requirements. As manufacturing works with the resulting process, its experiences can be fed back to design and industrial facilities management functions for future revision and enhancement of the system. With these three functions integrated, the firm establishes a base for making manufacturing into a strategic competitive weapon.

Integration Support Functions

Information Systems.   Mission: To facilitate the effective flow and use of information and to manage information as a strategic company resource.

Information systems is defined as the application of technology, usually electronic, for the purpose of collecting, processing, and distributing information. System inputs range in sophistication from punched cards to automated data capture. Data transmission and storage techniques range from holes in paper tape to light traveling in optical fibers. Equipment configurations range from centralized facilities to worldwide networks. These systems may be managed by a single department, or cooperatively managed by several organizations.

Despite variations in information systems, the intended functions and the responsibilities of those who build and maintain these systems are similar. Information systems share the objective of improving the management and use of information. Similarly, information systems share a common need for data capture, storage, processing, and output.

The thrust of systems development has begun to shift toward the use of information technology for achieving competitive advantage. The trends toward more sophisticated users, more capable hardware, and decentralized computer networks require an increasingly capable information systems employee. Proposed systems and modifications to systems must be evaluated with the objective of satisfying the organization's overall goals. New projects should take advantage of appropriate hardware and software and be structured to allow for integration with future technology. If information systems are to be effective, a larger and more senior cross section of the organization must understand, support, and contribute to corporate information systems development.

Human Resources.   Mission: To attract, deploy, and develop employee resources to the best advantage of the enterprise and its people.

Human resources in today's social and legal environment is responsible for much more than supplying the enterprise with an excellent staff. Many government regulations regarding employee rights and safety, as well as equal opportunity, labor relations, and tax laws, fall under the human resources umbrella. The evolving definition of the relationship between organizations and employees extends the human resource function into areas of employee development, training, employee involvement, and family services for employees and their families.

The human resources department is charged with balancing the needs of the organization, the employees, and the public. In addition, it must respond to shifts in internal management philosophy and global trends, including calls for reducing organizational layers and shifting toward customer service and information systems and away from traditional manufacturing practices.

Finance and Accounting. Mission: To maximize the value of the firm through the effective acquisition and management of financial resources and to provide financial information that fulfills external requirements while supporting internal functions.

The financial function traditionally has been charged with projecting the organization's future financial position based on its current position and the best available forecasts for sales and costs. In addition, detailed studies are undertaken to determine the advisability of proposed purchases, projects, and actions. The accounting function has been charged with maintaining accurate status of all assets, liabilities, and transactions with a financial impact. In practice, these two functions are often performed by the same employees. Tracking past performance is useful in projecting the future. Other functions performed by finance and accounting include government reporting and compliance, safeguarding of assets and information, providing cash management, and locating sources of capital.

The definitions of the accounting and finance functions are changing. Their roles are expanding and becoming more proactive. In addition to making projections and maintaining records, these employees are now more involved in formulating strategies, seeking alternative sources of capital, redesigning costing systems, and setting policies and procedures that support the company's overall objectives.

The relationship overlaps and interdependencies among departments and functions in organizations have never been greater. The world of corporate information systems, once limited to specialists, now includes most employees. Accounting and cost implications of decisions are also widely discussed. Human resources departments are continually involved in responding to organizational and work requirement change stemming from new technologies and philosophies in the work place.

Industry is moving toward integrating and interconnecting business technologies. This trend makes it more important than ever for management to fully appreciate the impact actions in one area will have on other parts of the organization.

TQM INTERFUNCTIONAL AND CROSS-FUNCTIONAL LINKAGES

As we move toward the millennium, the business enterprise shall be more fully integrated in terms of both interfunctional and cross-functional linkages. The trend toward flatter organizations, multifunctional work teams, customer satisfaction by design, and increased value (lower cost at higher quality) will require the "vertical stovepipe" type of business structure to change. The role of Total Quality Management (TQM) has already begun to change by moving from defect detection after the fact to process design and development that builds quality into products and/or services.

It is important for businesses to recognize that the key Integrated Resources Management activities are all impacted by Total Quality Management (see Figure 10–1). Not only can each of the CIRM functions be enhanced by applying Total Quality Management concepts and principles, but each of the other interactions—product and process design *and* manufacturing planning and control, marketing/sales *and* field service, and procurement *and* manufacturing planning and control—have synergistic opportunities to improve the entire organization.

Total Quality Management

Total Quality Management is a comprehensive, customer-focused system that many organizations are adopting so they can improve the quality of their products and services. It is a way of managing the organization at all levels, top management to front-line, for achieving customer satisfaction by involving all employees in continuously improving the work processes of the organization.

Many believe that the worldwide effort to improve the quality of goods and services through application of Total Quality Management principles represents a fundamental change in management style and philosophy that will dramatically alter the way successful enterprises (private and public) are managed for the foreseeable future. The impact of this movement on the way many U.S. companies are managed is

FIGURE 10–1
Total Quality Management Role in Integrated Resource Management

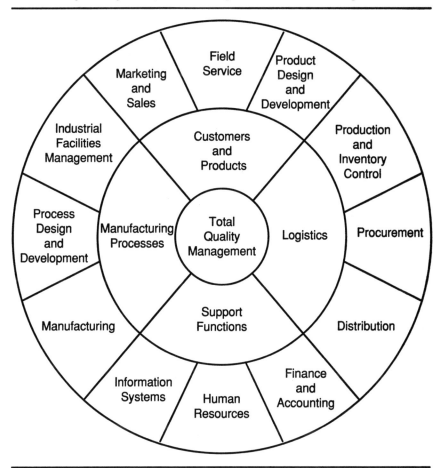

profound; results in market share, profitability, productivity, and worker involvement have been spectacular.

Chapter 6 has already described in detail the Total Quality Management activities shown in the central block of Figure 10–2.

To summarize, the three essential requirements or principles of Total Quality Management are (1) the pursuit of complete customer satisfaction by (2) continuously improving products and services through (3) the full and active involvement of the entire work force. These principles are met by integrating seven key operating practices:

FIGURE 10–2
Total Quality Management Interfunctional and Cross-Functional Linkages

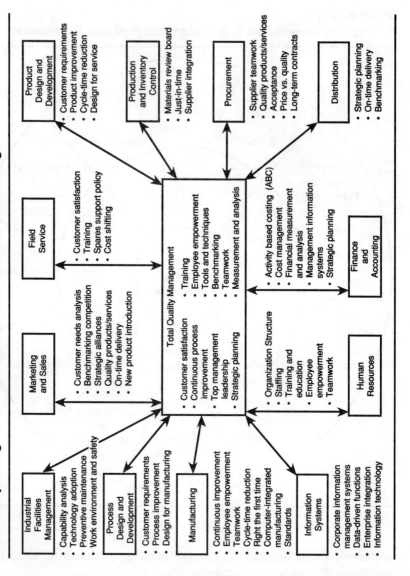

- Demonstrating personal leadership.
- Strategically planning the short- and long-term implementation of Total Quality Management.
- Assuring that everyone focuses on customers' needs and expectations.
- Developing clearly defined measures for tracking progress and identifying improvement opportunities.
- Providing adequate resources for training and recognition, which enables workers to carry the mission forward and reinforces positive behavior.
- Empowering workers to make decisions and fostering teamwork.
- Developing systems to assure that quality is built in at the beginning and throughout operations.

Total Quality Management provides synergistic improvements for marketing and sales, field service, product design and development, production and inventory control, procurement, distribution, finance and accounting, human resources, information systems, manufacturing, process design and development, and industrial facilities management. Total Quality Management has greater impact on some of these areas, such as product design and development, process design and development, and manufacturing. The impact of Total Quality Management on each of the CIRM elements is described in the following material.

Marketing and Sales.   Total Quality Management's first principle is satisfying the needs of your customers. This goal requires a dramatic change in the role marketing plays in your business. The traditional responsibilities of marketing have evolved: A focus on understanding customer needs and developing products and services that satisfy customer requirements is replacing the old approach of building or providing products or services the organization believes to be in its best interest.

Marketing also takes on a new role in looking at the competitors' products and services in a far more detailed and analytical way. The concepts of benchmarking that were formalized and implemented by Xerox Corporation are today being adopted by world-class organizations. The addition of benchmarking and quality function deployment to the new analytical-based efforts of marketing organizations helps assure that the customers' needs and wants are being incorporated in new product design and service opportunities.

New strategic alliances or contract team efforts are the trend in product and service marketing in large and small companies wishing to compete in the global marketplace. Major U.S., German, and Japanese companies have recently teamed up to research, design, and develop the next-generation super-computer chip. These types of strategic alliances will grow. However, the business participants will have to have comparable levels of "quality" performance for them to be effective in the marketplace.

In the 1980s, we experienced a market and consumer that believed that high cost meant high quality. As we enter the 1990s the market has changed to realize that adoption of Total Quality Management can produce high-quality products and services at lower costs. This dramatic change in creating "quality consumers" as well as "quality producers" directly impacts our approach at marketing and sales of new products and services. The global consumer expects reliable, high-quality products and services today more than ever before.

The provision of quality as the first strategic business priority is a given in the 1990s. However, quality alone is not enough. In addition to continually improving our quality we must also satisfy our customers by reducing the cycle time for delivering products and services. Global competition will set the standard for the time to bring new products to market. Not only do we have to focus on cycle time to introduce new products and services *faster,* we must—in an era of interrelated production processes and just-in-time systems—assure that we deliver *on time.* In the 1980s the interrelationships between supplier and user were not as strongly connected as they are today. When we agree to a promised delivery date in our sales effort we must assure that these real-time supply responsibilities are met. If your sales and production efforts do not communicate well, your competition will replace you in this global network of potential suppliers who do deliver on time.

We have seen in the automobile and consumer electronics industries the rapid development of new products. In many cases global competitors can bring complex new products to market in half the time they did just 10 years ago. If we can understand our markets better by incorporating Total Quality Management, quality function deployment (QFD), and concurrent engineering techniques into our extended marketing analysis efforts, then we can provide the right product or service to the market and ensure the continued satisfaction of our customers.

Field Service.   On-time, cost-effective, high-quality field service is critical to customer satisfaction. We have seen the days when copier companies or auto manufacturers designed field service to be a substantial part of the revenue stream rather than a service that assured continued operation of products that satisfied the customer. Even today we hear of excessive high cost for customer service, of the perception that reliability and quality were not designed into products that in effect were knowingly created to require high-cost service contracts, and — even in tight economic times — of the perception that companies are surviving in a slow sales era by increasing their field service hourly rates and "book" hours to repair products. These cost-shifting practices are being recognized today by "quality consumers" and rejected as unacceptable business practices.

In general we fail to provide our employees the level of training needed, both in technical and interpersonal communication skills. We focus on the on-the-job low-cost training approach rather than help our employees satisfy our customers by providing adequate training.

Today we have the opportunity to provide spare parts to almost any country in the world through reliable overnight-delivery services such as Federal Express. If used, this service greatly reduces the delay in satisfying our customers by quickly filling the logistics pipeline to meet their urgent needs. A down-side concern is that many local field service organizations have substantially reduced their on-hand supply of spare parts to reduce costs, and that situation does not assure customer satisfaction. By applying Total Quality Management tools and techniques we can better estimate the minimum stock we will be required to maintain for common problem areas. In order to ensure more reliable operation and provide customer satisfaction, we must not only stock appropriate levels of defective parts, but we must look more carefully at failed parts and communicate the reliability problems quickly to the manufacturers so these products can be redesigned.

Product Design and Development.   Product design and development focuses on the effective design of products that meet or exceed customer and market expectations. Today more than ever we are seeing the integration of Total Quality Management in the form of quality function deployment (QFD), concurrent engineering, and design for quality in new product design and development. In the 1970s and 1980s our enterprise designed what it thought the customer wanted, what our management wanted, or what our firm's production capability could provide. In today's global market, we have competitors that we have not even heard of in some cases. Therefore, we have to design and develop better products than the company "around the corner" from us. This goal requires that we understand the needs and wants of our customers and, accordingly, design and develop products to satisfy (form, fit, function, quality, cost, value) our customers.

We can no longer rest on our laurels in terms of new product development or improvement of existing products. We have to bring new and better products to market faster, at higher quality levels and at less cost than we did in the 1980s. With new product roll-outs, we must be able to respond to design defects or unanticipated customer concerns in a timely manner. When the new Saturn and Lexus automobiles hit the market, some annoying problems were found; the companies that manufacture these cars both responded rapidly in modifying or improving their design and development process for their vehicles in a way that demonstrated their ability to respond rapidly to customer concerns and improve their products.

Cycle-time reduction has been described briefly in terms of bringing new products to the marketplace faster. Studies have shown that it is cost-effective to spend additional product design and development funds on a product if you can gain market share by introducing your product faster. This bottom-line approach at improving profitability and gains in market share drives the current interest in applying concurrent engineering, multifunctional teams, Total Quality Management, design for quality, and use of computer-aided tools that speed up the design and development process.

All too often we have not communicated the design and development requirements to our manufacturing operations. Today we recognize that a better marriage between design engineers and production engineers is required. This communication process is enhanced by multifunctional teams of design and manufacturing personnel working directly together. Product design and development engineers understand that the total process is the key to delivering high-quality lower-cost products to the customer. This awareness has resulted in design engineers who understand the capabilities and limitations of manufacturing processes, and in the realization that design has to be accomplished in concert with manufacturing operations.

In the days of the Model T Ford, service of the car was rather simple. The parts were mechanical, there were few critical components, and in general the car could be serviced with conventional hand tools. Today we have mechatronics-integrated, complex computer-controlled cars. In some products the design and development has been deliberately complex to prevent customers from servicing their purchases. We are seeing a change in focus: companies are simplifying the new products where possible by concentrating on design for service considerations. Can you easily change the oil in your car, or has the car been designed so that an oil change is no longer required? These design-for-service approaches focus on providing modular replacement of parts, evaluation of the value to the customer in terms of the cost of servicing the product, and the physical-design attributes that simplify the ability of the customer to service the product.

Production and Inventory Control.   Production and inventory control focuses on the planning, scheduling, coordination, and control of supply materials and components that support sales/marketing and distribution requirements.

As described in the National Center for Manufacturing Sciences book titled *Competing in World Class Manufacturing,* Just in Time (JIT) is a company-wide philosophy oriented toward eliminating waste and improving materials throughout all operational functions. When implemented in manufacturing, JIT techniques provide ''the cost-effective production and delivery of only the necessary quality parts in the right quantity, at the right time and place, while using a minimum of facilities, equipment, materials, and human resources.''

The JIT tool kit includes management rules of thumb and techniques for purchasing of raw materials and parts, delivery of materials and parts to the point of assembly, and the manufacturing process itself as well as manufacturing interfaces with nonmanufacturing areas. It can become a springboard for developing integrated policies for manufacturing products and purchasing materials and components. The concept has received much publicity and has been evaluated or implemented by a large number of companies. Cycle-time reduction is one of the most effective methods of increasing overall productivity. While the heart of the JIT movement is the basic philosophy of waste elimination throughout the organization, many U.S. managers see JIT as only a series of special techniques that are applied to the manufacturing environment to improve efficiencies. JIT, however, must first be understood as an approach to business management and manufacturing from the perspective of better serving the customer.

Taiichi Ohno, the father of the Toyota Production System, defined JIT in terms of eliminating waste.

> The context of JIT, then, is the elimination of any process that is unnecessary. When viewed from this perspective, JIT is a common-sense approach to dealing with business, in general, and improving your competitive capabilities. Before attempting to implement JIT, any manufacturer aspiring to become world-class must first adopt the basic philosophy of JIT—waste elimination and, effectively, Total Quality Management.

Material requirements planning (MRP) and manufacturing resource planning (MRP II) are computerized manufacturing control systems that were originally developed by Joseph Orlicky in the early 1960s. Promoted and spread through the nation by the likes of Oliver Wight and George Plossl, MRP has become the single most widely implemented production planning and control technique in use today. The MRP process starts when items on the bills of material are "exploded," or multiplied, by a master schedule to determine material requirements on a time-phased basis. Next, stock on hand and material on order are subtracted from the exploded requirements to determine what else should be ordered. Although MRP logic is straightforward, a computer is required to manipulate the data. MRP is a push system, meaning items are produced at the time required by a predetermined schedule.

MRP II, like JIT, is much more than a system. It is a way of introducing an integrated style of management into a company. In fact, some view the integration of materials management and production control as a prerequisite to successful implementation. MRP II focuses all areas of operation on the same set of numbers in order to achieve synergy in operations. This synergy leads to the identification of corporate goals and an opportunity for translating those goals into individual targets. While MRP refers only to the systems aspects of production planning and control, an MRP II system can bring a company to a stage where it has control over all plantwide activities. Most literature today refers to MRP and MRP II concepts interchangeably.

Should MRP and JIT be used together in the manufacturing environment? The strength of MRP is planning; the strength of JIT is execution and quality improvement. Many companies believe that they must use either MRP or JIT exclusively, without realizing that together the two approaches are more powerful. The manufacturing environment itself will dictate the degree to which these techniques can and should be integrated. It is hard to imagine a manufacturer that applies JIT without innovative human resource practices, superior equipment maintenance, or outstanding quality. Likewise, superior product quality alone will not yield long-term success if material and production are poorly planned, resulting in long lead times and missed schedule dates. These key action programs are part of a holistic manufacturing strategy. Taken together, they form a set of mutually reinforcing manufacturing choices that are being driven by the changing competitive environments. Time and flexibility are becoming critical dimensions of competition, with quality at the foundation.

During the past decade a significant effort led by Dr. Deming has focused on supplier integration. Supplier integration can be defined as the reduction of the total number of suppliers being considered for procurement, and the move toward a longer-term, closer partnership with suppliers. Management information systems that directly link today's prime contractors and their suppliers almost make the different corporate structures disappear. This supplier integration effort has a common performance measurement in terms of providing reliable high-quality products and services to the partners in what could be a global supplier network.

Procurement. The nature of procurement has changed from a short-term focus on buying a quantity of parts that conform to an acceptable quality level (AQL) at the lowest cost to a long-term relationship between prime contractor and supplier. This new focus on procurement partnership extends to larger companies providing active guidance, training, and support to their smaller subcontractors. As noted above, the game has changed for procurement managers who now have to look at the long-term impact of their procurement decisions if they are to achieve procurement stability, simplicity, higher-quality-at-lower-cost production, and services that are delivered just in time.

Motorola's Supplier Partnership Growth Advisory Board breaks down communication barriers with its suppliers. The Motorola board includes about a dozen key supplier executives who advise Motorola about what it needs to do to continue its role as a world-class company.

After winning the Malcolm Baldrige National Quality Award in 1988, Motorola urged all suppliers to start implementing six sigma quality programs and to apply for the Baldrige Award themselves. Building a world-class supplier base demands the formation and cultivation of such relationships and open communications. Motorola and Xerox have devoted considerable energy and resources to educating their suppliers and developing their capabilities through training, hands-on technical assistance, and demonstrations.

Ford's Quality Is Job One program turned its zero-defects crusade outward to its suppliers. Ford is working with suppliers on meeting higher and higher standards. For example, any North American supplier who wants to obtain new business from Ford Motor Company must have a Q-1 award status from Ford. Procurement partnerships push quality excellence to success.

Distribution. Distribution focuses on receiving, storing, and transporting materials and products in order to meet your customers' requirements. The role of Total Quality Management in distribution is to maximize customer service and minimize distribution cost. The critical strategic issues facing enhanced distribution include whether your company should buy or lease transportation systems, utilize a subcontracted distribution network or create its own, and how the business can assure on-time delivery to satisfy your customers. These issues should be addressed as part of your unique strategic plan. Each business should look more carefully at its distribution management structure and the potential for productivity and quality of service delivery that can be made by warehouse and distribution system continuous improvement.

As we move more to global markets and global just-in-time distribution, the sophistication of our distribution approach and information systems must keep pace in terms of selection of transportation modes, information systems, and communication technology. We have gone way beyond the horse-and-wagon approach today. To satisfy our customers we have to provide what they want, when they want it!

As noted in the CIRM *Study Guide* distribution must also focus on the internal customer who is part of the production cycle. This means efficient information processes within the plant—from just-in-time material positioning for production to correct mailing labels for product delivery. In many cases we do not pay sufficient attention to the distribution operations. The global market demands improved responsiveness to our customers.

One tool, which was pioneered by Xerox, for improving overall operations is benchmarking. In his book on benchmarking, Robert C.

Camp has described benchmarking as a positive, proactive process of changing operations in a structured fashion in order to achieve superior performance. The benefit of using benchmarking is that you are forced to investigate external industry-best practices and incorporate those practices into your operations. As a result, your company can develop into a profitable, high-asset utilization business that meets customer needs and has a competitive advantage. The working definition preferred for benchmarking is this: Benchmarking is the search for industry-best practices that lead to superior performance. This definition is preferred because it is understood by operationally oriented business units and functions. If you know your operations thoroughly, then the effort to ensure that the best of proven practices are incorporated is a clear objective. The definition covers all possible business endeavors—whether a product, service, or support process.

The focus of benchmarking is on practices. Only through changing current practices or current methods of performing business processes will overall effectiveness be achieved. Practices must be understood before a benchmarking metric can be derived. Benchmarking metrics are seen as a result of understanding best practices, not something that can be quantified first and understood later.

The key to the benchmarking definition is achieving superior performance by pursuing the "best of the best" practices—best of class or best of breed—*regardless* of where they exist, whether inside one's own company or industry or outside one's industry. It is only this view that will ensure superiority rather than parity.

Benchmarking as a term should motivate you because it is a positive activity, perceived as a mechanism for improving operations and proactively searching for best practices. It will be only through the test of finding the best of the best in industry that you will be able to justify your own operation and be sure that you have performed to the ultimate standard.

Finance and Accounting. The role of finance and accounting is to maximize the value of your business through the effective acquisition and management of financial resources and to provide financial information that fulfills external requirements while supplying internal functions.

As Total Quality Management is applied throughout your business, it impacts all business functional activities—even the finance and accounting operations. With a multifunctional team approach the role of finance and accounting becomes more proactive in the strategic decisions of your business. By having early participation the finance people can understand and work with engineering, procurement, and production requirements more effectively.

Because Total Quality Management focuses on process improvement, new cost management systems are moving away from nondescript overhead accounts toward activity-based costing. Activity-based costing can be viewed as an evolutionary extension of the current two-stage cost accounting allocation procedures that are the basis for most modern cost accounting systems. Activity-based costing systems focus on the manufacturing activities (processes) performed in producing specific products. The cost of each activity is charged to specific products based on the actual consumption of materials and labor used. The implementation of Total Quality Management and activity-based costing enables you to achieve significant synergy and enhanced communication throughout your management organization.

As we move toward more high-quality, lower-cost products we will see the application of activity-based costing as a fundamental change in our traditional finance and accounting systems. Detailed product/process activity-based costing systems provide more realistic, useful financial measurement and analysis of your day-to-day business operations.

In addition to activity-based costing new management information systems are emerging that not only provide accounting data but include total integration of information from order entry to shipping-label preparation. Today, electronic data interchange not only impacts the definition of product design but it also is integrated as an element of the total enterprise management information system. In some cases, enterprise integration and management information systems are moving to a new level of data and information management called corporate information management. This trend in expanding the cross-functional linkages in finance, accounting, management, design, and production centers on computer-intensive functions. As the power, cost, and ease of use of computer technology continues to expand rapidly, the ability to manipulate and analyze the true costs of the product will allow your business to be even more competitive.

Human Resources. The role of human resources in a Total Quality Management organization has moved from the hire-and-fire clerical role to one of true personnel management. In Total Quality Management we are moving from top-down to bottom-up empowerment of your employees. We are seeing significant shifts in the type and level of training being applied in the business environment. The shift to participative management encourages the implementation of multifunctional teams where finance, design, production, marketing, work closely together rather than in closed organizational work functions.

In many businesses today, from General Motors to IBM, we see the downsizing/rightsizing and flattening of organizations. These often severe cuts are changing the organizational hierarchial structure and reducing the number of middle-level managers. This turmoil in the organization requires improved human resource approaches to assist in the continual growth and survival of your business. Therefore, today we see a more active intellectual and managerial role for human resource managers as part of the Total Quality Management implementation process.

One of the major efforts in Total Quality Management is awareness and tools/techniques training. All too often Total Quality Management training has been poorly created, poorly taught, and poorly applied. Human resources personnel have to participate in the design, selection of sources, and approach to Total Quality Management implementation in a manner that addresses the unique needs of your business. In many cases off-site training is poorly designed, not created or customized for your business, or taught in a time frame that cannot be applied directly in your organization. For that reason chain-training—where the top management learn and train their subordinates, who in turn train their personnel—is the most effective way of changing an organization's view toward quality.

Participative management, empowerment, and multifunctional teams are some of the most significant activities that human resource managers can develop and support in your business. We recognize today that the expert for a particular task is the worker on the line doing the task. We must encourage that "job expert" to communicate process improvements so that the overall quality of our products and services can be improved.

Information Systems.   Information systems are interfunctional and cross-functional communication linkages that facilitate the effective flow and use of information and support the management of information as a strategic business resource. In the finance and accounting area the use of corporate- or enterprise-wide management information systems is a growing information system activity. Information systems have evolved from payroll to accounting, to financial management, to today's enterprise management systems. We are able to have on our desk today the computer power that a decade ago took up a whole room along with their data processing staff specialists. Today we have the benefit of both large central computer power and desk-top information management systems.

Manufacturers use and store information on designs, inventory, outstanding orders, capabilities of different machines, personnel, and costs of raw materials, among other things. In even a modestly complex business operation, these databases become so large and intricate that complex computer programs must be used to sort and summarize the data efficiently. Management information systems (MIS) perform this function, providing reports on such topics as current status of production, inventory and demand levels, and personnel and financial information. Before the advent of powerful computers and management information systems, some of the information now handled by MIS was simply not collected. In other cases, the collection and digestion of the information required dozens of clerks. Beyond saving labor, MIS implementation allows for more flexible and more widespread access to corporate information. For example, with just a few seconds of computer time, a firm's sales records can be listed by region for the sales staff, by dollar amount for the sales managers, and by product type for production staff. Perhaps most importantly, the goal for MIS is that the system be so easy to use that it can be used directly by top-level managers.

Enterprise integration is a new approach to corporate information management and automation that includes a variety of product and process information and automation productivity technology initiatives under one system integration umbrella. Major programs or functional efforts that are included in enterprise integration include the following:

- Computer-aided acquisition and logistics support (CALS).
- Concurrent engineering/simultaneous product and process engineering.
- Product data specifications/national plan for intelligent product definition.
- Total Quality Management (TQM).
- Computer-integrated manufacturing (CIM).

Global manufacturing competitors have recognized the growing leadership in Europe and Japan in the field of system integration. The enterprise integration efforts reflect an understanding of the potential of global competition for product development and production that is truly world-class. The current vertically developed productivity programs could benefit from systems engineering integration. The enterprise integration concept provides a new vision for design, production, and support of new products.

Numerous companies, foreign and domestic, compete for market share in business. These businesses are geographically dispersed, multidisciplined competitors that establish partnerships and teaming arrangements under diverse management styles in order to remain leaders in national and international markets. The requirement for shared, accurate, and timely decision-making information at all levels of the enterprise is critical. Businesses need to infuse new technologies into their structures to survive. The "islands of automation" style of production technology is in turn creating "islands of information." The environment in which enterprise integration will succeed is complex, intense, and typical of a large business or government enterprise.

The time required to conceive and field a complex weapon system such as the B-1 bomber or a new car results in the product being deployed using yesterday's technology. Unless new approaches are used to develop, manufacture, and support design and production throughout the life cycle—including the best management tools such as Total Quality Management, quality function deployment, information integration, and participatory management and teamwork—and unless there are significant cultural changes within defense and commercial businesses, within a decade the United States, for example, could be confronted with an overwhelming dependency on foreign suppliers. The government is facing a future of diminishing budgets, resources that are strained to the limit, and increasing costs for highly complex and difficult-to-maintain systems. It is critical that the life-cycle cost, concept-to-delivery time, and complexity of systems be reduced, and that the industrial base productivity and support flexibility be increased. The role of enterprise integration is to facilitate the technical and cultural evolution or, in some instances, revolution that is so critical to our productivity needs in the coming century.

The introduction of enterprise integration technology as a support system cannot usually start with a clean slate. The systems installed in these businesses are a mixture of commercial and home-grown applications that have evolved along with the business and its computer systems. Many interfacing and integrating factors complicate the enterprise integration effort and therefore require the establishment of a succinct boundary definition. Specific architectures for integration based on enterprise integration guidelines are not application systems, but rather support systems that must meet the demands of both simple and complex applications for fulfilling the requirements of users and developers. For example, the average longevity of computer technology (hardware) is only 3 to 5 years, while computer applications (software) last 15 to 20 years. Because of the dichotomy between changing computer technology and user-specific requirements, companies are continually modifying their computer programs and systems.

Although many U.S. government agencies, including the National Institute of Standards and Technology (NIST) and the Department of Defense (U.S. Air Force and Navy), have spent hundreds of millions of dollars on the problems of integrating distributed, heterogeneous environments for many different application domains, they have yet to transfer true integration technology into the commercial marketplace and into the industrial base in order to significantly decrease the cost of systems. Many technical solutions have been prototyped, have demonstrated feasibility, and have claimed cost savings. However, the technology has not been implemented on a broad scale.

While government-funded software development projects result in public-domain software, no technical support and maintenance for this software is available. Because there is no long-term commitment to public-domain software, there is no organization to contact if a problem arises in implementing the technology and no one to maintain and evolve the technology. The government as well as the user organizations would prefer to buy integration products off the shelf complete with vendor commitment and support. Only when this becomes possible will the technology be implemented and the industrial base reap the benefits.

The research and development of enabling technologies is a substantial part of enterprise integration. The research not only pushes toward a more advanced true enterprise integration, but also feeds the solutions for the following issues: system performance, system adaptability and flexibility, system and data quality, data and knowledge acquisition, migration strategies from legacy systems to future systems, user interfaces for end users and developers, automated tools for system and data maintenance and monitoring, application development productivity, teamwork, cultural changes, support for distributed processing, support for knowledge and information processing (management automation), support for complex and heterogeneous data, and data security. The enterprise integration technologies for product development and implementation must make the transition to future integration projects.

Enterprise integration will help facilitate the development of existing manufacturing information and automation productivity improvement programs. Managers and engineers have not focused on what the total system business requirements are for their operation, and therefore they cannot develop manufacturing plans and development strategies for optimizing their information and automation implementation plans.

Manufacturing.   The mission of manufacturing is to plan and manage the effective use of resources (information, people, equipment, and investment) in order to produce goods that meet and exceed the customer expectations of quality, cost, and on-time delivery.

Manufacturing, industrial facilities management, and process design and development are most closely related and share one major objective: They must develop, implement, operate, maintain, and improve production systems that enable the firm to satisfy the needs of its customers at the lowest total cost. If the firm is to make a product or part within a process that performs well on the major dimensions of competition, the activities of these three areas must be coordinated, and cooperation between them must be established. These activities are driven by the need to ensure that the manufacturing system is best able to support and service the customer. These areas can achieve this objective by sharing information. Knowledge of equipment reliability traits and appropriate regulations can influence the processes designed and implemented by process design and development. The process designed can affect the staffing and skill requirements. As manufacturing works with the resulting process, its experiences can be fed back to design and industrial facilities management for continuous improvement and enhancement of the system. With these three functions integrated, the firm has established a base for making manufacturing into a strategic competitive weapon.

Achieving the highest levels of quality and competitiveness requires a well-defined and well-executed approach to continuous improvement of all operations and of all work unit activities of a company. Improvements may be of several types, such as (1) enhancing value to the customer through improved product and service attributes, (2) reducing errors and defects, (3) improving responsiveness and cycle-time performance, and (4) improving efficiency and effectiveness in use of all manufacturing resources. Therefore, improvement is driven not only by the objective of providing superior quality but also by the need to be responsive and efficient. Both achievements provide additional marketplace advantages. To meet all of these requirements, the process of continuous improvement must contain regular cycles of planning, execution, and evaluation. It must be accompanied by a basis—preferably a quantitative basis—for assessing progress and for deriving information for the next cycle of improvement.

In the discussion on human resources we briefly discussed teamwork. In manufacturing, in particular, teamwork and multifunctional teams have demonstrated significant improvements to the manufacturing processes. The empowerment of the work force and the peer pressure developed through teamwork have contributed to improved manufacturing profits, profitability, production, and products.

Multifunctional teams applied across the business, from marketing to manufacturing, have improved — one step at a time — the processes and quality, and have shortened the cycle time, allowing businesses to bring new products to market faster. Cycle-time reduction is becoming a strategic weapon in global competitiveness.

The application of Total Quality Management in the industrial base began in manufacturing. The design and production processes were defined better than the white-collar office tasks, or the creative process applied by scientists or engineers. Today we see greater adoption of Total Quality Management principles and practices in manufacturing. However, the Total Quality Management approach is now being applied to all elements of business.

It seems so simple to say, Do it right the first time; yet we see rework of 25 to 30 percent in many manufacturing operations today. If you understand the total process and continuously work at improving your processes throughout your operation, your rework will decrease, your quality will keep getting better, and your customers will be satisfied. The decision to change the work culture to one focused on *not* passing defective, poor-quality work from one work process station to another is a decision made by management.

Computer-integrated manufacturing (CIM) has existed in concept for many years. Although widely recognized for the major positive impact it can have on U.S. productivity, CIM is far from commonplace in American factories. The high costs of software development, maintenance, and integration (people and computer/hardware systems) are among the most prominent reasons for our slow evolution to CIM. Many computer packages have been developed that address specific manufacturing tasks like scheduling or process planning, but these packages fail to provide the "hooks" needed for total manufacturing system enterprise integration. These programs are developed by different vendors, on different hardware platforms, and they are not designed to be integrated with programs from other vendors, nor are they part of an overall CIM architecture.

Through a bottom-up approach in automation, we have seen a growth of islands of automation. Typical islands in industrial enterprises are the "product modeling" island, the "process modeling" island, and the "production" island. The product-modeling island typically deals with specialized hardware (work stations) for the manipulation of geometrical information of parts of products. The process-modeling island is concerned with more general, lower-capacity critical hardware (minicomputers, mainframes, and personal computers) for manipulating bills of materials, planning data, commercial data, and so on. The production island deals with specialized computer-controlled machines (e.g., punching, cutting, bending, milling, and drilling machines) and operations like automatic transportation and storage and positioning systems (e.g., robot systems). Integration of these islands of automation would require a global optimization of the business functions involved, instead of a suboptimization for every island.

Many industrialists have a futuristic vision of CIM that includes maximum use of coordination between CAD-CAM (computer-aided design and computer-aided manufacturing) tools, with few if any human workers, while others downplay CIM as a revolutionary change and emphasize that factories will only adopt automation as they deem appropriate. Most agree that the widespread use of CIM and virtually unmanned factories are already a reality in Japan and could be in place in the global manufacturing community by the turn of the century.

The essential difference between conventional factory machines and the automated production inherent in CIM is the latter's integration of all information system technology required for designing, producing, and delivering the product. The use of computers and information system communication networks allows machines to perform a greater variety of tasks than fixed automation allows, and allows for automation of some tasks previously requiring direct human control. In general, then, CIM can be defined as the application of information technology and production technology components in a way that supports the enterprise integration functions effectively, efficiently, and with a high degree of automation.

Information system components include all the software-based mechanisms for performing or supporting information processing functions in the "information system" of the enterprise. Concrete examples are CAD product modeling software, process planning software, and production control software. Automation system components include all the machines for performing or supporting the realization functions in the "real system" (the shop floor or factory) of an enterprise. Concrete examples are robots and numerical-controlled (NC) milling, punching, cutting, bending, and measuring machines that are controlled by the information system.

The enterprise integration functions of interest are those that deal with the complete product life cycle, from the product specification—via the part modeling (design), the process modeling (planning), and the time scheduling—to the production control and the actual production of the product, through logistic support and client service.

CIM includes a family of technologies that lie at the intersection of computer science and manufacturing engineering. "CAD-CAM" means that a switch from one task to another can be accomplished with relative ease by changing the (usually) computerized instructions; "automation" implies that a significant part of the functions can be performed without direct human intervention. The common element in these tools that makes them different from traditional manufacturing tools is their use of the computer for manipulating and storing data, and the use of related microelectronics core technology for facilitating communication of data to other machines in the factory.

These tools provide assistance in these general functions: in the design of products, in the manufacturing (fabricating and assembling) of products on the factory floor, and in the management of many factory operations. The three categories of automation technologies—tools for design, manufacturing, and management—are not mutually exclusive. In fact, the goal of much current research into computer-integrated manufacturing systems is to break down the barriers between the categories so that design and manufacturing systems become inextricably linked. However, these three categories help frame the discussion, particularly because they reflect the organization of a typical manufacturing firm.

Computer-integrated manufacturing systems can reduce waste, reduce levels of finished product inventory, and reduce the manufacturer's substantial investment in the products that are in various stages of completion, known as "work in process."

The vision of CIM is significantly different from its actual implementation. To date, most CIM demonstrations have taken place at major auto, aerospace, or defense contractors. Few medium- and small-size companies have adopted CIM or have been forced to adopt CIM by their customers. Thus the CIM technology implementation gap is substantial. For CIM to succeed we must develop manufacturing technology strategy and implementation tools that all levels (large, medium, and small business) of enterprise can adopt in a cost-effective manner.

World-class manufacturing centers have concentrated on the early development of standards for product performance and process uniformity. Japan has been the leader in developing standards for consumer and information system products, closely followed by the expanding integration of European organizations. The United States has traditionally developed new proprietary products, and only after long delays did the industry join national efforts to conform to universal standards. As a result, Japan and Europe have taken a leadership role in the global manufacturing market. An excellent example of Europe's commitment and leadership in enterprise integration is the Computer-Integrated Manufacturing–Open Systems Architecture (CIM-OSA) program.

Some years ago, computer-integrated manufacturing was only known to manufacturing experts, yet today it is a well-known and often-used term. Even today, however, the meaning of CIM is controversially interpreted, ranging from "catchword without meaning" to "humanless plant." Nonetheless, every enterprise that intends to keep its position in the global market must explore all possibilities if it is to keep its products and operations competitive. Among the many areas in which to concentrate quality efforts—such as labor costs, technology, teamwork, and education of employees—CIM is one of the most promising avenues for staying competitive.

Effective introduction of CIM requires skilled people, know-how, and structured implementation plans—in addition to the necessary investment capital and top management's full and active support for CIM. An enterprise-wide strategy for the introduction of CIM is a mandatory prerequisite if CIM is to succeed. Regardless of whether the introduction of CIM is accomplished slowly or quickly, regardless of which part of the enterprise is the forerunner in CIM's introduction, and despite the resistance of some of the people involved, a CIM model for the whole enterprise must be generated with engineering methods that support all steps of CIM introduction—from the very first concept down to the actual implementation.

Process Design and Development.   Total Quality Management is an integral part of process design and development. The mission of process design and development concentrates on the planning, coordination, and management of the production methodologies unique to your business. As Dan L. Shunk noted in his excellent book *Integrated Process Design and Development:*

> The world of process design and development has changed immensely over the past 10 to 20 years. Originally, in the serial fashion of design and manufacturing, process design and development was considered after the product was developed. But in today's integrated world, product design and process design are developed in a simultaneous, integrated fashion. In an attempt to understand how to develop integrated resource management for a successful 21st-century company, the role of process design and development must be understood.

The linkage between customer needs and requirements now are an integral part of the creation of process design and development systems that support both the external and internal customer. The application of concurrent engineering principles where multifunctional teams work closely together—not only in designing the product but in tying together the design and development of the production process—is the trend.

Process improvement on a continuous basis is one of the principle elements of Total Quality Management. First you need to fully understand your production processes, then you must simplify, integrate, and automate them in concert with your total enterprise integration effort. All too often we believe that we understand our process and its relationship with the cross-functional linkages; but to our surprise we have insufficient data to really appreciate the opportunity for real improvement. We have seen the rapid integration of design and production in our world-class facilities. This emphasis on breaking down the walls between design and production facilitates shorter cycle time, reduction of rework, improved quality, and enhanced worker communication.

The concentration on the total business enterprise has created new opportunities for consensus building by supporting design for manufacturing efforts within world-class businesses. In the past, we often left out the manufacturing functions in our competitiveness strategies. But now manufacturing is recognized as a critical part of the business. We now stress the conceptualization, design, development, and production of new products as an integrated effort. We can no longer compete if one element of the process is inferior to another stage of development. We must plan ahead by designing quality into our products, and by developing products that efficiently utilize our manufacturing capabilities.

Industrial Facilities Management.   The central mission of industrial facilities management is the installation and maintainance of plant, equipment, and facility environments required to support your business objectives. Industrial facilities management is a long-term support of the physical facility. The basic responsibilities include total quality maintenance procedures, administration and maintenance of buildings and grounds, environmental responsiveness, safety, and related support services.

Total Quality Management affects all elements of your business, including the continuous improvement and teamwork for your industrial facilities management staffs. Capability analysis is a basic part of Total Quality Management that determines whether the existing processes are inherently capable of meeting your requirements.

The Total Quality Management principles being applied today to industrial facilities management emphasize operator-centered preventive maintenance, industrial equipment designed for safety and maintainability, application of state-of-the art technology, and management practices and customer service.

I hope this book has convinced you of the vast potential Total Quality Management holds in store for businesses like yours. I also hope you feel confident enough now to go further, to take the next step and become your company's integrated resource management Total Quality Management advocate.

CHAPTER 11

ACT NOW!

LEAD YOUR TOTAL QUALITY MANAGEMENT TEAM

No matter who we are in an organization, we can fall into the trap of thinking that our business is too big to be affected by our individual actions. That perception is common and frustrating, and fortunately, it is a false one. Only through the collective efforts of individual members do companies change; companies are incapable of changing themselves.

Whatever your position in your business, your efforts to perform a job and to improve that performance directly affect the influence you will have in the organization, the control you will have over your personal situation, and your ability to manage and lead. Combined with the efforts of others, your effectiveness directly influences the business's overall ability to meet its mission and ultimately affects our performance as a global competitor. Furthermore, how we perform today will also affect future generations.

Total Quality Management is a means for improving personal effectiveness and performance and for aligning and focusing all individual quality efforts throughout your business. It provides a framework within which you may continuously improve everything you do and affect. It is a way of leveraging your individual effort and extending its effect and its importance throughout your organization and beyond.

MAKE THE DECISION TODAY

You have examined in this book the need to adopt the Total Quality Management strategy for improving your business competitiveness. The costs and benefits presented here show that your business cannot afford to wait—that you must act now if you want to improve your level of quality performance. Now that you have read about the different philosophies of quality improvement from Crosby, Deming, and Juran, you will find that an amalgam of these principles and practices can be created that will meet your specific needs. The Malcolm Baldrige National Quality Award and Deming Prize have set the scene for self-assessment; and the companies that have won quality awards have described their experiences and the lessons they have learned in improving the quality of their products or services. Approximately 200 questions were raised so you can perform your own armchair assessment of how your company or organization is doing in terms of quality. The Total Quality Management methodology has laid down the basic steps you'll take in aggressively and continuously improving your operations. And in this book you have examined the tools and techniques you and your staff need in order to understand your level of quality, to show areas of improvement, and to act.

It is now up to you. Do it!

APPENDIX A

ADDITIONAL READING

Aubrey, Charles A. II, and Patricia K. Felkins. *Teamwork: Involving People in Quality and Productivity Improvement*. Milwaukee, Wis.: Publisher's Quality Press, 1988.

Bennis, Warren, and Burt Nanus. *Leaders: The Strategies for Taking Charge*. New York: Harper and Row, 1985.

Crosby, Philip B. *Quality Is Free: The Art of Making Quality Certain*. New York: McGraw-Hill, 1979.

Crosby, Philip B. *Quality Without Tears: The Art of Hassle-Free Management*. New York: McGraw-Hill, 1984.

Deming, W. Edwards. *Out of the Crisis*. Cambridge, Mass.: MIT Center for Advanced Engineering Study, 1982.

Ealey, Lance A. *Quality by Design: Taguchi Methods and U.S. Industry*. Dearborn, Mich.: ASI Press, 1988.

Ernst & Young Quality Improvement Consulting Group. *Total Quality: An Executive's Guide for the 1990s*. Homewood, Ill.: The Dow Jones-Irwin/APICS Series in Production Management, 1990.

Garvin, David A. *Managing Quality: The Strategic and Competitive Edge*. New York: The Free Press, 1988.

Harrington, H. James. *Excellence—The IBM Way*. Milwaukee, Wis.: Publisher's Quality Press, 1988.

Harrington, H. James. *The Improvement Process—How America's Leading Companies Improve Quality*. New York: McGraw-Hill, 1987.

Hickman, Craig R., and Michael A. Silva. *Creating Excellence*. New York: New American Library, 1984.

Hunt, V. Daniel. *Quality in America*. Homewood, Ill.: Business One Irwin, 1992.

Hunt, V. Daniel. *Computer Integrated Manufacturing Handbook*. New York: Chapman and Hall, 1989.

Hunt, V. Daniel. *Robotics Sourcebook*. New York: Elsevier Science Publishing Co., Inc., 1988.

Hunt, V. Daniel. *Mechatronics—Japan's Newest Threat*. New York: Chapman and Hall, 1988.

Hunt, V. Daniel. *Artificial Intelligence and Expert Systems Sourcebook*. New York: Chapman and Hall, 1986.

Hunt, V. Daniel. *Smart Robots*. New York: Chapman and Hall, 1985.

Imai, Masaki. *Kaizen: The Key to Japan's Competitive Success*. New York: Random House, 1986.

Ishikawa, Kaoru. *Guide to Quality Control*. White Plains, N.Y.: Kraus International Publications, 1982.

Ishikawa, Kaoru. *What Is Total Quality Control? The Japanese Way*. Englewood Cliffs, N.J.: Prentice-Hall, 1985.

Juran, Joseph M. *Juran on Leadership for Quality: An Executive Handbook*. New York: The Free Press, 1989.

Juran, Joseph M. *Juran on Planning for Quality*. New York: The Free Press, 1988.

Juran, Joseph M. *Juran's Quality Control Handbook*. New York: McGraw-Hill, 1988.

McGregor, Douglas. *The Human Side of Enterprise*. New York: McGraw-Hill, 1985.

Michalak, Donald F., and Edwin G. Yager. *Making the Training Process Work*. New York: Harper and Row, 1979.

Peters, Tom. *Thriving on Chaos*. New York: Alfred A. Knopf, 1987.

Scherkenbach, William W. *The Deming Route to Quality and Productivity*. Rockville, Md.: Mercury Press, 1988.

Scholtes, Peter R., et al. *The Team Handbook—How to Use Teams to Improve Quality*. Madison, Wis.: Joiner Associates Inc., 1988.

Walton, Mary. *Deming Management at Work*. New York: Putnam, 1990.

Zemke, Ron, and Dick Schaaf. *The Service Edge: 101 Companies that Profit from Customer Care*. New York: New American Library, 1989.

Walton, Mary. *The Deming Management Method*. New York: Dodd, Mead and Company, 1986.

APPENDIX B

KEY TERMINOLOGY

These key terms include the "quality" definitions that are presented in the American Production and Inventory Control Society (APICS) CIRM interim dictionary of terminology. These definitions are marked with an asterisk. Special recognition is given to the APICS Educational and Research Foundation for the development of the key terminology list.

acceptance sampling Sampling inspection in which decisions are made to accept or not accept product or service. It also is the methodology that deals with procedures by which decisions to accept or not accept are based on the results of the inspection of samples.

appraisal costs The costs associated with inspecting the product to ensure that it meets the customer's (either internal or external) needs and requirements.

average outgoing quality limit (AOQL) The maximum expected quality of outgoing quality over all possible levels of incoming quality, following the use of an acceptance sampling plan for a given value of incoming product quality.

best of class When overall performance, in terms of effectiveness, efficiency, and adaptability, is superior to all comparables.

brainstorming A technique used by a group of people for thought generation. The aim is to elicit as many ideas as possible within a given time frame.

cause An established reason for the existence of a defect.

common cause A source of variation in the process output that is inherent to the process and will affect all the individual results or values of process output.

control The set of activities employed to detect and correct deviation in order to maintain or restore a desired state. It is a past-oriented approach to quality management.

correction The totality of actions to minimize or remove variations and their causes.

corrective action   The implementation of effective solutions that result in the elimination of identified product, service, and process problems.

cost of quality   The sum of the cost of prevention, appraisal, and failure. The key financial measurement tool that ties process control and process optimization into a total process management effort. It can be used both as an indicator and a signal for variation (more often, for patterns of variation), as well as a measure of productivity and efficiency.

cross-functional teams   Teams similar to quality teams but whose members are from several work units that interface with one another. These teams are particularly useful when work units are dependent on one another for materials, information, and the like.

culture   A prevailing pattern of activities, interactions, norms, sentiments, beliefs, attitudes, values, and products in an organization.

customer   The recipient or beneficiary of the outputs of your work efforts or the purchaser of your products and services; may be either internal or external to the organization. The customer is the recipient that must be satisfied with the output.

data   Information or a set of facts presented in descriptive form. There are two basic kinds of data: measured (also known as variable data) and counted (also known as attribute data).

defect   Any state of nonconformance to requirements.

Deming Prize   In 1950, W. Edwards Deming was invited to Japan by the Union of Japanese Scientists and Engineers (JUSE) to lecture on the applicability of using quality control in manufacturing companies. The impact of Deming's teaching was widespread and swift to take root. In 1951, JUSE instituted the Deming Prize to honor Deming for his friendship and achievements in industrial quality control. Today, Japanese companies wishing to improve the level of quality within their organization compete for the Deming Prize to achieve not only the honor and prestige of winning, but also the improvements that come from implementing his quality principles.

deviation   Any departure from a desired or expected value or pattern. The standard deviation is used as the measure of spread for almost all industrial frequency distributions.

effectiveness   How closely an organization's output meets its goal and/or meets the customer's requirement.

efficiency   A process characteristic indicating that the process produces the required output at a perceived minimum cost. Ratio of the quantity of resources expected or planned to be consumed in meeting customer requirements to the resources actually consumed.

external failure costs The costs incurred when an external customer receives a defective product.

failsafe techniques The inclusion in the design and production process of simple automatic checking devices that catch common errors—sometimes called fail-safe production methods (or *poka-yoke* in Japan).

fishbone analysis A diagram that depicts the characteristics of a problem or process and the factors or root causes that contribute to them.

force field analysis A technique involving the identification of forces for and against a certain course of action. The *nominal group technique* could be used in conjunction with force field analysis. The group might prioritize the forces for and against by assessing their magnitude and probability of occurrence. The group might then develop an action plan to minimize the forces against and maximize the forces for.

form-fit-function As part of configuration control, Engineering Change Notices (ECNs) typically support drawing/component changes that do not affect the form, fit, or function of the component in relation to the system in which it is used.

frequency distribution Frequency distribution of a discrete variable is the count of the number of occurrences of individual values over a given range. Frequency distribution of a continuous variable is the count of cases that lie between certain predetermined limits over the range of values the variable may assume.

functional administrative control technique A tool designed to improve performance through a process combining time management and value engineering. The process involves breaking down activities into functions and establishing action teams to target and solve problems in each function.

functional organization An organization responsible for one of the major organizational functions, such as marketing, sales, design, manufacturing, and distribution.

gainsharing A reward system that shares productivity gains between owners and employees. Gainsharing is generally used to provide incentive for group efforts toward improvement.

goal A statement of attainment/achievement that one proposes to accomplish or attain with an implication of sustained effort and energy directed to it over the long term.

guideline A suggested practice that is not mandatory in programs intended to comply with a standard.

hypothesis An assertion made about the value of some parameter of a population.

input   Materials, energy, or information required to complete the activities necessary to produce a specified output (work product).

internal failure costs   The costs generated by defects found within the enterprise, prior to the product reaching the external customer.

maintainability   The characteristic of equipment design and/or installation that provides the equipment the ability to be repaired easily and efficiently.*

materials review board (MRB)   Where disposition of nonconforming materials is at issue, a materials review board acts at the quality-control agency to make or coordinate the making of the required decisions. This board is composed of a concerned process-control engineer, representatives of the design engineering and purchasing departments and, when the material involved is used on products for purchase by government service, the resident government inspector.

mean time between failures (MTBF)   The average time between successive failures of a given product.

measurement   The act or process of measuring to compare results with requirements. A quantitative estimate of performance.

military standards   The (U.S.) federal government standards of performance for products procured for military systems. These standards include quality standards, performance requirements, statistical sampling requirements, and component specifications.

need   A lack of something requisite, desired, or useful; a condition requiring provision or relief. Need is usually expressed by users or customers.

nominal group technique   A tool for idea generation, problem solving, mission and key result area definition, performance measure definition, and goals/objectives definition.

normative performance measurement technique   Incorporates structured group processes so that work groups can design measurement systems suited for their own needs. This approach considers behavioral consequences of measurement to foster acceptance of measurement effort.

objective   A statement of the desired result to be achieved within a specified time. By definition, an objective always has an associated schedule.

output   The specified end result. Required by the recipient.

outputs   Materials or information provided to others (internal or external customers).

---

*APICS/CIRM definition

Pareto analysis   Used to classify problems or causes by priority. It helps high-light the vital few as opposed to the trivial many. It also helps to identify which cause or problem is the most significant.

performance   Term used both as an attribute of the work product itself and as a general process characteristic. The broad performance characteristics that are of interest to management are quality (effectiveness), cost (efficiency), and schedule. Performance is the highly effective common measurement that links the quality of the work product to efficiency and productivity.

plan   A specified course of action designed to attain a stated objective.

policy   A statement of principles and beliefs, or a settled course, adopted to guide the overall management of affairs in support of a stated aim or goal. It is mostly related to fundamental conduct and usually defines a general framework within which other business and management actions are carried out.

population   A large collection of items (product observations, data) about certain characteristics of which conclusions and decisions are to be made for purposes of process assessment and quality improvement.

prevention   A future-oriented approach to quality management that achieves quality improvement through curative action on the process.

prevention costs   The costs associated with actions taken to plan the product or process to ensure that defects do not occur.

problem   A question or situation proposed for solution. The result of not conforming to requirements or, in other words, a potential task resulting from the existence of defects.

process   A system in operation to produce an output of higher value than that of the sum of its inputs. A process is also defined as the logical organization of people, materials, energy, equipment, and procedures into work activities designed to produce a specified end result (work product).

process average   One of the most useful measures of central tendency. It is obtained by dividing the sum of the values in a series of readings by the number of readings.

process capability   Long-term performance level after the process has been brought under control.

process control   The set of activities employed to detect and remove special causes of variation in order to maintain or restore stability (statistical control).

process flow analysis   A technique for identification and analysis of key processes. The technique identifies areas and methods of possible improvement. It is particularly useful for roadblock removal.

process improvement   The set of activities employed to detect and remove common causes of variation in order to improve process capability. Process improvement leads to quality improvement.

process management   Management approach comprising quality management and process optimization.

process optimization   The major aspect of process management that concerns itself with the efficiency and productivity of the process — that is, with economic factors.

process owner   A designated person within the process who has authority to manage the process and responsibility for its overall performance.

process performance   A measure of how effectively and efficiently a process satisfies customer requirements.

process review   An objective assessment of how well the methodology has been applied to your process. Emphasizes the potential for long-term process results rather than the actual results achieved.

product genealogy   The historical record of the components, fabrication, testing, and quality audit status of a component or total product.

productivity   Ratio of outputs produced (or service transactions) to inputs required for production/completion. Productivity is an expected outcome of quality and a necessary companion to improving service.

quality   The extent to which products and services produced conform to customer requirements. Customers can be internal as well as external to the organizational system (e.g., products or services may flow to the person at the next desk or work area rather than to people outside of the immediate organization). The Federal Quality Institute defines quality as meeting the customer requirements the first time and every time. The Department of Defense defines quality as conformance to a set of customer requirements that, if met, result in a product that is fit for its intended use.

quality circles   A group of workers and their supervisors who voluntarily meet to identify and solve job-related problems. Structured processes are used by the group to accomplish their task.

quality function deployment (QFD)   A disciplined approach to solving quality problems before the design phase of a product. The foundation of QFD is the belief that products should be designed to reflect customer desires; therefore, marketers, design engineers, and manufacturing personnel work closely together from the beginning to ensure a successful product. The approach involves finding out what features are important to customers, ranking them in importance, identifying conflicts, and translating them into engineering specifications.

quality of working life   The extent to which the organizational culture provides employees with information, knowledge, authority, and rewards in an effort to ensure that employees perform safely and effectively, are compensated equitably, and maintain a sense of human dignity.

quality teams   Also referred to as performance action teams or quality improvement teams. These teams might be composed of volunteers who meet regularly to review progress toward goal attainment, plan for changes, decide upon corrective actions, and so on. Members are usually from the same work unit.

range   The difference between the maximum and the minimum value of data in a sample.

reliability   The probability of a product performing its specified function under prescribed conditions without failure for a specified period of time. It is a design parameter that can be made part of a requirements statement.*

requirement   A formal statement of a need and the expected manner in which it is to be met.

requirements   What is expected in providing a product or service. The "it" in "do it right the first time." Specific and measurable customer needs with an associated performance standard.

roadblock identification analysis   A tool that focuses on identifying roadblocks to performance improvement and/or problems that are causing the group to be less productive than it could be. This tool utilizes the nominal group technique to identify and prioritize performance roadblocks. Action teams are formed to analyze barriers and develop proposals to remove roadblocks. The proposals are implemented, tracked, and evaluated.

root cause analysis   The bottom line of a problem. Often, problems present themselves only as symptoms. Symptoms do not explain problems, they point to them. A root cause is the reason for the problem or symptom. Root cause analysis, then, is a method used to identify potential root causes of problems, narrow those down to the most significant causes, and analyze them using other Total Quality Management tools.

sample size   A finite number of items taken from a population.

Scanlon committees   Committees comprising managers, supervisors, and employees who work together to implement a philosophy of management/labor cooperation that is believed to enhance productivity. A number of principles and techniques are involved, with employee participation being a major component.

---

*APICS/CIRM definition

simulation The technique of observing and manipulating an artificial mechanism (model) that represents a real-world process which, for technical or economical reasons, is not suitable or available for direct experimentation.

special cause A source of variation in the process output that is unpredictable, unstable, or intermittent. Also called assignable cause.

specification A document containing a detailed description or enumeration of particulars. It is a formal description of a work product and the intended manner of providing it (the provider's view of the work product).

standard deviation A parameter describing the spread of the process output, denoted by the Greek letter sigma, σ. The positive square root of the variance.

statistic Any parameter that can be determined on the basis of the quantitative characteristics of a sample. A descriptive statistic is a computed measure of some property of a set of values, making possible a definitive statement about the meaning of the collected data. An inferential statistic indicates the confidence that can be placed in any statement regarding its expected accuracy, the range of applicability of the statement, and the probability of its being true. Consequently, decisions can be based on inferential statistics.

statistics The branch of applied mathematics that describes and analyzes empirical observations for the purpose of predicting certain events in order to make decisions in the face of uncertainty. Statistics, in turn, are based on the theory of probability. The two together provide the abstraction for the mathematical model underlying the study of problems involving uncertainty.

statistical control The status of a process from which all special causes of variation have been removed and only common causes remain. Such a process is also said to be stable.

statistical estimation The analysis of a sample parameter in order to predict the values of the corresponding population parameter.

statistical methods The application of the theory of probability to problems of variation. There are two groups of statistical methods. Basic statistical methods are relatively simple problem-solving tools and techniques, such as control charts, capability analysis, data summarization and analysis, and statistical inference. Advanced statistical methods are more sophisticated specialized techniques of statistical analysis, such as the design of experiments, regression and correlation analysis, and the analysis of variance.

statistical process control A systematic philosophy of doing business by continually reducing variation around a target value. A disciplined way of identifying and solving problems in order to improve performance. It involves use of fishbone diagrams to identify causes and effects of problems. Data are then collected and organized in various ways (graphs, fishbone diagrams, Pareto charts, and/or histograms) to further examine problems. The data may be tracked over time (control charts) to determine variation in the process. The process is then changed in some way, and new data are collected and analyzed to determine whether the process has been improved.

statistical quality control   A systematic methodology of manufacturing products or services by continually monitoring the state of the product or service based on a target standard of quality.

strategy   A broad course of action, chosen from a number of alternatives, to accomplish a stated goal in the face of uncertainty.

subprocesses   The internal processes that make up a process.

suppliers   Individuals or organizations or firms that provide inputs to you. Suppliers can be internal or external to a company, firm, or organization.

Taguchi methods   Genichi Taguchi's approach to quality improvement, which focuses on how to evaluate quality, how to improve quality cost effectively, and how to maintain quality cost effectively. Using the Taguchi "loss function" approach, all quality improvements are measured in terms of cost savings. Cost and quality improvement become one and the same.

team building   A process of developing and maintaining a group of people who are working toward a common goal. Team building usually focuses on one or more of the following objectives: (1) clarifying role expectations and obligations of team members; (2) improving superior-subordinate or peer relationships; (3) improving problem solving, decision making, resource utilization, or planning activities; (4) reducing conflict; and (5) improving organizational climate.

timeliness   The promptness with which quality products and services are delivered, relative to customer expectations.

total employee involvement   Teamwork-based efforts in which employee involvement teams meet regularly to discuss ways to improve the work place, the production process, and the lines of communication within an organization. Employee involvement flows from the bottom up rather than from the top down in an organization.

total quality control   Concept originated by Armand V. Feigenbaum, who defined TQC as an effective system for integrating the quality development, quality maintenance, and quality improvement efforts of the various groups in an organization so as to enable production and service at the most economical levels which allow for full customer satisfaction.

Total Quality Management (TQM)   A set of activities with the purpose of continuous process improvement and the objective of total customer satisfaction. The core concepts of Total Quality Management include standardization, the efficient use of materials, the critical role of top management, design specifications control, reduction of defect rates, statistical process control, and effective use of human resources as part of teams.

transactional analysis   A process that helps people change to be more effective on the job and can also help organizations to change. The process involves several exercises that help identify organizational scripts and games that people may be playing. The results help point the way toward change.

variable   A data item that takes on values within some range with a certain frequency or pattern. Variables may be discrete—that is, limited in value to integer quantities (for example, the number of bolts produced in a manufacturing process); discrete variables relate to attribute data. Variables may also be continuous—that is, measured to any desired degree of accuracy (for example, the diameter of a shaft); continuous variables relate to variables data.

variance   In quality management terminology, any nonconformance to specifications. In statistics, it is the square of the standard deviation.

zero defects   Not a motivation program, but a method for communicating to all employees the concept that everyone should do things right the first time, without failures or defects.

APPENDIX C

ISO 9000 UPDATE

Sara Hagigh of the U.S. Department of Commerce has recently updated in *Business America* a profile of the implementation status and fundamental elements of ISO 9000. Significant portions of this *Business America* report are included in this appendix to provide an update on ISO 9000.

Suppose your business is interested in exporting to the European Community (EC). As of January 1, 1993, you may be required to have some type of product approval, which includes designing your product to certain standards and certifying that your product meets the necessary standards.

A variety of EC certification options—such as manufacturer's self-certification, third-party certification, and registration of a manufacturer's quality system—are offered as part of the certification process. For regulated products (those subject to an EC directive or regulation), certification requirements are spelled out in individual directives. For many regulated products, a manufacturer may self-certify that a product complies with a directive's requirements. Examples of directives permitting self-certification include machinery, toys, and electromagnetic compatibility. The self-certification option is greatly facilitated when a manufacturer meets European standards that are being developed by European regional standards organizations. Other directives may require a third party to be involved in the certification process. Examples include medical devices and simple pressure vessels.

While manufacturers may be familiar with self-certification and third-party certification options, new procedures for product approval are emerging in the EC that may be unfamiliar to exporters. One such certification option, which has gained a great deal of attention, is registration of a manufacturer's quality system to ISO 9000: Standards related to quality assurance issued in 1987 by the International Organization for Standardization. Although a legal requirement in only a small number of directives, ISO 9000 is becoming increasingly important commercially for gaining access to EC markets. Manufacturers of construction products need to be familiar with European technical approvals provided by the European Organization for Technical Approvals (EOTA). For the unregulated sector, a framework for product approval is developing under the new European Organization for Testing and Certification (EOTC). This appendix will elaborate on these emerging approval procedures. All exporters to the EC are encouraged to consult applicable directives to ensure compliance with certification and approval requirements.

ISO 9000: BACKGROUND AND UPDATE

Nowhere is the confusion on EC conformity assessment so apparent as in questions relating to ISO 9000. Under EC legislation, certain products will require ISO 9000 registration as part of the product certification process after January 1, 1993. Highly regulated, high-risk products will be affected—for example medical devices, telecommunications terminal equipment, gas appliances, and personal protective equipment. Outside of regulated product sectors, ISO 9000 registration is becoming important in Europe as a competitive benchmarking marketing tool. Sectors where purchasers are likely to generate pressure for ISO 9000 registration include aerospace, automobiles, computers, electronic components, and measuring and testing equipment. ISO 9000 registration may also be a competitive factor in all 911 product areas (regulated or not) where safety or liability are concerns.

   ISO 9000 is a series of five standards (ISO 9000–9004) used to document, implement, and demonstrate quality assurance systems. The series describes three quality system models, defines quality concepts, and gives guidelines for using international standards on quality systems. Contrary to what many believe, ISO 9000 does not apply to specific products and does not guarantee that a manufacturer produces a "quality" product. The standards are generic and enable a company to assure (by means of internal and external third-party audits) that it has a quality system in place that meets one of the three published standards for a quality system.

An important idea to keep in mind is that the strong level of interest in ISO 9000 is being driven more by marketplace requirements than by government regulations. Purchasers in Europe are increasingly requesting ISO 9000 registration from suppliers. European consumers are often more aware of the importance of quality in their purchasing decisions. Manufacturers may find their competitors obtaining a registration to one of the three ISO 9000 standards, forcing them to consider ISO 9000 to remain competitive. This trend is not surprising, as the original standards were published in 1987 to meet the need for product quality in purchasing agreements. Three of the five standards in the series (ISO 9001, 9002, and 9003) define different quality system models and deal with contractual obligations between buyer and seller.

ISO 9000 registration provides certain advantages for a firm in marketing its product. A registration may serve as a means of distinguishing different classes of suppliers. If a European purchaser is choosing between two suppliers and one has an ISO 9000 registration, the supplier with the registration will have the competitive edge. In sales to the EC, manufacturers may be subject to far-reaching product liability and product safety laws, both of which place the burden on the manufacturer to have a well-documented quality system and to continually monitor product safety. The EC's strict liability law makes the manufacturer liable, regardless of fault or negligence, for harm to a person or object caused by a faulty or defective product. A manufacturer with a well-documented quality system will be better able to prove that products are defect-free and thus minimize liability claims. Another advantage is that quality systems registration may permit manufacturers to limit third-party involvement in product testing and approval.

NEW DEVELOPMENTS IN ISO 9000

One of the most difficult decisions for manufacturers seeking an ISO 9000 registration is choosing a registrar to audit and certify their quality system. A commonly asked question is, "If I register my quality system with Registrar X, will this be accepted in Europe?" Although guarantees are always difficult to give, a manufacturer with an ISO 9000 registration from a registrar who is accredited by a group that meets appropriate international guidelines is more likely to gain acceptance in the EC market. Since the onset of the ISO 9000 "craze," a large number of registrars have surfaced in the United States, many of whom have no credentials or proof that they are competent to perform quality system audits to acceptable standards. To ensure acceptability in the EC marketplace, many U.S. registrars have begun to seek accreditation from European entities (primarily the RvC, Dutch Council for Certification, in the Netherlands) or to enter into some form of contractual arrangement with European registrars of quality systems.

An alternative now exists for quality registrars seeking accreditation in the United States. The Registrar Accreditation Board (RAB), an affiliate of the American Society for Quality Control (ASQC), was established in November 1989 to accredit registrars of quality systems. RAB has accredited three quality system registrars (Quality Systems Registrars Inc., AT&T Quality Registrar, and ABS Quality Evaluation Inc.). In a move to strengthen this program, an agreement was signed with ANSI on December 13, 1991, creating the American National Accreditation Program for Registrars of Quality Systems. The joint program, operating under a joint ANSI/RAB committee, accredits registrars of quality systems. RAB administers the program, performing actual site inspections and audits of quality registrars to determine whether registrars meet appropriate international criteria for registering companies to ISO 9000. If RAB determines that a registrar is competent to perform ISO 9000 registrations, the registrar is accredited under the joint program.

ANSI coordinates the program's due process procedures, operates a final appeals process, conducts periodic program reviews, and is the focal point for dealings with the U.S. government and international organizations. The agreement does not affect previous RAB accreditations, although a review of the three RAB-approved programs will occur. To provide recognition of registrations made by registrars accredited under the ANSI/RAB program, ANSI and RAB are seeking recognition of the program by European accreditation bodies.

European regional standards bodies are developing additional standards that will address how to apply ISO 9000 to specific industries. An example is the EN 46000 series, which concern European standards for quality assurance systems in the medical device sector. When these standards are complete, they will replace the ISO 9000 series (EN 29000 series, the European equivalent to ISO 9000) for device exports to Europe.

ISO 9000 has also gained ground in several U.S. government agencies. The U.S. Food and Drug Administration (FDA) moved toward incorporating ISO 9001 into its Good Manufacturing Practices (GMP) for medical devices by the end of 1992. Current GMP regulations govern how devices are manufactured, and FDA believes adopting ISO 9001 would increase the scope of GMP regulations, take advantage of design control and service elements of ISO 9001, and meet the needs of a growing international marketplace. The new GMP regulations will be regulatory requirements, and will delete the voluntary language of the ISO 9000 series. The U.S. Department of Defense also plans to replace its MIL-Q-9858A and MIL-I-45208A quality system standards with the ISO 9000 standards. The Defense Department is currently making changes to the Defense Federal Acquisition Regulations that would allow the official use of ISO 9000 by its contractors. It has indicated that it will accept ISO 9000 from its contractors but would not require it. Other U.S. agencies considering the ISO 9000 include the Federal Aviation Administration (FAA) and the National Aeronautics and Space Administration (NASA).

EUROPEAN ORGANIZATION FOR TESTING AND CERTIFICATION

Outside the areas covered by EC legislation, mutual recognition of national requirements is intended to be the operative principle for the EC market. In April 1990, the EC created an organization to facilitate the mutual recognition process: the European Organization for Testing and Certification (EOTC). EOTC's role is to promote the mutual recognition of conformity assessment activities (including test results, certification procedures, and quality systems assessments) in the nonregulated product sector in the EC. Additionally, EOTC will provide technical assistance to the commission on implementation of EC legislation in the regulated sphere—notably in preparing mutual recognition agreements with third countries. EOTC is designed to encourage technical equivalency among various testing and certification entities in the EC, thus avoiding waste caused by multiple certifications. Some areas where EOTC coordination may take place include electrical components, aircraft parts, and measurement and control instruments.

Structurally, EOTC includes a council, sectoral committees in industry disciplines (such as steel and medical), specialized committees along functional lines (such as testing and certification), and agreement groups. Agreement groups, attached to each sectoral committee, are the principal grouping within the EOTC charged with developing agreements that establish technical equivalence between conformity assessment entities. Agreement groups will be open to non-European interests on equivalent terms to European participants. Sectoral committees, although not open to direct non-EC participation, will place a priority on establishing dialogues with similarly organized sector groups in the United States and elsewhere.

EOTC is in an experimental stage and will move to an operational phase as soon as guidelines for recognition of agreement groups and sectoral committees begin to be applied. Currently, one agreement group has been recognized by EOTC (in the area of accreditation of calibration laboratories) and several applications are pending. The EOTC Council approved the application of the European Committee for Information Technology Certification (ECITC) to become a sectoral committee. No specialized committees have been formally established, although the European Organization for Quality (EOQ) and the European Committee for Quality System Assessment and Certification (EQS) have been given observer status in EOTC.

One area of uncertainty is EOTC's role in the regulated product sector. Although the organization will be a key entity for conformity assessment in the nonregulated sector, many believe the EOTC will also become active in the regulated sector. In recent discussions, Machado Jorge, EOTC's executive director, said the organization would not play a direct role in the implementation of new approach directives, and, should an overlap exist between the work of notified bodies in the regulated sector and agreement groups in the nonregulated sector, EOTC would concentrate its activities on the nonregulated issues involved. Questions remain about how far the EOTC will extend into the regulated sector. Answers will only be known as the organization continues to evolve.

EUROPEAN ORGANIZATION FOR TECHNICAL APPROVALS

The Construction Products Directive (Council Directive 89/106) is one of the more complex of the EC's new approach directives, both in terms of the number of products within its scope and the nature of standards work to be undertaken. Consequently, the directive provides for an interim method for allowing products to enter the European market, known as

European Technical Approvals (ETAs). The group providing such approvals is the European Organization for Technical Approvals (EOTA).

A nonprofit organization officially established on October 10, 1990, the EOTA has essentially replaced the UEATC (European Union for Technical Approvals in Construction), a 1960 organization that established technical means by which construction and building products met requirements through "fitness for purpose assessments." The new EOTA (statutes have been prepared and application for association status will be made shortly) will act as an umbrella organization for participating member-state bodies—presumably the national members of the former UEATC. Applications for ETAs will normally go through the member-state bodies.

A European technical approval is a supplementary method for construction products to gain the certification mark and therefore enjoy free circulation throughout the EC. An ETA is a favorable technical assessment of the fitness of a product for its intended use. ETAs are granted when there is/are (1) no harmonized European standard, (2) no recognized national standard, (3) no mandate for a harmonized standard and the EC Commission determines that a standard could not be developed, or (4) products that differ significantly from harmonized or recognized national standards.

Proposals for ETAs are authorized by the Standing Committee on Construction, created in the directive. After securing ETA authorization, the CE mark can be affixed to the product. ETAs are valid for a five-year period, with one additional five-year extension. After this time, standards will have been developed for the product in question, and ETAs will no longer be needed.

Several questions have been raised concerning the relationship between EOTA and the Commission. The Commission role will be limited to participation in certain EOTA committees and to providing funding for developing ETA guidelines.

SUMMARY

European technical requirements are developing rapidly as the EC zeroes in on its target. This appendix has highlighted the quality assurance area and several new EC organizations involved in technical approvals. Manufacturers must know legal requirements for selling products outlined in

TABLE C–1
Revisions to ISO 9000

Existing Standards

9000:	Quality Management and Quality Assurance Standards—Guidelines for Selection and Use
9001:	Quality Systems—Model for Quality Assurance in Design, Production, Installation, and Servicing
9002:	Quality Systems—Model for Quality Assurance in Production and Installation
9003:	Quality Systems—Model for Quality Assurance in Final Inspection and Test
9004:	Quality Management and Quality System Elements—Guidelines

New Standards (All Adopted, Some Published by ISO)

9000–3:	Guidelines for the Application of ISO 9001 to the Development, Supply and Maintenance of Software
9004–2:	Quality Management and Quality System Elements, Part 2—Guidelines for Services
10011–1:	Guidelines for Auditing Quality Systems, Part 1—Auditing
10011–2:	Guidelines for Auditing Quality Systems, Part 2—Qualification Criteria for Auditors
10011–3:	Guidelines for Auditing Quality Systems, Part 3—Managing Audit Programs
10012–1:	Quality Assurance Requirements for Measuring Equipment, Part 1—Management of Measuring Equipment

Two additional draft international standards (DIS) are being considered by ISO TC 176. They are (1) DIS 9004–3: Addendum to 9004 on Processed Materials, and (2) DIS 9000–2: Generic Guidelines for the Application of ISO 9001–9003 (additional information to assist companies in satisfying the requirements of ISO 9001, 9002, and 9003).

Additional Documents under Consideration

Guidelines for Quality Improvement (to be 9004–4)
Guidelines for Quality Plans (to be 9004–5)
Guidelines for Configuration Management (to be 9004–6)

Strategic Plan for Revision of ISO 9000

"Vision 2000: A Strategy for International Standards Implementation in the Quality Arena During the 1990s," a long-range plan developed by ISO TC 176.

Source: "Business America," U.S. Department of Commerce, February 24, 1992.

EC directives as well as track the status of European standards and certification requirements.

Companies are encouraged to contact the Commerce Department's Single Internal Market Information Service (SIMIS) at (202)-337-5276 to order directives, to obtain various guides for doing business in the EC, and to ask questions pertaining to any aspect of EC 1992. Additional information on ISO 9000 can be obtained from the National Institute of Standards and Technology (NIST). A recent publication, "Questions and Answers on Quality, the ISO 9000 Standard Series, Quality System Registration, and Related Issues (NISTIR 4721)," provides helpful information for exporters. Companies interested in obtaining a copy of NISTIR 4721 can send a self-addressed mailing label to The Standards Code and Information Program, A-629, Administration Building, National Institute of Standards and Technology, Gaithersburg, MD 20899.

The ISO 9000 standards series on quality assurance (see Table C–1), issued in 1987, is reviewed approximately every five years, with the first scheduled revision having occurred in 1992. Minor changes will be made to the ISO 9000 standards in 1992 with more extensive revisions planned for 1997. ISO Technical Committee 176 is responsible for revising the standards, the same committee which drafted the original ISO 9000 standards. The American Society for Quality Control (ASQC) is in charge of the U.S. Technical Advisory Group to ISO TC 176.

INDEX

About APICS

APICS, the educational society for resource management, offers the resources professionals need to succeed in the manufacturing community. With more than 35 years of experience, 70,000 members, and 260 local chapters, APICS is recognized worldwide for setting the standards for professional education. The society offers a full range of courses, conferences, educational programs, certification processes, and materials developed under the direction of industry experts.

APICS offers everything members need to enhance their careers and increase their professional value. Benefits include:

- Two internationally recognized educational certification processes—Certified in Production and Inventory Management (CPIM) and Certified in Integrated Resource Management (CIRM), which provide immediate recognition in the field and enhance members' work-related knowledge and skills. The CPIM process focuses on depth of knowledge in the core areas of production and inventory management, while the CIRM process supplies a breadth of knowledge in 13 functional areas of the business enterprise.
- The APICS Educational Materials Catalog—a handy collection of courses, proceedings, reprints, training materials, videos, software, and books written by industry experts . . . many of which are available to members at substantial discounts.
- *APICS The Performance Advantage*—a monthly magazine that focuses on improving competitiveness, quality, and productivity.
- Specific industry groups (SIGs)—suborganizations that develop educational programs, offer accompanying materials, and provide valuable networking opportunities.
- A multitude of educational workshops, employment referral, insurance, a retirement plan, and more.

To join APICS, or for complete information on the many benefits and services of APICS membership, **call 1-800-444-2742 or 703-237-8344.** Use extension 297.

Other titles in The Business One Irwin/APICS
Library of Integrated Resource Management

INTEGRATED PRODUCTION AND INVENTORY MANAGEMENT
Revitalizing the Manufacturing Enterprise
Thomas E. Vollmann, William L. Berry, and D. Clay Whybark

Discover how to slash production and distribution costs by effectively monitoring inventory. *Integrated Production and Inventory Management* explains the inventory control processes that optimize customer service and improve purchasing forecasts and production schedules.
ISBN: 1-55623-604-2

PURCHASING
Continued Improvement through Integration
Joseph R. Carter

A complete, integrative resource for purchasing goods and services in the United States and abroad! As free trading zones open up around the world, the possibilities for sourcing nationally and internationally expand with them. This guide will help you enrich the buyer-supplier relationship that can lead to higher-quality products from suppliers and more lucrative contracts from buyers.
ISBN: 1-55623-535-6

EFFECTIVE PRODUCT DESIGN AND DEVELOPMENT
How to Cut Lead Time and Increase Customer Satisfaction
Stephen R. Rosenthal

Effective Product Design and Development will help you steer clear of long development delays by pointing out ways to detect design flaws early and by showing how to empower the entire work team to recognize time-absorbing mistakes. You will discover how to shorten the cycle of new product design and development and turn time into a strategic competitive advantage.
ISBN: 1-55623-603-4

INTEGRATED PROCESS DESIGN AND DEVELOPMENT
Dan L. Shunk

Shunk's book is a no-nonsense, reader-friendly guide that not only defines the information requirements for integrated process design but also outlines the procedures you must take to achieve it. You will discover ways your company can benefit from new and future technological trends, value-adding through design, value-added tracking, and more.
ISBN: 1-55623-556-9

FIELD SERVICE MANAGEMENT
An Integrated Approach to Increasing Customer Satisfaction
Arthur V. Hill

How do companies like 3M and Whirlpool consistently rate highly with customers in areas of field service repair? Hill, an established researcher and consultant in service operations management, examines their tactics and offers practical strategies to manage field service for high-quality results.
ISBN: 1-55623-547-X

Available at fine bookstores and libraries everywhere.